DISCOVERY OF A VICTIM

Sergeant Bell looked to his right and saw something that looked like a trash bag. It was about a mile from where Doug Gissendaner's car was discovered. He hadn't seen it before. Fleetingly he thought it was probably nothing and he started to drive on, but something made him stop the vehicle. He walked up into the woods. As he went up the embankment, he saw a large hole on the other side and thought it would be the perfect place to hide a body. He walked on. As he got closer, he thought whatever he was looking at looked more like a person than a trash bag. The way it was bent over with its back to him made him think perhaps it was someone hiding. Fear overpowered him. A person hiding meant only that he had done something wrong, and Bell was out in the middle of nowhere by himself. He slowed his pace and set aside the fear. He walked closer. In a small clearing, about one hundred yards off the road, was the body of a man, hunched over on his knees, his face in the dirt. The man wore a black jacket, blue jeans, hiking boots. Flies circled the body, but there was no smell. Bell stopped about twelve feet from the body, knowing he did not want to disturb a crime scene. He couldn't tell anything about what the man looked like, but he knew he had found the man he had been hunting for so long. He couldn't get a signal from his cell phone, so he went back to his truck and drove toward the paved road to call his office.

"Call C̶̶̶̶̶̶̶̶̶̶, C̶̶̶̶̶̶̶̶," dispatcher.

"̶̶̶̶̶̶̶̶̶̶̶̶̶̶̶̶̶̶̶̶̶̶̶̶̶̶̶̶̶̶̶̶ been

lo̶̶̶̶

FIRST WE'LL KILL MY HUSBAND

LYN RIDDLE

PINNACLE BOOKS
Kensington Publishing Corp.
http://www.kensingtonbooks.com

Some names have been changed to protect the privacy of individuals connected to this story.

PINNACLE BOOKS are published by

Kensington Publishing Corp.
850 Third Avenue
New York, NY 10022

All Kensington Titles, Imprints, and Distributed Lines are available at special quantity discounts for bulk purchases for sales promotions, premiums, fund-raising, and educational or institutional use. Special book excerpts or customized printings can also be created to fit specific needs. For details, write or phone the office of the Kensington special sales manager: Kensington Publishing Corp., 850 Third Avenue, New York, NY 10022, attn: Special Sales Department, Phone: 1-800-221-2647.

Pinnacle and the P logo Reg. U.S. Pat. & TM Off.

ISBN-13: 978-0-7860-1720-1
ISBN-10: 0-7860-1720-1

First Printing: August 2008

10 9 8 7 6 5 4 3 2 1

Printed in the United States of America

The Crime

Chapter 1

Barrow County lies just north of Atlanta; yet in the winter of 1997, it remained a place of piney woods and small towns. With less than seven thousand residents, Auburn was a small burb. It wasn't the county seat or much more than a crossroads for U.S. Highway 29 and Georgia Highway 8. Tiny Auburn was known for being a speed trap for students going to and from the University of Georgia, in Athens. It was a blue-collar town. Men most likely worked as truck drivers or in some sort of construction, and women, if they worked at all, oftentimes taught school or served as someone's secretary. Married couples filled the small ranch houses in the few subdivisions that broke up the expanse of woodlands and pasture.

Kelly Gissendaner and her husband, Doug, moved to Auburn just before Christmas in 1996. The house on Meadow Trace Drive, a short street of modest homes on bigger than normal lots, was the first home they had owned in six years of marriage. They had lived with her mother in nearby Winder, Georgia, and on army bases. Their three children did not know what it was like to have their own rooms, to have some sense of permanence. Many relatives lived in neighboring towns and counties, and so the children had roots, but no real home. Kelly lived all her life in the area; Doug moved there as a young boy. Kelly Gissendaner worked in nearby Suwanee in the office at a distribution center owned by Rooms To Go, a low-price furniture store in which customers can buy an entire room as displayed and have it delivered within a day. Doug worked the assembly line at Pro Shocks, a manufacturer of shock absorbers for race cars in Lawrenceville, the county seat for neighboring Gwinnett County. Neither husband nor wife had education beyond high school. They were as likely to change jobs as to stay. Especially Kelly. She was twenty-nine and had worked four jobs during the past two years, including a few months of service in the United States Army. She was discharged after she became pregnant with the youngest of her three children, Cody.

The house the Gissendaners bought was yellow, with rust-colored shutters. It had three bedrooms and two baths, one of which was in the master bedroom, a true luxury to Kelly, who was used to living in the cramped space of a mobile home and sharing a bathroom with whoever was living there at the time. The bedroom closest to the living room went to Kayla, the middle child. The boys, Brandon and Cody, would share the bigger room across from the master bedroom. The eat-in kitchen was big enough for Doug and Kelly to cook together. The living room was not overly large, but served its purpose primarily as a place for the family to watch television. A carport, sized for one vehicle, braced one side of the house. The

Gissendaners didn't have much, but they were able to fill the children's bedrooms with beds and dressers. The living room and dining room could be described as utilitarian. Spare, simple clusters of furniture cast off by other families or from family members. Kelly framed school pictures of the children and a church portrait of Doug to hang on the walls. She placed a few knickknacks on shelves and end tables. It would never be featured in *Southern Accents,* but it belonged to them. Them and the bank, which charged higher than normal interest because late payments decimated their credit score.

When they moved in, all the rooms needed paint. The large front yard looked more like a pasture than a lawn. Weeds sprouted where shrubs usually grew. Doug happily did the work. It was for his family. He prided himself a family man. It was all he ever wanted from his life. To be like his dad, a caretaker, a hardworking man who spent all his free time doing for his wife and children. To Doug, the children offered security, and in his moments of introspection, a reason to live. Brandon was ten, Kayla six, and Cody three.

They had lived in the house for three months on February 8, 1997, when Kelly woke up after a night out with her girlfriends. The children had spent the night with her mother. Doug had not come home. Kelly called Kathy Nesbit, a friend from Atlanta Church of Christ. Kathy was still sleeping when the phone rang before seven o'clock.

"Is Doug there?" Kelly asked.

Kathy did not know what Kelly was talking about. Doug left around ten o'clock the night before, she told Kelly.

"He's not home?" Kathy asked, struggling to take in what her friend was saying.

"No," Kelly said flatly.

Kathy explained she cooked dinner and Doug ate with her and her husband. Then Tom, Kathy's husband, and Doug worked on their cars. About ten o'clock, Doug said he was going to go on home, even though Kelly was out for the night. He was tired. He told them he had to get up early on Saturday to do some work for the church, Kathy said.

Kelly hung up and dialed her in-laws. Sue Gissendaner, Doug's mother, answered. She and her husband, Doug Sr., were eating breakfast in the kitchen of their Buford, Georgia, home, about sixteen miles northwest of where their son lived. Their white Colonial-style house served as the rallying point for the three Gissendaner children and three grandchildren. The cozy rooms full of comfortable sofas and chairs, and a kitchen of maple-colored cabinets and a round oak table, offered an "Ozzie and Harriet" touchstone.

The elder Doug leapt from his chair at the kitchen table when he noticed the alarmed look on his wife's face. He picked up an extension to hear his wife say, "What do you mean he didn't come home?" Sue Gissendaner viewed her son as the most structured man she knew. He worked; he went home. It was not even half past seven on a Saturday morning. Where else would he be but home?

"Is it possible he ran out of gas? Did he have enough gas in his car?" the mother implored.

"I think he had plenty of gas," Kelly answered.

"Did he have his insurance card?"

"Yes," Kelly said, and explained Doug had been at the Nesbits'.

"Did you call them?"

"Yes."

"Call the police station and hospitals," Sue Gissendaner demanded.

Kelly called the local hospitals and called Kathy again to ask her to call the police. Kathy didn't understand why Kelly asked her to call, but she didn't question it. She just wanted to help her friend. She was so anxious about Doug's whereabouts, it didn't occur to her that police would take a missing persons report only from a family member. She made the call, but the dispatcher said Kelly had to call on her own. Central dispatch received Kelly's call about ten o'clock. Officer D. H. Kunihro took the information and typed up a standard incident report. Name. Age. Height. Weight. Driving a 1994 Chevrolet Caprice. Hasn't been heard from since the night before. Only valuable item on his person, a wedding ring.

Sue and Doug Gissendaner Sr. did not know what to say to each other. After thirty-four years of marriage, and raising a son and two daughters, they believed they had been through most of the highs and lows of life. They felt they had come out the other side. Nothing out of the ordinary had scarred their lives. Now their son was missing. They called their daughters, Lee, four years younger than Doug, and Jennifer, seven years younger. Doug Sr. decided to drive over to his son's house while Sue waited for Lee to come home. She still considered the house her children's home, even though they had had homes of their own for some time.

Kelly was alone when her father-in-law arrived. Doug Sr. thought she seemed nervous, but not frantic. His wife and daughters were frantic.

He looked at Kelly and asked point-blank: "Have you been fighting again?"

"No, everything was going fine," she said. She looked down.

Doug Sr. didn't believe her. He knew there had been trouble in the past between her and his son. He blamed Kelly for most of the problems. And he didn't think people had the capacity to change all that much, despite their best efforts. Kelly had never shown him a best effort for anything.

He left to look for his son. He spent most of the day searching. He drove the route between the Nesbits' and Auburn. He drove from his house to Auburn, to Pro Shocks, back to the Nesbits'. He scoured the ditches along the road and peered into the woods. He drove slowly. Nothing. He looked for the car. He looked for his son.

Meanwhile, Kathy Nesbit got dressed and drove the twelve miles to Kelly's house. The women attended the same Sunday school class at Atlanta Church of Christ. They grew close quickly, largely because their husbands did. Kelly was doing laundry when Kathy arrived. The women hugged, the six-foot-tall Kelly engulfing Kathy.

"I just need to do the laundry, just to keep busy," Kelly said, pushing back her dark, coarse hair.

"Well, I don't think I could help you anyway, 'cause I'm shaking too much," Kathy said. She wondered about her friend's demeanor. Kelly didn't seem too upset, she thought, but then people handle stress in all sorts of ways. She was not one to judge.

Chapter 2

In 1997, Luke Edwards Road weaved through neighboring Gwinnett County, past horse farms and land that would one day look profitable to subdivision developers. An abandoned house and a home owned by a longtime resident that folks called "Black Jim" were the only structures on the main road to Luke Edwards. A never-paved section offered teenagers privacy in a wilderness of loblolly pines and dense undergrowth. It drew people looking to discard broken-down water heaters and washing machines. And poachers found what they were looking for in any manner of wildlife or shooting targets.

It was Sunday, February 9, midmorning, when James Bell angled his patrol car onto the dirt road, looking for poachers. Deer season had ended on New Year's Day and turkey wouldn't start for another month. It had been cold overnight, but the sun warmed the woods to a relatively comfortable 40 degrees. Bell, a sergeant with the Georgia Department of Natural Resources (DNR), drove about fifty yards before he saw a Chevrolet Caprice in the middle of the road. It had been set on fire, perhaps days earlier. Nothing smoldered and the smell of wet ashes was not prominent. Bell could barely tell the color, yellow, perhaps, or silver. He did not know. The color had been burned off the top and the sides and the numbers and letters on the Georgia license plate were masked by soot. E, maybe an F, SN231.

Bell, who had been with the DNR for twenty years, skirted the car and drove on. Another car was parked down the hill, close to a bridge. He questioned the occupants, who said they were out for a walk. Bell took down their names. He knew the area well. He patrolled it regularly for poachers, and not six months before, he had gotten into an altercation with some people who were making a lot of noise in the woods. When he stopped, they sped off in their car and the subsequent chase drew in three law enforcement agencies before the suspects wrecked their car. Authorities discovered they fled because they were driving a car stolen from the mayor of a small town nearby. The area drew people practicing witchcraft and grave robbers, who haunted a nearby cemetery. Bell made a habit of driving down the road once or twice a week.

He drove back to the burned car. The ground was singed beneath it and around it. A pine tree nearby looked like it had been struck by lightning, its needles brown. Bell looked inside the car and saw destruction. Obviously, the fire began inside. What once was upholstery looked like the inside of a fireplace. The plastic on the dash had warped from the heat. Everything was gone, but about half of the trunk. But there was one clue remaining. The vehicle identification number was legible. The area was so remote, Bell had trouble getting a radio signal or reception on his cell phone. He managed to get a nearby county law enforcement agency on the phone to relay the identification number.

Corporal W. V. Morgan, of the Gwinnett County Police Department (GCPD), soon arrived. Morgan told Bell the vehicle number was traced to a guy named Warren Gunter in another county. They reached Gunter by phone. He told authorities his nephew Doug Gissendaner paid him $500 for the 1994 model a few weeks earlier. And that's not all Morgan told Bell. Gissendaner's wife, Kelly, had reported him missing the day before.

"Foul play," Bell said immediately. Initially he thought the car had been stolen and the fire was set to get rid of it. It could have been abandoned and kids playing in the woods torched it for fun. Teens often drove all-terrain vehicles (ATVs) along the bumpy, hilly road.

Gwinnett County police officers knew an abandoned car and a missing husband added up to a possible homicide. Morgan stayed with the car as the identification officers began to process the scene. Officers found no sign of struggle, no footprints around the car. No weapons. No chance of fingerprints in the burned-out hulk. The ID techs, as they're known, took pictures and prepared to have the car towed to the impound laboratory for further testing.

Doug Davis, a sixteen-year veteran of the Gwinnett County Police Department, and an investigator with the major felony unit, was on call that afternoon. He and his wife had just gotten home from Hebron Baptist Church in Dacula, Georgia, when the call about a burned vehicle, out in the middle of nowhere, came in. Davis had been in law enforcement almost twenty years by that time and had worked in the funeral home business for close to a decade. His wife was used to a Sunday-afternoon change in plans. He would serve as lead investigator.

Davis grew up in Gainesville, Georgia, thirty miles north of Auburn on Lake Lanier. He had been a center on the high-school football team and a catcher on the baseball team. By the time he was twenty-one, he was married, the father of one of the two sons his wife would ultimately bear. He was in the first graduating class of Gupton-Jones College of Funeral Service and worked as a funeral director before deciding to go into law enforcement.

"I wanted to try something new," he said. He had been working what seemed like twenty-four hours a day at the mortuary. He took a job first as a patrolman, then as a motorcycle officer with the Gainesville Police Department (GPD). Three years later, he went back into the funeral business, lured by the offer of more money. In 1981, he joined the Gwinnett County Police Department as a patrol officer. He'd been out of college eleven years and was now in a whole new career that would take him through just about every facet of police work.

Davis rode out to the scene and looked the car over. He knew only what was obvious: somebody burned it for a reason. He wasn't sure why it was parked there. He didn't know what he had. A missing husband and father. A burned car. Did Gissendaner commit suicide? Was he murdered? Had he been kidnapped?

All there was to do was to go back and look at the

Gissendaners' lives, to look at where they started. And then try to figure out where they ended up.

Members of the media had already started prowling the area. Television choppers puttered overhead. The police department set up a makeshift command post at the point where the pavement ended and the red clay road began. Lieutenant Mike Reonas, the criminal investigations division supervisor with the Gwinnett County Police Department, briefed the media. He had served in any number of law enforcement capacities in twenty years with the department, including leading two precincts and conducting internal investigations. He had been a member of a SWAT team. Reonas was known as a policeman who told it straight.

"There's nothing left. That really hurts us," he told the media.

Davis called the Gissendaner home, and Maxine Wade, Kelly Gissendaner's mother, answered. He didn't let on that the car had been found. He simply asked about Doug Gissendaner. Had he returned? Not yet, Wade told him.

"I'll be there shortly," he said. He and fellow investigator Troy Hutson drove to police headquarters to review the missing persons report filed the day before. They asked Officer Jim Kelly and Investigator Robert Evans to fly over the area in the department helicopter. The officers were in the air within the hour and used a heat-seeking scope to survey the dense woods. They searched for an hour, but found no evidence of a human in the woods.

The missing persons report had the particulars, but no real leads. Doug was wearing a gray tank top, jeans, hiking boots, his wife had reported. A

Tasmanian devil was tattooed on his upper right arm. He left the home of a friend and did not arrive at his own house.

Mrs. Gissendaner stated that this is out of character for her husband, the officer wrote in the report.

Davis was ready to tell the family about the car. The Gissendaner home was full of people at midafternoon when he and Hutson arrived. Kelly Gissendaner sat in the small living room with her mother, father-in-law, Doug Sr., and some friends. Kelly had just returned from taking her children to the circus. They had planned to go before Doug went missing, so she decided to keep life as normal as possible for the children. Doug Sr. wondered about that decision. It didn't seem right. He had spent the day handing out missing person flyers and posting signs anywhere he could think of, anywhere people would allow them to be hung.

Davis told the group that the Caprice had been found. It was burned and on a dirt road, out in the country. Kelly hugged a church friend and collapsed into a chair. She put her hands to her face and wept. But within fifteen minutes, she composed herself.

Doug Sr. thought she seemed nervous. His suspicion of her grew, but he didn't think she could actually harm his son. In fact, he didn't know what to think about any of it. Kidnapping seemed unlikely. While he made a comfortable living selling ball bearings, his net worth remained in the middle-income range, perhaps upper middle. His house wasn't worth more than $200,000, even in the north Atlanta suburbs. His son's income hovered around the barely making-ends-meet side of the economy. Sometimes it wasn't even paycheck to paycheck. Doug Sr. still held on to hope that his son was all right. Perhaps he had stopped to help someone. He was always helping people. Perhaps the person stole the car. Perhaps the person beat him up and he was unconscious in a hospital. The worst he could think of was that his son had been beaten and left in a ditch. But in the father's mind, his son would come to and wander to safety.

Doug Sr. excused himself to call his wife. Sue was at home with his brother and his brother's wife. The car has been found, he told her, describing the location and its condition. She threw down the phone, screamed and ran out of the house. She darted down the street like a crazed animal. She ended up at a neighbor's house, hysterical. She didn't say the words aloud, she didn't tell her husband, but she knew then, her only son was dead. She believed he had burned to death in the car.

The senior Gissendaner's reaction was to drive to the place the car was found and search some more. He traced the route his thirty-year-old son should have driven home the night before. He drove and drove. He would not give up. It was his second day of driving through the woods and small towns of north Georgia. He and daughter Jennifer had spent almost all of the day before combing the two-lane highways of Gwinnett and Barrow Counties looking for Doug. They rode together well into the night. There were long periods of silence. They made small talk. They remembered family times together. He and Jennifer stopped at every convenience store they crossed and checked the malls for his car. Now the car had been found and Doug set out to search for the son he believed was wounded someplace along the road.

A salesman, Doug Sr. was no stranger to driving along all sorts of roads. This time, though, was a frenzied trip to a place he had never been before. The abject fear of the unknown. He was a brawny man, on the tall side, with a head full of light reddish brown, graying hair. He wore glasses, like his son. He had an easy smile and his calloused hands showed the years working with wrenches and grease as he pursued a pastime he shared with his son, auto repair.

Back at the house, Davis, the investigator, asked Kelly, "Ma'am, may I speak with you privately?" Like many men who investigate death, Davis had a courteous, quiet manner. He had been schooled in the ways of interviewing and he had the added bonus of being a true Southern gentleman. He knew when to use "ma'am" and "sir."

Kelly led him into the only room where they could talk privately, her bedroom. She told Davis what she had told police the day before. Her husband had been at the Lawrenceville home of the Nesbits. She motioned toward the living room and said Kathy Nesbit was in there now. Kelly said Doug arrived at the Nesbits' about five-thirty, after he had finished his shift at Pro Shocks.

Kathy Nesbit had fixed fettuccine, salad and iced tea for Tom and Doug. Then the men worked on Tom's truck, and Doug changed the spark plugs on Doug's Caprice. He left about ten o'clock to make the fifteen-minute drive home.

"Have you and Mr. Gissendaner had any marital problems in the past?" Davis asked.

"No," Kelly said emphatically.

She told Davis she spent Friday night with

three friends from work. They ate pizza at one friend's house and later the four of them went to a local dance club to celebrate a birthday. Kelly said she took a pill when she got home about midnight. She had intended to take a pain pill, but she apparently got a sleeping pill by mistake. She dozed off. It was about seven when she woke up and realized her husband was not in the bed with her.

"I checked the entire house," Kelly told Davis. "Then I called the Nesbits. They told me Doug left about ten."

"Are there any guns in the house?" Davis asked. "No."

She told him she also called Doug's parents. He was not there, either. Then she called her mother.

"Did Doug have on any jewelry?" Davis asked Kelly.

"A gold watch with a black face, a gold wedding band and a silver-blue Buford High School, Class of 1985, ring," she answered, handing him a sign the family made announcing Doug's disappearance. They had taken them to area stores and around the neighborhood. Davis watched her as she spoke. He looked into her eyes. She averted his gaze. It was a sign of untruthfulness, he knew. She became a suspect.

Kelly estimated her husband had no more than $150 with him. She said she knew that because he called her on his way to the Nesbits' home and told her he had deposited his check and kept that much out to pay a finance company bill the next day. They didn't have any credit cards, but they did have a debit card through NationsBank. She had already checked. It had not been used, Kelly said.

"You may want to contact Bell South and put a

trace on your phone," Davis said, handing her a business card and asking her to call if she heard anything at all.

It was after five in the evening when Davis talked with Kathy Nesbit at the Gissendaner home. She confirmed what Kelly Gissendaner said. The couples had known each other for almost a year and had been good friends. The last thing she said to Doug was to tell Kelly "hi."

Doug was wearing a gray tank top and he threw on his black jacket before he left.

The Nesbits had helped distribute the flyers detailing Doug's disappearance. Brett Brantley, the Gissendaners' next-door neighbor, thought it was odd how quickly they assembled the flyers.

Davis and Hutson drove back to headquarters, the back-and-forth driving and talking and searching of a difficult investigation just beginning. A criminal investigation is like putting the pieces of a puzzle together in the dark, with some of the pieces missing. Follow the trail. Reach a dead end. Talk to someone else. Always looking for that one mistake. Criminals always do it. At least one mistake in any crime. At least. Davis and Hutson didn't know for sure that a crime had been committed, because they had no body, but instinct told them one had been.

Davis had called Lance Wrecker Service to get the Caprice to the crime scene bay. Soon after the car was backed into the crime scene bay, investigators began processing it. Davis would have a report soon. He'd know if they uncovered any evidence that would lead him to something else. He wanted to talk to Tom Nesbit. It was almost eight o'clock when he and Hutson arrived at the Nesbit home. Nesbit told virtually the same story as his wife, but added that Doug told him he intended to go straight home, take a shower and get in bed. He had to get up early on Saturday to hand out flyers for their church at the Chamblee MARTA Station, Atlanta's commuter train service. It was an outreach of the church, trying to get people to visit the rapidly growing denomination.

Like many young couples in the South, the Nesbits and the Gissendaners became acquainted through their church. The Nesbits, in their mid-thirties, were a bit older than the Gissendaners, but they shared common interests, especially the men, who liked to work on cars. Kathy thought Kelly seemed like a sweet girl.

When Davis arrived back at the Gwinnett County Police Department, he had a report on the car. A quart jar of burned material was all that would be sent to the evidence room. It wasn't much, if anything. The car was taken to the wrecker company's secure storage area. And Davis went back to square one.

It seemed unlikely that they would turn up anything, but the officers drove to Pro Shocks, where Doug had worked for about two years, to see if he was there. They already knew Doug Gissendaner had not had any trouble with the law. All evidence pointed to his being a God-fearing family man. Perhaps he just went to work for some reason and something happened while he was there. As expected, he wasn't there.

Doug's parents remained convinced their son had stopped to help someone stranded on the roadway and was perhaps lying wounded in a ditch. They had seen their son's helpful nature over and over again. He was a gentle soul who wanted to help people in need. And he was an especially gifted mechanic.

Their other theory was he had been in an accident and was left unconscious in his car. After the car was found, both situations looked unlikely to investigators.

First thing Monday morning, Davis and Hutson organized a foot search of the woods along Luke Edwards Road. It was raining, the kind of drenching downpour that regularly engulfs the South on summer days. The only benefit was the clouds tended to keep the temperature from dropping too low. This day it rose into the 50s. The search began about ten o'clock and included six law enforcement agencies, search dogs, helicopter pilots flying routes overhead and Gissendaner's friends. They scoured the area, up and down ravines, into the woods and along the road—six hours of search about half a mile in either direction from where the car was found. They walked some three hundred yards into the woods on each side. Nothing. Doug Gissendaner Sr. searched, too. It had been his only activity for three days. He barely slept. If he was home, he preferred his lounge chair, where he could hear if the front door opened. He believed his son would walk through it at any moment.

In the end, the searchers found nothing of use: three door handles, five automobile bulbs, a small light frame, a gas cap, a filament, a metal emblem from a car, a tag frame and a long wooden-handled shovel.

When the search ended, Doug Sr. got into Davis's detective car, a white Lumina. Doug Sr. said he wanted Davis to know his son and daughter-in-law's marriage had been troubled from the beginning. He thought she had told authorities otherwise.

"During Desert Storm, Doug was in Turkey," Doug Sr. began. "They went there to keep the Iraqis out. While Doug was over there, Kelly saw other men." He looked at Davis. Doug and Kelly separated for about ten months, he said.

"I don't know why he went back with her," the father said. "It was her idea to get that house they live in." The parents thought their son was extending himself financially and refused to help him. His son and daughter-in-law had had financial problems in the past, the father told the cop.

Doug Sr. was a planner and a doer. He didn't know how to just sit and wait. His wife was an emotional wreck. Her children were her life. She could barely stop crying. Nothing terrifyingly bad had ever happened in her life or his.

That afternoon, Davis and a newly formed team of investigators began sorting through the Gissendaners' lives. They flagged their checking account, gathered phone records, talked to Doug's boss and Kelly Gissendaner's friends. At about four-thirty, a man called to say he and a friend had been on Luke Edwards Road on Saturday and saw the burned car. They drove about two miles down to the river, where they saw a man of slight build, with dark hair, wearing an army jacket. A blue Areostar van was parked near the rocks. When the man spotted them, he left in a hurry.

Davis and Hutson returned to the scene, but the lead proved fruitless. Kelly Gissendaner and the friends she was with Friday night were at the scene. Kelly got into the patrol car with Davis.

"I don't know anything more than I've already

told you," she said, but she agreed to his request for a taped interview the next day.

Kelly Gissendaner gave interviews to various news media that Monday, too. To the *Atlanta Journal-Constitution,* she speculated that her husband's Good Samaritan nature probably got him in trouble.

"I'm at a total loss," the newspaper quoted her as saying. *"I've been racking my brain trying to think of anything."*

To a local newspaper, the *Banner Eagle,* Kelly said, "If he was where he could get to [a] phone, he would call."

To the *Gwinnett Daily Post,* she said a reward was offered for information leading to an arrest in the case. She wanted to be sure whoever killed her husband was convicted, she said, adding that she knew he was dead because he had not come home. The statements drew notice from Davis and other investigators.

Tuesday morning, a crime scene technician went to Lance Wrecker Service to look through the car once again. He found a piece of glass coated with a rust-colored substance, a piece of fabric and what looked like a shell casing. He also found a dog tag, keys and a key ring and some small tools.

Davis headed to the Gissendaner home as scheduled. He set up the tape recorder and began with the standard questions: name, address, Social Security numbers, then went straight to questions about the Gissendaners' marriage.

"Doug and I have known each other probably eight and a half, nine years," Kelly said. "We got married in September of '89, and we've been married for seven years."

They were married in Gwinnett County and lived there all their married lives, except for the time he was in the army in Germany and she was in the army in Virginia. Doug was a tanker, she said. She worked on a watercraft. They bought their house in December, and before that, they lived with her mother.

She had worked at Rooms To Go's corporate office in Suwanee for about eight months; Doug at Pro Shocks in Lawrenceville for two years.

"Let's go back to Friday," Davis said. "What time did y'all leave to go to work?"

"I left, probably between seven and seven-ten, because I clocked in at seven-thirty, so . . ."

"What was the—what time was he going in?"

"He leaves, he usually leaves shortly after I leave, because he takes the kids to school and Cody to day care, and then he goes on to work. He has to be at work by eight-thirty, so he always leaves just shortly after I do, if he's not leaving at the same time I am."

"And when y'all get through at work, does he pick the kids up, or do you pick the children up?"

"It just depends. If I have to work late, he'll pick them up. If I get off at four-thirty like, you know, like regular hours, I'll go pick them up from the day care. Friday, he didn't drop Cody off at day care, he dropped him off at my mother's and then my mom went and picked [up] the other two at school, because they had plans to stay over there. It was her off day."

She explained that she went out with friends Friday night and Doug went to the Nesbit home.

"So about [what] time did you get home?" Davis asked.

"The house was exactly the way I left it," she

responded. "When I left, I forgot to turn the porch light on, so, of course, it was still off and I left my car lights on so I could see to get my key in the door so I could unlock the door, and I flipped my lights on and everything was exactly the way I left it."

"After work, did you come home and change or—"

"Yes, I did."

"Okay."

"I was in the house probably ten minutes, you know. I had been to H and R Block to go redo my taxes, and Pamela had started paging me because they were so long, so I didn't even do them, and then I came home, changed, and I was here ten minutes, long enough to change clothes and freshen up my hair, clothes and makeup, and I was gone."

"You have any idea what time that was?"

"She paged me, it had to be about six-thirty, because we were supposed to be at Kerri's by seven, and I know I came straight home and I did my hair and I left, 'cause we were already running late."

"So when you left, you didn't turn [on] any lights or anything?"

"No, uh-uh."

Kelly explained she talked to Doug at lunchtime, probably between noon and one o'clock.

"Did you call him, or did he call you?"

"He called me."

"Can you tell me what the general conversation was about?"

"General conversation with him was about my plans on Friday night, about his plans on Friday night, about . . . ah . . . we have some stuff to do on Saturday morning, so we kind of went over what we needed to do there, and that was basically it. I was real busy, he was real busy. It was a very short, five- or ten-minute conversation."

"When you came home Friday night, how was the house?" Davis asked. "You said it was, I mean describe it, I mean was it dark, light, or what?"

"It was dark," she said, her demeanor even. Davis looked at her with a steady gaze. She did not meet his eyes. Just as she had done in the initial interview, Kelly Gissendaner looked away as she described her evening. She offered more detail, though, than the first time Davis met with her.

"It was exactly like I left it," she said. "No porch light on, again, like when I got out of the car, I left my car lights on so I could see to open the door, and when I turned on the lights, no one, no one, had been here, no sign of nothing of even him coming, 'cause I thought maybe if he would've came home and changed. There would be no reason for him to come home and change and go back out, but . . ."

"Okay. Did you call anyone when you got home to see where Doug was at?"

"No, I didn't. No, because it's, you know, it's not unusual for him to get wrapped up in working on something and lose track of time. He's done it several times before, so it's nothing unusual."

"Okay. What did you do when you got home?"

"I came in. I have endometriosis—I thought what [I] was taking was a pain pill, which actually was a sleeping pill, and went to bed and went to sleep and did not know that he was not here until seven o'clock the next morning. When my alarm went off and he wasn't in the bed, I got up and I went and looked in the living room, looked in the kids' room to see if maybe he had fell asleep in one of the beds, and, ah, 'cause I was in the middle of my bed, and when he wasn't, I opened the back door to see if his car was here and he wasn't home. So that's when I called Kathy to find out what time he left there and they told me he had left the night before at about ten or ten-thirty. So then I called his mother to see if they had heard from him and she said no, and then I called my mother and she said she hadn't heard from him, so that's when his dad came on down here and we started trying to find out where he was at."

"And what, about what time did y'all call the police?"

"Um, we called the police . . . well, Kathy Nesbit called the police probably around eight. She was on the phone with them to see if they had any reports of any accidents, um, if anybody had been locked up under his name. She called the Gwinnett County and the Barrow County. I was on the phone calling all the hospitals while she was doing that, just to see if he had came in, was in an accident or . . . nothing there, so finally after she got off the phone with . . . she'd called Gwinnett County [and] was on the phone with them for a long time and then Barrow County. She called me back and said that Gwinnett County said that I needed to call and file a missing persons report and that happened between nine o'clock and ten o'clock, somewhere 'round in there."

"In the past, have you and Doug had any problems?"

"We've been divorced once, and remarried, and we've been separated, um, near divorce and we got back together and basically got our lives involved in church, and that's basically what saved our marriage."

"How long have y'all been remarried?"

"Around three years."

"Three years?"

"Uh-huh."

"Have y'all had any problems in those three years?"

"No. No, just regular, a couple of arguments, I mean nothing that's been big."

"Doug hasn't made any mention of his policy, has he?"

"No," Kelly said. "We had a lady come out and do our physical on life insurance on Wednesday, because he and I both talked about life insurance since we were back together." Kelly Gissendaner said the insurance agent told them it would be four weeks until they learned whether they'd be able to get the insurance.

Davis asked whether it was out of character for Doug to disappear for days without calling.

"He may forget to call for a couple of hours, but not four or five days, no way. You know, he's a very family-oriented man, does not drink, does not do drugs. If he's not with me, he's with his kids. He's always with, you know, one or the other. It's very rare that, you know, it's very weird for him not to have the kids with him. The only time the kids are not with us is when they're staying with my mom and they spend a lot of time with her on her off days, 'cause she doesn't get to see them."

"Can you think of anything else that might help us locate Doug?"

"No. I have tried to rack my brain over and over and over again."

"Where do you think Doug may be?"

"I don't know," she said, looking away from Davis. "All I can think is, is he hurt somewhere and he can't get to a phone, or something bad has happened, 'cause he would've called me by now. If he was to [a] point where he could get to a phone, he would've called me or his parents."

Kelly Gissendaner and Davis reviewed the routes Doug could have taken. Then Davis asked, "Do you know about how much money Doug makes an hour?"

Apparently not hearing the question correctly, Kelly answered: "Doug would've had anywhere from one hundred to a hundred and fifty dollars on him, because we had a bill that we were going to pay Saturday after we had done all we planned. We were going to help out HOPE for Kids with our church."

She said her husband was to pay a bill at Covington Credit. The bill was never paid.

"Can you think of anywhere else he may have went?" Davis asked.

"The only other thing, when he left Kathy's. Maybe he stopped by the store to get gas or . . . I don't know. That would've been the only place, 'cause Kathy said he was covered with grease when he left there."

"If he purchased gas, would he pay for it [with] cash?"

"Yes, he would pay for it with cash."

Finally Davis asked, "At this time, can you think of anything else that may come to mind?"

"Nothing."

It was three-twelve in the afternoon. Doug Gissendaner had been missing for almost four days.

The investigative team, which by now included a dozen officers, split up to interview Kelly Gissendaner's friends. Kerri Otis, Kelly's supervisor, said the girls came to her house around seven. They ordered pizza and watched television. Another friend decided she wanted to go dancing, so they went to The Shack, a club on Jimmy Carter Boulevard, where they danced for about an hour.

"On the way home, Kelly said she had a feeling something bad was going to happen," Otis told Investigator Dave Henry. "I didn't really think anything about it at the time."

Kelly immediately left when they arrived back at Otis's home.

"Did Kelly ever tell you about any marital problems between her and Doug?" Henry asked.

"They were having problems about three months ago, but I think they've worked them out," she said. "Kelly was involved with a guy named Greg."

"What's his last name?"

"I don't know," Otis responded.

Another friend who had been with Kelly Gissendaner on Friday night told the same story: pizza, television, dancing. She also knew about a guy named Greg, but she didn't know his last name. Kelly Gissendaner and Greg had been involved in October or November, the friend said, and Kelly told her he had made threats about Doug. The boyfriend was mad because Kelly went back to her husband, the friend said. The third friend not only knew about Greg, but also knew he had taken Kelly Gissendaner to a motel, a Holiday Inn Express, the previous November to spend the night with him.

Kelly called Davis again, shortly before eight that night. She said Shane Brookshire, her brother, had been out searching the woods for

Doug. He found a knife. Davis went to the Gissendaner home and picked up a Gerber folding knife, with a black handle. He sent it to the property room, but he doubted it helped advance the investigation any more than the door handles found earlier.

He left headquarters, weary from what seemed like twenty-four-hour days since Sunday, but he went to see Doug's parents at their Buford home. It was close to ten o'clock when he climbed the stairs to the Gissendaners' front door. He knew they were up. He knew they could not sleep from worry. He just wanted to let them know what he knew up to that point. All he could think of was what it would be like to have a missing son. It was hard as an investigator with children of his own to block out the fear associated with not knowing where your child is, whether he is even alive.

Police knew nothing of Doug's whereabouts, but they were starting to assemble a portrait of the Gissendaners that was nothing like the happy family Kelly Gissendaner wanted them to see. Yet, suspecting someone is involved in a murder and proving it are two different things. Police had no evidence Kelly Gissendaner knew anything about where her husband was or why he had not come home. She was nothing more than a wife worried about a husband acting out of character.

Chapter 3

Kelly Gissendaner decided to go back to work on Tuesday. Doug Gissendaner Sr., on the other hand, didn't think for a moment about going back to work. Instead, Doug Sr. traversed the roads of Gwinnett County, continuing his desperate crusade. As he drove, he wondered about his daughter-in-law's apparent ease with returning to life as usual. Taking the children to the circus while their father was missing seemed weird to him. Going back to work, even worse. She didn't seem to feel the same sort of anxiety he and his wife felt. She didn't seem sad. But he couldn't imagine, either, that she would hurt Doug physically. There were more than enough emotional hurts, but she had never wounded Doug, as far as Doug Sr. knew.

By Wednesday afternoon, Henry and Davis had run down dozens of leads, added page after page to their casebook, but considered themselves no closer to figuring out what had happened to Doug Gissendaner than they were on Sunday when his car was found.

Two officers went to Rooms To Go to meet

with Kelly's friend Pamela Kogut. She told the details of their Friday night out and also that she spent time with Kelly after everyone realized Doug had not come home. She also told them about a guy named Greg that Kelly had been seeing when she and Doug were separated. She didn't know his last name, but he lived in Cumming and his sister lived in Auburn. Pamela told the investigators that she took Kelly to the Holiday Inn Express in Winder, Georgia, so Kelly could spend the night with Greg. That was in November 1996, she said.

Doug's supervisor at Pro Shocks was interviewed that morning as well. He said Doug had a $15,000 insurance policy and that he had received a check for $269.51 the day he disappeared. He had another check coming.

The supervisor was asked whether Doug was friends with any coworkers.

"He pretty much kept to himself," he said.

Davis and another officer went that afternoon to the Holiday Inn Express to meet with the manager. They scoured the ledger for anyone who checked in on November 8, 1996, the date the friend remembered she had taken Kelly to meet the guy she called Greg. They found a woman named Belinda Leicht, a local woman. It seemed odd for a woman who lived nearby to check into such a place, so investigators thought she might be tied to the mysterious Greg—perhaps she was the sister Pamela had told them about. Belinda Leicht checked into room 215 and paid cash.

The next day, Kerri Otis called the police. Kelly Gissendaner had called her the night before, Otis said, and reported that a man named Greg Owen had made threats against Doug Gissendaner.

Police now had a last name. Records showed Belinda Leicht was indeed his sister. They had a motel record. They had subpoenaed the telephone records of the Gissendaners and Nesbits. They had a jar of ashes. It all added up to not much more than a lot of suspicion. And Doug Gissendaner was still missing.

Police traced Owen through a credit report and found out he and Leicht had lived together in Auburn. His criminal record was sparse, one arrest for drunk driving in Lawrenceville two years earlier. Piece by piece, a portrait was coming together, but police were not quite sure what the picture would look like once it was complete.

On Thursday morning, Kelly called Davis and asked to meet with him when she left work after lunch. Thirty minutes later, Doug Gissendaner Sr. called Davis and asked to meet him. Davis met Doug Sr. in the parking lot of Dacula City Hall that afternoon.

"Kelly had a Cavalier and the engine burned up," Doug Sr. said. "It cost fifteen hundred dollars to fix it. I wonder if Kelly didn't pay for it and whoever fixed it hurt Doug."

She was terrible with money, Doug Sr. said. She had ruined his son's credit rating. Often she didn't pay bills on time, if at all. His son managed to scratch his way back to some semblance of financial security, but it was a long stretch of rock-strewn road that Kelly kept throwing boulders on. Every time he'd get ahead, Kelly would manage to mess it up.

Davis and Hutson went back out to the Gissendaner home that afternoon at about three-thirty. They recorded another interview with Kelly Gissendaner in the master bedroom.

"Basically, what I called you about this morning," Kelly began earnestly, "when Doug and I were split up before, Doug and I have been divorced once, been remarried, we were split up again about to go through another divorce. In the meantime, while we were split up, I had been seeing a guy named Greg Owen. Him and I split up before Doug and I ever got back together. I had some death threats, you know, him threatening to kill him, said that he would get me one way or the other. Just one night, he called my house one hundred thirty-something times 'cause my mom has caller ID, this is when I stayed with her. Doug and I eventually did get back together, Greg knew nothing about it. I mean, I'm sure he probably does now, 'cause his sister worked with me for a little while before she got fired from Rooms To Go, so—"

Davis interrupted: "What is her—what is his sister's name?"

"Belinda Leicht."

Davis tried to keep her focused. He asked for more information about Greg. He asked what Greg did for a living. He wanted to keep the talk feeling more like a conversation and less like an interrogation, to see if he could trip her up. In every domestic situation, the closest family members become the first suspects. In this case, Kelly's demeanor indicted her, in Davis's opinion. That was purely opinion at this point, though.

She said she didn't know for sure what Greg did for a living.

"When I was dating him, he worked with a guy and they worked with dynamite, blasting rock is all I know, and I don't even know. The guy's first name was Pat, that's all I know."

Then, curiously, Kelly changed course, as if she was going back to a prepared script.

"I did start seeing Greg again after Doug and I got back together, for a very short period of time. I was with him on November the eighth."

She said she went out to Cherokee, North Carolina, for two days the next day with her girlfriends, the same ones she was with the night Doug did not come home. That day in November was the last time she saw Greg, she said, although she had talked to him on the phone a time or two.

She looked down and said she and Doug were not getting along because they were living with her mother. But then she blurted out, "We were happy." She rarely looked Davis in the eye.

She said she stopped the relationship with Greg when she and Doug started trying to work out their marital problems. She wanted a life with Doug and the children. They both wanted their life back on track, she said.

But Owen kept paging her, she said. She even changed the number so he couldn't contact her, but his sister gave him Kelly's work number.

"I never gave it to him," she said. "He never had my home address here or my home phone number, 'cause I never gave it to him."

It was obvious to Davis she had said what she wanted to say. She was ready to stop talking. He needed her to keep talking. He asked when Kelly ended the relationship with Owen.

That was the previous December, she said. The first of the month before she and Doug bought the house on Meadow Trace. He asked about recent contact. Again she admitted she had talked with Owen. He called her at work and asked about her kids, her health.

"It was very brief, very short conversations," she said. "He one time did apologize for everything he said to me. He said, 'I was mad because I knew I was losing you and that was my way of trying to get you back,' because he did threaten to kill himself and the whole nine yards, but . . ."

"Anytime during the time you were seeing him, did he ever make any conversations toward hurting Doug?"

"No. No. None whatsoever. No."

"None at all?"

"None at all. The only thing he ever said to me was that he would pay me back one way or the other."

She told Davis about staying with Owen at the Winder hotel the previous November. Davis asked again whether she had been with Greg since then. She said she had not, but then revealed something new.

"I've seen him a couple times. It's just he was over at his sister's when I went over there. I've seen him and that's basically been it. 'Cause him, his sister and I were good friends."

"Since you broke up with him in December?"

"No, December was the last time I saw him."

He asked when the last time she had spoken with Owen. She said it had probably been three weeks since she spoke with him.

"Is that by telephone?" Davis asked. He was trying to keep her off-guard. Ask a question, get an answer, ask another way. A liar can't keep up. He believed nonconfrontational interviewing worked better than in-your-face accusations. He was trying to build her trust. He didn't have a lot of facts to go on. If she was involved, she was certainly the key that could unlock the mystery of Doug's whereabouts.

"It was by telephone, yes."

"Home or at work?"

"At work," Kelly replied.

"He called you or you called him?"

"He called me."

"Okay. Did at any time did he try to contact you other than the telephone at work?"

"No, no, he has never called here."

He asked about her pager and again she told him she had changed the number, but Greg got it anyway. Kelly gave Davis the number and said she still had the beeper, but she hadn't used it.

"He's paged me several times within, you know, I said I talked to him three weeks ago was the last time I talked to him. He has paged me several times within that time period and I haven't returned the call. I just basically got [to] where I just stopped even carrying the pager."

"When's the last time he paged you?"

"It may have even been Friday the last time he paged me." Friday, the day her husband did not come home.

Davis asked about Greg's car. He asked where Owen lived, but Kelly said she didn't know. All she knew was it was in Cumming, and that when she was with him, he worked with a guy named Pat. She didn't think he worked with Pat anymore because his sister said he was working in Cumming.

"How did you meet Greg?"

"Through Greg's sister. And she was my boss at International Readers League when I worked there before I came to work. After International Readers League, I went to Juno Lighting, and after Juno Lighting, I went to Rooms To Go."

He tried to keep her talking. He asked whether she was in the service when she met Owen. And she said again she met him while she was working with Belinda at International Readers League.

"And your last contact that you know of that he may have tried to contact you was Friday?"

"Uh-huh, 'cause he, if I'm not mistaken, my pager went off Friday. I can't remember. It was Thursday or Friday the last time my pager went off with his . . . his number in it."

"Has he tried to contact you since Doug has been missing?"

"No, no, he has not."

"How about Belinda?"

"No, I haven't talked to her, either."

"When's the last time you talked to Belinda?"

"Belinda, the last time I talked to her was, I'm trying to think, um, January fifteenth, somewhere around in there."

Kelly Gissendaner explained she and Owen were together for eight months to a year, during the time she and Doug were divorced. She felt she and Owen would marry, but they had problems. He drank too much and was arrested for driving under the influence. He lost his license and was on probation.

"He had just a lot of stuff going on that I didn't approve of, not in front of my kids, and that's why I ended the relationship."

She went to live with her mother, she said, and the weekend after she broke up with Owen, she and Doug began the road to reconciliation.

"We were in church and we had started going to church in the meantime with me seeing Greg, and Kayla wanted to go by and ask her daddy to go to church one Saturday, and so he started going to church with us and we started working things out, 'cause I never—I guess I never stopped loving Doug. There's just, I guess when you been with somebody for eight years . . ."

"But you and Greg had a special relationship?" Davis asked.

"I don't know if it was special, I think it was just that I, because I was on the rebound, 'cause I started seeing him very shortly after Doug and I broke up. Doug walked out on me right after I started to work at International Readers League, 'cause we were having some problems. He came home from work one day while I was still at work and packed his clothes and left."

"What was the reason he left you?"

"Just, he said he couldn't deal with things at the time. There was just a lot, we were living with my mom, there was a lot of pressure there, there was a lot of pressure from the kids and just everything going on at the time. We were in Amway at the time, and there's just a lot of pressures coming in on all of us and we were in the process of trying to get an apartment in Buford, so we were staying with my mom until then."

She told Davis she didn't remember what month that was, but it was late 1995.

"So that was back after y'all had got back from the service?" Davis asked.

"Yeah, I was already out and home. I got out of the army in '93."

He asked if she had anything else she wanted to tell him, but Kelly said she just wanted him to know about Greg.

"He can be crazy," she said.

Then Davis asked her about other men she was involved with. Was she in a relationship with someone at work? Kelly admitted there was one, a one-night stand. It was while she and Doug were having problems. Then she confessed to another. One guy named Ethan (pseudonym), she said, who didn't work there any longer. She couldn't remember his name. Then there was someone named Bill Johnson (pseudonym), who moved to Nebraska. She looked a bit guilty. She knew how it sounded to someone like Davis. He was obviously a family man, obviously a straight shooter. She said demurely she was just trying to be honest.

It did not shock Davis. He had seen a lot in two decades of law enforcement.

"I don't want you to think, 'Well, she was running around on him,' this was in the time that him and I were having major problems and I thought we were gonna . . . we were headed down the same road we had come from. Doug and I have had problems in the past, I mean—"

"Every marriage has problems," Davis said, looking at her sympathetically as he tried to earn her trust.

"Yes, I know. But those are the only three people that, you know, like I said Ethan, number one—"

Davis didn't let her finish her list. He asked if Kelly had told her friends during the weekend in Cherokee, North Carolina, that Greg said something about harming Doug. He wanted her to think Owen was the main suspect. She said she didn't recall telling her friends anything about Greg harming Doug or about anyone harming Doug for that matter.

"If I did, I don't remember. I mean, I don't . . . we talked about a lot up there and, you know, with Pamela, Pamela and I are like sisters and

I tell her everything. So at one point during the conversation, I may have. I don't remember. . . . I really, like I said, we talked about so much up there."

Davis asked about staying in the Winder motel with Owen. He wanted to know who got the room. Kelly said Greg's sister signed for the room. He also asked if there were other places she had been with Owen. She said she had not.

Davis turned the tables on her and stated bluntly, "In the back of Doug's car, we located a shovel." The shovel had actually been found in a search of the area near where the car was found.

"We had been doing yard work, here in the yard on the weekends when it was nice. Actually, there was—maybe I haven't looked—but there was two sitting out in our garage out in the . . . where his tools are at. There were two shovels sitting out there and I haven't looked to see if anything's gone from out there, but he had borrowed . . . I don't know whether he had borrowed the shovel from my mom or my dad or who he borrowed it from, but I know we had been doing some yard work up around the dog pen and, you know, around here."

"How about the light fixtures in the back? It's a light fixture that goes to a ceiling fan or something."

"We had taken the ceiling fan down out of here and he was taking them to the dump. There should've been probably some, it was racks back there that came out of our old dishwasher, some wires that came off of his old windshield wiper motor. . . ."

Davis wanted to get more information about Owen. Kelly Gissendaner explained the last time she talked to him, the conversation was essentially about him wanting to know how her kids were.

"When did he tell you that he wanted to get even with—"

"With me? Oh, that was when we first broke up. That was way back in, last year."

Davis went back over the breakup with Owen. He was testing her. Was she telling the truth? Would she change some of the details? He wanted to know whether Greg kept calling her. She said he called for the first week at her mother's house, but not at work. She said she screened her calls to see who it was before she answered.

He asked what else she had to tell him. Was there something he had not asked about, something that might lead him to Doug?

"I'm trying to find a reason that someone might want to do harm to Doug," Davis said.

"I know, I know, and that's what, that's all I'm trying to do, too. And I don't, I mean, I don't know if he had anything to do with it, but any avenue at this point is the only thing I'm looking at."

"Y'all . . . y'all have life insurance, is that correct?"

"No, we don't."

He asked about benefits from the service and insurance on the house. Kelly said she didn't think her husband had any insurance from the service and didn't know how much the house insurance would pay.

Davis showed her a booking shot taken by the Lawrenceville Police Department (LPD) after a DUI arrest and she identified the man as Owen.

"Okay," Davis said. "And this is the guy you had a relationship with at one time?"

"Yes."

"And y'all at one point were gonna get married?"

"Yes."

"When you told him that . . . you were leaving him to go back to Doug, what was his reaction?"

"I never really told him I was leaving him to go back to Doug because that wasn't the plan. It was just that we had problems and there was a lot of things he was doing that I didn't like around the kids."

Davis couldn't shake her. She relayed the same information time and again. Could she be telling the truth?

"Okay, and after he found out that you were going back to Doug?"

"He started threatening to kill me and kill himself, and told me he would get even with me or he would get me one way or the other is basically what he said."

"Kelly, at any point did he ever threaten Doug in any way?"

"Not that I recall."

Davis asked again about the lights on at the house that night and she said no lights were on. She explained that Doug always parked his car outside the carport so she could park inside. She also said her children were at her mother's house that night. She explained again about coming home after work, changing clothes and going out with friends. She drank about a half a glass of Seven and Seven and a bottle of Mudslide.

"What do you think happened to Doug?" Davis asked, trying another tactic. It was a standard interrogation tool. Get the suspect to guess what happened.

"Don't know whether he stopped on the way home to help somebody. I personally don't think he ever came home. There was no evidence to prove that he was ever here. I mean, like I said, when I left I left the lights off. When I came home, the lights were off."

"Is there a possibility that he could have come home and before he got in the door, somebody jumped him?"

"Not that I know of. Doug was, I mean, he knew how to fight. So my thing is if he came in my house and somebody jumped him, Doug would've defended himself and something would've been out of place."

"How about outside?"

"That I don't know. That I don't know, but there was, it was raining hard when I came home, 'cause I remember I had a hard time seeing. All the way down 85, I kept telling Pamela, you know, I don't feel good. I need to go home and I did. I had a bad feeling."

She said she didn't know why but a nagging feeling overcame her that something bad was about to happen. She wanted to go home. Pamela told her the feeling probably stemmed from the news earlier in the week that a friend's dad was dying of cancer.

"She said, 'I know you've been really upset about that.' Pamela said she had had similar feelings that something was wrong with her mom."

She rambled on about bad feelings and what Pamela said; then Davis stopped her and asked who the friend with cancer was and where Juno Lighting was located.

"Do you think personally that Doug could've got home and somebody jumped him out in the yard?"

"It's a possibility. I can't say for sure."

"I mean you know him better than I do."

"Yeah, yeah. I don't . . . I think if, there's too many, I don't know. I just feel that there's too many neighbors here that someone would've had to have saw something, you know, and I asked my next-door neighbor over here if he was home and he said he was home all night and didn't hear anything. So . . ."

Davis asked permission to have technicians come to the house and check the house with luminol for cleaned-up blood. The substance would illuminate chemicals in blood that cannot be cleaned up with everyday household cleaners.

"Okay," she said. "That's fine, and I was wondering why, you know, if y'all think somebody has been here in this house."

"That shouldn't have been?" Davis asked.

"Or shouldn't have been or, you know, met my husband outside. Then I guess it's run through my mind, too, that's why all this is being put in the house."

"We'd like to, our purpose is, we'd like to have permission from you, just oral permission. We just want to look."

"Okay, that's fine."

"You said something that, you know, you said you didn't see anybody anywhere near it—"

"Uh-huh."

"Our folks might can see something—"

"That I can't. They might can pick up on anything. I don't know, but, yeah, that's fine. My thing is Doug. I want to find out what happened to my husband."

"We would, too," Davis responded. "We'd like to know exactly where he's at and exactly where, what happened to him."

"I have three kids I have to explain it to every night."

"I know, where their daddy is. If there's something that we're overlooking, we need to know."

He asked again about conducting the tests, which might tell them something they don't already know.

Kelly Gissendaner said, "Like I said, again, I guess that's why. I guess it might have crossed my mind a few times, too, and that's why I had my door locks changed because I don't know where his keys are at. I don't know where Doug's at. I don't know what information they have, whether they have my address or whether they have his father's address, and then last night is the first night I've spent in my house alone. And I know all night long, I was . . . every little noise I heard, I was jumpity."

"What's your feelings about Greg?" Davis said, guiding her along.

"As far as whether I think he did this or not, or just feelings period?"

"Feelings period."

"Greg and I were friends, you know, that's why he, I guess, he called me all the time, 'cause when we left, when I said this was the last time, he told me he cared about me, and, you know, 'I don't want to lose your friendship. Can we be friends?' That's fine. That's the only reason I talk to him," Kelly stated.

"But he's still mad because you—"

"He never let on to me that he, like I said, if he made remarks to me, I guess I just blocked them out and—"

"I guess my feelings are that he had made remarks to you that he was . . . he was gonna get

back at you one day and after y'all had been together for over a year."

"Yeah," Kelly answered.

"Anyone else we need to talk to?"

"No, that's basically it. That's . . . and, you
know, like I said, I finally sat down last night and
had a moment to myself where there wasn't nine
hundred people running in and out of my house,
so I could think and I could try to figure out what
happened, I guess, to the point of trying to explain something to these kids every night."

"Well, we certainly are going to try to find
Doug. We hope he's okay when we find him."

"Me too," Kelly said. "I mean that's our prayers
every night. That's my kids' prayers. How do you
explain to a three-year-old that sits there and says,
you know, 'I prayed every night for my daddy to
come home and he's not here. Please bring him
home or find him before or, you know, before
I come home from school, or at least by the time
I get home from school.' I mean how do you explain to a three-year-old when he says, 'My daddy's
lost and can't find his way home.' How do [you]
explain to him why his daddy's not here?"

"I wish I knew how I could explain it to him,"
Davis said.

They had been speaking for a little more than
an hour when Davis turned the tape recorder off.

Technicians arrived about six hours later,
around ten in the evening after obtaining a
search warrant. Kelly Gissendaner was there
with two friends. The luminol test was a last
resort for investigators, because the chemical
reaction destroys other evidence in a crime
scene. And it is not all that reliable. Often the
test incorrectly shows evidence of blood because

some household products, such as bleach, cause
the same reaction. But the test can also lead investigators to other evidence, such as bloodstains on the wood floor underneath carpet.

Investigators with the Gwinnett County Police
took out their gear and sprayed luminol in various
sections of the entryway and outside. Luminol is a
powdery substance made of nitrogen, hydrogen,
oxygen and carbon mixed with a number of liq-
uids, including hydrogen peroxide. The chemical
causes the iron in hemoglobin to glow bluish
green under ultraviolet light.

They were prepared to videotape whatever
they found. But after two hours of spraying and
searching, they found nothing.

Calls came in to investigators, and chance
meetings brought more information. A coworker
of Doug's ran into an officer at a convenience
store. He confided that Doug had complained
that his wife's ex-boyfriend was giving him a "hard
time."

By the following Saturday, there was still no
sign of Doug Gissendaner. Davis and two other
officers walked the Gissendaners' neighborhood
at dusk. No one reported seeing anything. No
one heard anything.

Friends decided to conduct another search
the next day. More than two hundred people
turned out. Bell, the DNR officer who found
Doug's car, was there. He had been to the scene
and down the road many times during the past
week. He had driven over to a nearby cemetery
and anywhere else he could think of where
somebody would do something mean to someone else. He wasn't sure what drove him to continue. The mystery, perhaps? The family? He had

three children of his own and had worked hard all his life, beginning with a $1.45-an-hour job as an orderly in a Waynesboro, Georgia, hospital when he was still a high-school student. Like Doug, he was an army veteran.

Bell told a colleague, "That body has got to be here someplace."

The group decided to extend the search four miles, walking along the shoulder, peering into ditches and up the bank to the deep woods of loblolly pines and scrub oaks. They searched for more than four hours. They found rusted car doors and illegally dumped building materials, beer cans and plastic cups. Litter lined the rutted road like townspeople at a parade. They found billfolds, none of which belonged to Doug. Driver's licenses. But no one found any sign of Doug Gissendaner. No clothing, no sign of struggle—just garbage, north Georgia red clay and piney woods.

Friends gathered at Kelly Gissendaner's home, including coworker Pamela Kogut, one of the women Kelly had been with the night before. Kelly told Pamela she had been to a fortune-teller. A man and a blond woman were standing over her husband, the fortune-teller said, and he would be dead if he was not found by 11:00 A.M., Sunday.

Police continued interviewing friends and business associates of the Gissendaners'. They heard time after time that Doug Gissendaner was the kind of man who would help anyone in need. He was a former soldier, and at thirty years of age, he was in good condition, hefty, in fact, and more than six feet tall. He felt comfortable in his surroundings. Even though he had seen war, he was home, and home was safe.

Davis went to the Gissendaner home that evening. A friend who had organized the search was there with other people. Davis asked to see Kelly. Davis was told she was asleep.

"I'll speak with her later," Davis said, and walked away. Kelly Gissendaner was a woman who stood out in a crowd, almost six feet tall. She met people's greetings with a sure distance, a coldness. In the South, there's a saying about someone who keeps her distance. You say you can't get any closer to her than her elbows. Folks felt that way about Kelly Gissendaner. She seemed pleasant, nice enough, but she kept most people at arm's length.

Stan Hall, who worked as a police investigator for a time before moving to the district attorney's office to run the Gwinnett County Victim Witness Program, met with Doug's parents. They seemed a typical American family, and investigators found nothing in their background or their son's that would lead them to believe he would end up a victim of foul play. Sue Gissendaner, Doug's mother, said she felt close to her son and his wife and couldn't imagine what had happened. But she confided there had been tension between Doug and Kelly. They had been divorced for a time, but they had been remarried about two years when Doug went missing. And two of the children were fathered by other men, the two boys, the youngest and the oldest. The middle child, Kayla, was Doug's, yet family and friends told investigators Doug treated all the children as his own.

By Tuesday, February 18, Doug Gissendaner had been missing eleven days. His wife had given interviews, told about a reward, told about her husband's good nature. One reporter had asked for a photograph the newspaper could publish. Kelly walked to the wall and pulled a framed picture of Doug off and handed it to her.

"It's the only one I have," she said.

The reporter responded she didn't want to take such an irreplaceable object.

Kelly said, "It's okay. You can take it."

Investigators worked full-time on the case, and had already assembled a hefty file. They were well on their way to what would become four full binders of material. Davis and Henry decided it was time to see Owen's sister, Belinda. She and Kelly Gissendaner were good friends. They met when Belinda hired Kelly to work at a telemarketing company and soon began socializing. Belinda and Kelly had the same wacky sense of humor and passed many lunch hours together laughing. They went out for drinks. Kelly usually drank beer and loved to dance. She had the essence of a free spirit, which Belinda wondered about, since her friend had three children. Belinda felt close to the middle child, Kelly and Doug's daughter, Kayla, who was five.

Next to Kelly, Belinda's short stature and small frame looked even shorter and smaller. At twenty-seven, Belinda wore her curly brown hair long and was at home in jeans and T-shirts. Despite her small size, she had the force of a powerful woman, the kind who did not tolerate people who mistreated her, who was more apt to attack than draw back. She had already beaten up any number of boys by the time she graduated from Spartanburg High School in Spartanburg, South Carolina. She studied cosmetology after high school and had held a number of jobs in a variety of businesses through the years. By the time she met Kelly, she was on her second marriage. She didn't judge Kelly for having a failed marriage. Doug and Kelly Gissendaner were separated when Belinda and Kelly were the closest.

One day at work, Kelly noticed a picture of Belinda's brother, Greg, on Belinda's desk. Looking at his brown hair and blue eyes, Kelly thought he was cute, so Belinda introduced them. As she spoke to investigators after Doug Gissendaner's disappearance, she emphatically remembered the date: September 22, 1995. A month after they started dating, Greg asked Kelly to marry him. But six months later, they broke up. Belinda again knew the date: April 21, 1996. She knew another date: October 18, 1996, the day Kelly Gissendaner came back into their lives. Kelly asked Belinda to meet her at the bar in the Suwanee Holiday Inn. Kelly was always fun and Belinda missed her friendship. She went. Kelly asked about Greg, and Belinda ended up giving her his pager number. Belinda would regret her decision for a long time.

Years later, Belinda, who had gone back to using her maiden name, would say she still had so many regrets when it came to Kelly Gissendaner. One was letting Kelly come to her home in October 1996 because it led to her reuniting with Greg. Belinda regretted renting a motel room for Kelly and Greg the next month. Belinda told Investigator Henry her brother went with Kelly to Virginia in January for a few days. She was under the impression Kelly was attending a child support hearing for her youngest son. She told Henry how to find her brother. Greg, who delivered furniture, was now living in an outbuilding at the home of a friend in Cumming.

Davis collected Belinda's date book, in which she wrote down everything she did every day. He wanted to make copies to use as evidence of the motel visit and Belinda's driving her brother to meet Kelly.

Next on the list of interviews was Greg Owen. The trail seemed to be leading toward him. Two officers went to Owen's home, which was little more than a toolshed. Owen wasn't surprised to see them and agreed without hesitation to go with them to Gwinnett County Police headquarters in Lawrenceville. They were not going to give Owen the benefit of talking to them at his home. They wanted him on their turf, to keep him off-balance. They had a statement from Kelly that he had made threats against her. Could he have possibly directed his anger at her husband?

Gwinnett County's law enforcement operation is not a typical arrangement. The county police enforce laws while the sheriff's office runs the jail and provides protection in the courthouse. They work from different offices.

Owen shuffled into the police department's building with the officers at about six-thirty. As with most interrogation rooms, Gwinnett County's was designed to keep the suspect on edge. It's classic police procedure for the actual interrogation to begin long before any questions are asked. It begins with a straight-backed chair to keep the suspect feeling powerless and uncomfortable. The room was sparse. Besides a chair for Owen, there was a table and chairs for the detectives. It's designed to isolate the suspect, with the hope he will feel closed in and want to do what he needs to do to get out of there as soon as possible. Davis would continue the method he used with Kelly Gissendaner, to avoid confrontation and keep things conversational. He wanted to build Greg Owen's trust. Davis gave him a Mountain Dew.

The interview began fifteen minutes later, at about 6:45 P.M. Owen, a slightly built man of twenty-five, said he met Kelly Gissendaner in September 1995 and dated her until the following April.

He told the same story his sister did about her involvement in his relationship with Kelly. He and Gissendaner got back together in October 1996. They saw each other about every weekend, he said.

Davis looked at Greg Owen and said, "Did you know Kelly was having relationships with other men?"

Surprise swept over Owen's face, perhaps the first show of emotion all night, and he said simply that he did not.

"When was the last time you saw Kelly?" Davis asked.

"I talked to her on the phone Friday night. Called her at work from a pay phone to tell her I was on my way home."

He asked her to go out with him. She said she couldn't. She had plans with friends. He stayed home, instead, with a friend. Owen said he did not know about Doug's disappearance until a friend told him on Sunday. Investigators pressed him on his relationship with Kelly. He said he was sad to lose her, but he would never hurt her or himself. He looked meek and nonconfrontational. Investigators were dismayed that Owen didn't yield any new information.

When the officers drove Owen home after midnight, Ricky Lee Barrett, a teenager who lived in the house, told them he and Greg were together from eight o'clock, Friday night, until midnight. They watched television and drank some beers. Owen had some Jack Daniel's, too. Barrett said he fell asleep about half past midnight. The next morning, a friend picked up Owen before nine o'clock to go to work.

Greg Owen had an alibi.

Chapter 4

Twelve days after Doug was reported missing, Sergeant Bell, of the Department of Natural Resources, was once again patrolling Luke Edwards Road. This time, he wasn't looking for poachers. He was looking for Gissendaner's body. He told himself he'd go once more and he'd be through. He had already been out there so many times he could not count them. He drove down the road and, as always, didn't see anything suspicious. He turned around and headed back toward the paved road. That was it, he thought. His search for this guy he had never met was over.

He looked to his right and saw something that looked like a trash bag. It was about a mile from where Doug Gissendaner's car was discovered. He hadn't seen it before. Fleetingly he thought it was probably nothing and he started to drive on, but something made him stop the vehicle. He walked up into the woods. As he went up the embankment, he saw a large hole on the other side and thought it would be the perfect place to hide a body. He walked on. As he got closer, he thought whatever he was looking at looked more like a person than a trash bag. The way it was bent over with its back to him made him think perhaps it was someone hiding. Fear overpowered him. A person hiding meant only that he had done something wrong, and Bell was out in the middle of nowhere by himself. He slowed his pace and set aside the fear. He walked closer. In a small clearing, about one hundred yards off the road, was the body of a man, hunched over on his knees, his face in the dirt. The man wore a black jacket, blue jeans, hiking boots. Flies circled the body, but there was no smell. Bell stopped about twelve feet from the body, knowing he did not want to disturb a crime scene. He couldn't tell anything about what the man looked like, but he knew he had found the man he had been hunting for so long. He couldn't get a signal from his cell phone, so he went back to his truck and drove toward the paved road to call his office.

"Call Gwinnett County," he told the dispatcher. "Tell them I have found the item they have been looking for."

The woods along Luke Edwards Road were a particularly forlorn place to die, especially on a February night at midnight. The red-dirt strip of road showed few car tracks but many prints from deer and dogs left behind as they loped through the woods. Winter cold came fast as the sun sunk below the horizon shortly after six and the wind picked up, rustling the gangly pines and offering the only sound. Isolation. There was no moon on February 7 and frigid rain fell much of the night.

Years later, Bell would say, "It's a puzzlement to me, the way I found that body. I almost passed it up, and it was there all along, and I had never seen it."

The mystery of Doug Gissendaner's disappearance was unraveling. Police roped off the woods with crime scene tape, and the identification unit came back to Luke Edwards Road. Davis and the other law enforcement officers stayed outside the tape and watched quietly as the unit worked.

Police called Assistant District Attorney (ADA) Phil Wiley, a twenty-one-year veteran of the district attorney's office. His name suited him. He had the agile, wily look of a fox, the determination of a man who worked a blue-collar job— probation officer—for seven years before going to Atlanta Law School at night. He had been interested in criminal law for a long time and knew he could never be on the side of the accused. He had no interest in defending someone he knew was guilty, and, conversely, as a prosecutor, he could not try someone he believed was innocent.

"Never have, never will," he said a few years later when talking about the Gissendaner case. The Gwinnett County District Attorney's Office gets about 4,500 cases a year and presents about 3,500 to a grand jury.

Wiley grew up in north Georgia and had not strayed more than a hundred miles to find a place to call home. He was familiar with the horse farm country where the body was found. He had already heard of Doug Gissendaner's disappearance on the news.

"You never know what's going to happen with a missing person," he said later. He learned the police were focusing on the wife, not necessarily as the killer but as someone who knew more than she was saying. He saw his job at the scene as trying to keep the press away. Television crews and print journalists huddled at the spot where the dirt road met the pavement, far enough away to keep them from seeing what investigators saw. A man had been out in the woods for twelve days. Even though it had been cold most of that time, it was not a preserved body. He had shared the space with all sorts of animals.

Wiley thought, *That's got to be one of the most horrible ways to die.*

The crew began processing the scene after dark. Huge lights illuminated the dank woods. Police cars jammed the dirt road. The police photographer took pictures of the body, hunched over in the leaves with most of the back exposed when the jacket rose up. The photographer took about an hour, and when he finished, a policeman took a black wallet out of the back pocket of the man's blue jeans. As expected, it contained a driver's license for Douglas Morgan Gissendaner. Davis and another detective stepped over the crime scene tape when the ID unit was done and removed the body. It was work Davis had done many times before, but it was sad work nonetheless. About twenty minutes later, Doug's body was driven to the morgue.

Davis went to Kelly's house first to tell her a body that resembled Doug had been found. He told her where and that he would be back in touch once a positive identification was made. That would come after the medical examiner conducted an autopsy the next day. Davis then went to the home of Doug and Sue Gissendaner Sr. This was unlike most other times he had to tell parents their child was dead. He had gotten to know the Gissendaners over the course of more than a week. He found them to be honest, hardworking people, a nice couple. On the ride over, he thought about how he would tell them. What words would he use. He wanted to be professional. He wanted to be kind.

He climbed the stairs as he had done so many times before. He rang the doorbell. Politely they asked him in. He dropped his news as gently as he knew how. He had sat with family after family in his years as a funeral director. But as always, despite how soft his voice was, the news exploded like fireworks. Sue crumpled. Doug Sr.'s eyes welled. Davis reiterated what he had told the wife, now widow. Positive identification had not yet been made, but Doug's wallet was in the pocket of the man found in the woods on Luke Edwards Road. It wasn't far from where his car was found, Davis told them. The glimmer of hope in an incomplete ID was little consolation to the Gissendaners. They knew son, father and husband was gone.

The autopsy began about nine-thirty the next morning. Dr. Steven Dunton, the medical examiner, was in charge of finding out how Doug Gissendaner spent his last moments. Dunton's assistant removed a black nylon jacket with a Pro-Formance Shocks patch. Inside a pocket were eight ACDelco spark plugs, a white pen and a NationsBank receipt showing a deposit of $219.71 on the day Doug Gissendaner disappeared. He had fifty-four cents in one pocket of his blue jeans and thirteen cents in the other. No money was inside his Dale Earnhardt wallet.

Dunton found four stab wounds in the scalp, neck and left shoulder. The deepest was to Doug's shoulder, going in about five inches. He surmised a single-edge knife—four to five inches long—was used. There was no trauma to the brain, the doctor said.

Dunton compared Doug's dental records to the body and concluded the dead man on the table was indeed Doug Gissendaner.

Chapter 5

It was days and days before police released Doug Gissendaner's body to the family for burial. As much as they were grieving and wanted to honor their son's memory, Doug Sr. and Sue knew it was not their place to make the funeral arrangements. That would be up to Kelly, but they would be there to help her with whatever she needed. She chose Flanigan Funeral Home in Buford. It was one of the few mortuaries that hadn't been bought by one of the nation's major funeral home companies. It was started in 1990 by Junior and Sharon Flanigan, and the couple worked there side by side—he as a funeral director and embalmer and she as the secretary. Junior Flanigan started working in the funeral business in 1969 as a sophomore at North Gwinnett High School. He drove the ambulance, which at the time was a duty for all funeral homes in the county. The dream of owning a funeral home dawned for him as a young man and he served his time at Patterson Funeral Home in Atlanta, one of the largest in the region.

He had the easy, soft-spoken manner folks

want in the man taking their loved one to a final resting place. He told every customer he was there for them. He wanted to give individual service, compassionate service, to make a difficult time easier.

"Every day's a different day in the funeral business. Every family's grief is different." It was a refrain his employees heard regularly. He grew up in Buford and knew the community intimately. That was the service he wanted to provide the people he had lived among all his life. Even when he worked in Atlanta, forty miles to the southwest, he lived in Buford. There was no other place to open his business when the time came. He chose South Lee Street, just off busy Buford Highway.

Flanigan did not know the Gissendaners and did not often handle funerals for murder victims, but he approached the event as he would any other. He expressed sympathy for their loss and guided them into the arrangement room off the foyer in the warmly appointed Colonial-style building.

Doug's parents, his sister, and Kelly sat with Flanigan around a wooden conference-room table. Kelly seemed stoic. Sue Gissendaner cried. They gave him the information for the death certificate and the obituary. The children were to be listed as Doug's children. When Flanigan asked how many death certificates they would need, Kelly answered quickly.

"Ten," she said.

Doug Sr. looked at Sue in surprise. She knew what he was thinking. How would Kelly know so quickly how many death certificates she needed? They certainly did not know. Did this woman who married their son and bore their only grandchild research how many certificates she'd need when her husband died? Doug Sr. pushed from his mind an idea that had been brewing for days. He knew Kelly could be mean, but to have something to do with her husband's murder? No, it wasn't possible.

They talked about who would speak and what music Kelly wanted. Kelly wanted her preacher, Don Burroughs, to do the primary eulogy, and the Gissendaners' pastor from First Baptist Church of Buford would give remarks as well. Visitation would be from seven to nine on Saturday night and all day Sunday. The funeral would be in the chapel at eleven o'clock, Monday morning.

Kelly Gissendaner arrived unexpectedly at the funeral home on Saturday morning. She told Junior Flanigan she wanted to see her husband's body, which was lying on a dressing table in a holding room. There was nothing Flanigan could do to make Doug's body look more like Doug or even a man. It was mauled and decomposed. The casket would be closed. An open casket wasn't even discussed, but Kelly wanted to see him anyway before they put him in the oak casket they had selected.

Flanigan described her as "very cool, nonchalant."

Saturday evening came and the family gathered to receive friends. The first of what would ultimately be five hundred people came through the door and down the wide hallway to the visitation room to speak to the Gissendaners. Sue sat in a wing-back chair most of the time, unable to do anything but grieve. The casket was covered in a spray of flowers.

Kelly Gissendaner arrived early Sunday morning, but it was afternoon before Doug's parents got to the funeral home. It had been a grueling evening for them. People continued to come to pay their respects through the day. Visitation is important in the South, and people will stand in line for hours to do their duty. That was the way with the people of Buford, where it wasn't unusual to have two days set aside for visitation.

The family gathered at Flanigan's on Monday, February 24, to say good-bye to Doug. He'd been dead for more than two weeks. Doug's widow, his parents, his younger sisters, his children, all sat together in the chapel as the minister from Atlanta Church of Christ spoke. Doug and Kelly had been attending the church for a short while, and had made some friends, many of whom sat vigil with Kelly during the long days of his disappearance. Burroughs talked about Doug and his goodness, his acts of kindness and how he had gotten involved in the ministry of the church. He talked about salvation, and because Doug was saved, the minister said he knew Doug was in heaven. He spoke long and hard.

Doug Sr. grew weary. The minister had been speaking for more than an hour. Doug Sr. gestured that it was time to wind it up. He tried to get the minister's attention. Finally he raised his arm and drew his hand across his neck. "Cut it," Doug Sr. wanted to yell.

The Reverend Bobby Owens, of the First Baptist Church of Buford, offered brief remarks to the family.

Kelly Gissendaner read a poem she wrote. It ended with the verse: *I want to go to heaven's gates, and if I wash my sins away, I know it won't be too late.*

Then came the strains of a Garth Brooks song, "The Dance," a song about loss, a song about being grateful for not knowing how painful an end could be, because if the vocalist had known, he might have missed their time together. Doug Sr. and Sue appreciated the sentiment, but the idea of playing a country music hit at a funeral seemed a bit bizarre for their Baptist upbringing.

The Gissendaners and law enforcement officials wondered about the ending of Kelly's poem. Was it some sort of clue about Kelly Gissendaner's involvement in her husband's murder? Was she tipping her hand? Despite a lack of hard evidence, she had become their prime suspect. They weren't looking for anyone else.

When the funeral ended, they all got into their cars for the sixty-mile trip to Timber Ridge Cemetery, in McDonough, Georgia, Sue's hometown, where Doug would be buried. The trip down was quiet, and when Doug Sr. and Sue and their daughters arrived, they walked solemnly to their seats under the tent. Kelly had not yet arrived. Many of the Gissendaners' friends were there, huddled under the tent at the grave site. Sue Gissendaner had known some of them since childhood. Her father was a longtime and much beloved principal in the town of about eight thousand people.

Pallbearers brought the casket and laid it on the bier. And the Gissendaners waited. More time passed. They wondered what had happened to Kelly. Could something bad have happened to her? A wreck? Traffic? She should have been right behind them. An hour passed, and finally the Gissendaners saw the car pull in. Kelly and some church friends moved quickly to the grave site. Kelly Gissendaner looked like a distraught cartoon character. She waved her hands and gestured and looked sad. Her in-laws returned a steely stare while Sue Gissendaner's family minister began the short graveside service, which ended in her son's body being given over to the earth near her beloved father.

When the service ended, Kelly Gissendaner stood and walked to her husband's casket. She pulled out a Matchbox car with flames painted on the hood and placed it on top of the casket. She collapsed into Sue Gissendaner's arms, crying.

Later, Doug Sr. and Sue learned their daughter-in-law was late because she stopped at a Cracker Barrel restaurant for lunch and then spent time shopping in the restaurant's store. They were astounded. It scored high on the list of unbelievably inconsiderate things they had seen people do.

The Families

Chapter 6

Families brought together by marriage sometimes form an uneasy alliance, while work mates stand in for relatives considered odd or lacking. Family members, however extended, twist through each other's lives like licorice. For better or worse. A trip to the grocery store can feel like a family reunion. In many small towns, people go from the delivery room to the grave knowing virtually the same folks. They play together, work together, grieve together and, most especially, worship together. And when young people get married, their families often know each other or know people who do. "Who are your people?" is a question posed of the rare stranger. And next, "where do you go to church?"

Sue Mobley grew up in such a place: McDonough, Georgia. Her father, Tombs Mobley, was the high-school principal. He ruled with an iron fist and a loving smile. Where others would bring out the paddle to punish wayward students, Mr. Mobley, as he was known by practically everyone in town, would simply look at the student like he was an unfathomable disappointment. He'd talk to them about their waywardness. "Do you realize . . . ," he would start his speech. He'd talk about the infraction, why it should never happen again, how it relates to character and being a good person. Before long, the student would feel lower than the bottom rung of a chain-link fence. More than one child wanted to cry out, "Just go ahead and beat me." Yet, he had a great sense of humor. He could laugh at himself, although only outside of the school hallways. He served as principal for forty years. His first students were the grandparents of his last.

His pastimes were basketball and golf and he took them into the schoolhouse with him. He worked as a basketball coach for years. He also believed the family was the backbone of America. No law and order without it, he would say. When a family dissolved, it weakened the world for everyone, he said. *Family*. Mr. Mobley protected his fiercely.

The Mobley household, forever rambling through a big white Victorian near downtown, was an active place. The First Baptist Church of McDonough centered their world. Sunday-morning worship, Sunday-evening prayer meeting, Wednesday activities. As a young girl, the woman who grew up to be Sue Gissendaner went to Girls in Action (GA), an organization sponsored by the Southern Baptist Convention's Women's Missionary Union. Girls must be six to take part. First grade and GAs, Sue was excited. She could be a GA for all her elementary-school years. (The organization exists to forge a love for missions, to help young girls see God's hand in the world and to figure out their

place in it. It offers a lifelong map for doing for
others in God's image.)

She never had a problem with her father
being principal. He was beloved and that carried
over to her throughout her high-school years.
For college, Sue chose Tift College of Education,
where she enrolled at the Forsyth, Georgia,
campus with the goal of being an educator like
her dad. Two years into her classes, Sue decided
she would rather work. She got a job as a teller in
a bank and was living at home.

In January 1963, her best friend, Nancy, asked
if Sue would go out with her boyfriend's best
friend. His name was Doug Gissendaner and he
was a student at North Georgia College. He
wanted to be a pharmacist and chose the college
in Dahlonega, not for the Military College or its
scenery in the Blue Ridge Mountains, but because his brother and sister went there. The population of the gold-rush town of Dahlonega
doubles to eight thousand when school is in ses-
sion. Its location in the middle of the Chatta-
hoochee National Forest draws students who
hike, climb mountains, hunt and fish.

Doug had little time for that. He was a worker.
He had been working most of his life. His father
was a farmer, who instilled in him that passion
for work. The elder Gissendaner went only as far
as the ninth grade, but he provided for his family
and remained steadfast in his desire to see that
all his children would go to college.

Doug's mother was a teacher who had set that
career aside to work in a peanut-processing plant.
The money was better. It was hard work, but she
shared her husband's desire to put all three children through college. Years later, they would

remain in awe that their parents managed to do so.

Doug Gissendaner helped out by working each summer. He graded peaches at the Federal Inspection Service. He went to Ohio to build a pipeline. Whatever it took.

He had transferred to the University of Georgia by the time his friend Curtis Martin asked him to go on a blind date with this girl named Sue. She drove the hour and a half to Athens for dinner and a movie. They clicked. Doug thought she was attractive and fun. Sue thought the same of him. They saw each other about every weekend; she usually went to Athens.

Within a few months, they knew they belonged together. They decided to get married the next November. Her parents had their reservations. He still had two more years of school and they were so young. However, they liked this young man who seemed earnest and hardworking. They knew he would be a good provider.

Ten months after their blind date, Doug Gissendaner and Sue Mobley were preparing for their evening wedding at the First Baptist Church of McDonough. That morning, Sue and Doug decided they needed to hide the car they would drive after the ceremony. They didn't want *Just Married* or *Doug & Sue 4ever* painted all over their Corvair. Or worse, they feared someone would throw a dead fish into the backseat.

Sue was driving the Corvair; Doug was following. They were traveling out into the countryside down a gravel road. At one point, Sue slammed the brake, bringing the car to a halt, but not before it slid into a tree. The car they didn't want scratched or scraped was now wrecked.

"It shook her up pretty good," Doug Sr. remembered many years later. "It shook me up pretty good, too."

They went ahead with the ceremony.

For some reason—perhaps the accident, perhaps the momentous occasion with all their family and friends assembled in the church on Macon Street in her hometown—Sue started to cry during the ceremony. And she cried. And cried some more. She didn't sob, but tears streamed down her face like a summer afternoon shower.

"Are you sure you want to go through with this?" the minister quipped. The knot of friends and neighbors—many of whom remained close through the decades to come—laughed.

And, of course, she did want to continue. In Doug Gissendaner, she had found a man of integrity, who shared her sense of family, a man she could count on.

When the minister told Doug he could kiss his bride, Doug and Sue started laughing. They knew laughter was a great way to begin a marriage.

For the first two years, Doug was in school and Sue worked as a bank teller in Athens. Doug had changed his major to business. When he graduated, he was hired at International Harvester, in Atlanta. They happily struggled through those first years. Doug Gissendaner knew how to plan and to save. His bills were paid on time, his savings account grew. He positioned himself and his wife for the years to come when children would center their world and Sue would stay at home to care for them.

Two years after they were married, Sue found out she was pregnant. It was an uneventful nine months before the December 1966 birth of their son. They named him Doug after his father, but they chose something different than Doug Sr.'s name for a middle name. Douglas Morgan Gissendaner was born at Crawford Long Hospital in Atlanta, twenty-one inches long, eight pounds two and a half ounces.

"All boy," the proud father told his friends.

He was a happy child. Little Doug would sit in his high chair with a Kleenex box, pull one out and throw it up in the air, laughing like he had seen the greatest comic on earth. Cars caught his attention early on, and he would crawl underneath any car his dad or a friend was working on. Sometimes all he'd have on was a diaper, but he thought he was a mechanic. "That boy is talented with his hands," Doug Sr.'s mechanic friends would say.

Doug Sr.'s job took the family to Mississippi. Little Doug was six. The family built a house and had just moved in when Doug became fast friends with twins down the street. One afternoon, he came in covered in mud and missing one of his new boots.

Sue yanked out the garden hose and started spraying him to get the mud off, all the while fussing and fretting.

"What have you been doing?" the mother demanded, and launched into a tirade worthy of her lecturing father as she squirted water on her son.

"There was this big monster . . . ," Doug began, and threw his arms up in the air to denote something bigger than Sasquatch.

Sue could not help but laugh. It turned out he had ridden his bicycle into a drainage ditch. They laughed about it for years.

Sue and Doug imparted their values to their

children with a firm hand and a loving touch. The two ideas were not disparate in any way to them. Family centered their lives.

When little Doug started playing baseball, he had trouble seeing the pitch. Sometimes it would hit him in the face before he saw it. His teachers, too, wondered about him. They said he wasn't cooperating. He wouldn't read in class.

That's when the parents found out their son was dyslexic. He was fitted for glasses. A tutor taught him skills to help him read. Some words he could make out with no problem. Others he turned around or saw in reverse. He learned to compensate for his problem. He worked and worked. Little Doug would sit at the kitchen table while his mother prepared dinner and he would struggle over his schoolwork. It was a homey kitchen of dark wood cabinets and country furnishings, with a small dining area that included a sliding glass door to the deck. His attitude toward his studies was as determined as his father's toward work. "Work hard and you will succeed" was his father's mantra.

And even though he worked diligently, he was self-conscious about his learning disability. He thought he was not smart. He had a hard time learning to read.

When little Doug was four, his sister, Lee, was born. Then three years later, another sister, Jennifer, was born. They lived in a white Colonial-style home in a quiet neighborhood in Buford, Georgia, north of Atlanta. When they moved there, they were decidedly in the country. Within years, they would be within walking distance of the Mall of Georgia, one of the biggest shopping centers in the state.

Their lives revolved around each other. The elder Doug traveled frequently with his work as a salesman. He sold self-lubricating ball bearings and traveled across the Southeast. Regularly, it was Sue and little Doug with the girls at home. The son had a happy demeanor. Not much worried him. And that, in turn, caused his sisters to think they could get through most anything. Their brother would be there to protect them, to make everything seem right again. It was a happy house, full of children and animals. Mickey, the golden retriever, Tigger, the tiger-striped cat, and Dusty, the mutt.

The house was a comfortable one, nothing trendy. La-Z-Boys and well-used end tables. An entertainment center held the television, which was the family's main amusement. Pictures of the children at all ages covered the top and filled the heavy wood fireplace mantel. Visitors could mark each one's evolution with a simple scan of the room.

The family regularly traveled to McDonough to spend Sundays with Sue's family. Or to see the Gissendaner clan. It wasn't only their core group they considered family. It was the extended family that belonged to them and shaped them. They also took in one of Doug's friends, Teddy Beam. He lived with the Gissendaners for several years. There was always room for everyone they loved.

In high school, young Doug took auto mechanics. He retained his love of working on cars. He'd tinker awhile and then fuss when it wasn't going right. He'd buy a car, then another, and work on them in the basement. A 1957 Chevy was a labor of love he shared with his dad. It was a beat-up, run-down wreck when they got it. They primed the engine and painted the outside. Father and son did all the work except the upholstery, bringing the car to near perfect condition, enough to win trophies in area car shows. It was matador red with an India ivory interior. Smooth. The only time the father would let the son drive it was to back it out of the driveway.

The Gissendaners wanted their son to go to college. He had other ideas. He was tired of struggling with reading and writing. He wanted a job. He wanted to work with his hands. He graduated from Buford High in 1985 and went straight to work at a series of blue-collar jobs. He was a working man and that's what he wanted.

Four years later, his sister followed him across the stage to receive her Buford High diploma, and the next fall, she enrolled in her father's alma mater, the University of Georgia. About that same time, Doug's friend Teddy introduced him to a friend of his sister-in-law's, Kelly Brookshire.

Chapter 7

Anger. Alcoholism. Divorce. That was the fabric of Kelly Brookshire's early life. Her mother, Maxine, knew only brute strength and drunken living from life on a farm with six brothers, two sisters and parents who would just as readily get a switch to beat them as to feed them. The children missed day after day of school when their father forced them to pick cotton, grueling days of stripping the white bolls from the prickly stalk under the hot Georgia sun. Maxine was nearly grown when the family got its first indoor bathroom. They lived with need and want as constant companions but their father always had money for booze. A favorite pastime was sitting on the front porch cussing at passersby.

Maxine married Larry Brookshire, her second husband, in 1967. They lived with his mother and brother. Within a week of their marriage, Maxine was pregnant. They were both working in a chicken plant. Maxine quit when she was three months pregnant. She stopped smoking, but continued drinking. Maxine and Larry had used speed together before she became pregnant, but she stopped.

After Kelly was born the next year, they stayed on with Edna Brookshire, Larry's mother. Just like Maxine's first husband, Larry Brookshire liked to drink and he continued to do speed. Maxine liked a beer now and then, too, and it led to fights. Larry would hit Maxine. Several of her relatives say they regularly saw bruises on her body.

A son, Shane, was born to them in 1969. Maxine went back to work and Larry's grandmother and aunt took care of Kelly and Shane.

By 1971, the marriage was over. Maxine had been having an affair. Kelly was three years old. Eight days after the divorce was final, Maxine married the paramour, Billy Wade, a Vietnam veteran whose service left him scarred and angry. According to court records, he was even more abusive than Larry Brookshire had been. Fights were an almost daily occurrence. Wade frequently accused Maxine of cheating. He would hold her down, bruising her arms and shoulders. Folks outside the house did not know what was happening, because Wade did not mar her face or anyplace someone could see the evidence of abuse. He threatened to kill Maxine and her children. The only time, it seemed, he would be silent was when he would pass out on the floor drunk.

During the fights, Kelly usually scooped up her brother and hid with him in the hall closet or under a bed. At night, she lay awake, listening to Wade's threats from the bedroom next door. She would not sleep until they ceased. At some point, she feared, she would need to help her mother flee from a burning house or to step in and protect her mother. Sometimes her stepfather would lock the children in their room while he beat their mother. Kelly was always afraid. Thunderstorms, loud noises, being surprised, all caused her to cry and to shake.

Typically, Billy Wade would throw Maxine to the ground and sit on her as he punched and spit on her and pulled her hair. Maxine would spit back and try to claw him with her fingernails.

"Go ahead and leave, you slut," he mocked her. "You bitch. You whore."

Maxine would run to the car. He'd chase her down, throw open the hood of the car and jerk the wires out.

"I'll kill y'all one night while you're sleeping," he would say. The next night, he might say, "I'll burn down the house with all of you in it."

He kept a shotgun behind the door of his bedroom. The shells were in the dresser drawer.

One day when Kelly was nine, Billy and her mother were outside the house and started arguing. He punched Maxine. She clawed at him ferociously; he started to bleed. His blood was all over her clothes. Then Maxine picked up a wheel and flung it into the windshield of Billy's truck. The children watched, growing increasingly frightened. It was lasting longer than most fights.

Kelly ran to a neighbor's house. The neighbor called the police. The deputy offered to take Maxine and the children to safety, but he did not arrest Wade. Maxine told the officer simply, "I have nowhere to go." And so she stayed.

Once, Billy Wade purposely turned on his truck, knowing a cat had crawled inside the engine to get warm. The children sat helplessly as the engine ground up the animal.

"That's one less cat to deal with," he sneered.

Kelly was about ten when Wade came home one night and checked the odometer of Maxine's car. It seemed she had driven more miles than he expected. He called her a whore and accused her of cheating on him. Maxine went to leave, but the brake lines of her car had been cut. The next morning, she went into the woods, and when she came out, he harangued her again, accusing her of cheating.

"Bitch! Whore!" he screamed.

"I'm going to kill him," she said, and went to get his shotgun. She intended to end it for good, but the shells had been moved. That same day, Maxine heard sirens coming from the direction of a neighbor's house, where Kelly had slept the night before. Maxine and Kelly ran over to find the neighbor in the front yard yelling, "I shot him. I shot him." Their neighbor said he had choked her and tried to rape their daughter, so she shot him. Kelly saw the dead body, struck down with a .22. Bullet holes marred the walls.

Kelly was not immune from Billy Wade's temper and jealousy. When she left her bicycle in the driveway, Wade came after her.

"I'm going to beat your ass," he screeched as he called for her to come outside. Meekly she stepped from the house. He grabbed her neck and choked her. She gasped for breath.

"You'll remember next time," he said.

Maxine didn't say anything to Kelly when Billy Wade finally released her and she went back inside the house. Kelly felt alone in the world.

Wade used a belt, a switch, a flyswatter, a hand. If he wasn't beating her, he was ignoring her or calling her names. He told her she was stupid. She was ugly and worthless.

"Your daddy don't want you, that's why you're here with me," he would say. "No one wants you." It was an especially tough statement for the teenage Kelly to hear.

Kelly's mother, too, was excessive with her discipline, once using a hickory switch on Kelly with such force it broke and lodged in Kelly's leg. Maxine Wade took on the persona of the abused spouse. She was jumpy and irritable. She couldn't sleep and lived in constant fear of being beaten. She was emotionally unavailable to her children. Years later, Maxine would say she remembered precious little about her children's elementary- and middle-school years. She spent all her time making sure the house was picked up and dinner was ready when Wade got home so he wouldn't get mad. She also forced the children to stay outside.

Billy Wade would not allow the children to have contact with Larry Brookshire. And when an aunt tried to deliver Christmas presents from their father, Billy turned her away with an angry snarl.

School proved difficult for Kelly. She could not concentrate. She didn't do homework. Even her days in elementary school brought daydreaming and distraction. Her teachers said she had a hard time attending to tasks, but she tried and was cooperative. By third grade, she was already below grade level in reading, and before long, spelling and math. All she could think of was whether her family would live to see the next day. Would Wade kill her or her mother? She couldn't sleep. She was also angry that her mother stayed with Wade.

When Kelly was ten, she learned Wade was not her biological father. Her aunt secretly took her to see Larry Brookshire. Kelly longed for some semblance of a father-daughter relationship with him,

but instead she found only distance. He seemed
cold to her. Brookshire had remarried, and his
wife had a daughter. Kelly had been away too long.

About the same time, her mother rented a
U-Haul one morning after Billy Wade went to
work. They packed their things. And finally Maxine did what Kelly had been begging her to do for
at least three years. She left. They moved to Athens
until the divorce was final and then to Winder,
Georgia.

At North Gwinnett High School in Suwanee,
Kelly Brookshire might have been a student, but
she didn't feel part of Bulldog pride. She didn't
wear the red and black. She didn't hang out with
friends at the local McDonald's. She felt alone.
And she felt worthless.

By the time Kelly was a teen, she believed all
the adjectives Billy Wade had used for a decade
to describe her. But the people she passed in the
school hallway knew nothing of her inner turmoil. She presented a demeanor of a girl who was
just a high-school kid in a small Southern town.
Not a care in the world. Kelly, however, couldn't
bring anyone home from school, couldn't have
boys come to the house or to pick her up there
for a date. Prom was out of the question. Instead
of rooting for Bulldog football, Kelly was working
at a local McDonald's. She was sixteen when she
got her first job. The next year, she went over to
Play It Again Sam, a video store, to work.

Maxine married again briefly, but that was as
sorry a union as the other three. Before long, it
was her and the two children living in a trailer in
Winder. Kelly continued to keep to herself in
school. To cover her pain of not belonging, she
acted the class clown. The other students looked

down on her, called her "trailer trash" behind her back. Even some mothers considered Kelly not good enough to be friends with their children.

In her senior year, Mitzi Smith noticed Kelly, always alone, seemingly forlorn. She thought Kelly looked like a "sleeper kid," one of those teens you just don't see. Mitzi asked Kelly to sit with her at lunch. They talked. They passed notes. They got together a couple of days a week after school.

Mitzi soon began suspecting Kelly might be pregnant. It seemed obvious to Mitzi, but Kelly tried to hide it. But before long, the pregnancy was school news. And students looked down on Kelly even more. Kelly told Mitzi she didn't know who the father was. It could be either one of two guys—a fellow student or someone Kelly refused to name. Mitzi was not as concerned about who the father was as she was about the baby. Kelly had not been to a doctor. Mitzi pestered Kelly until she made an appointment.

For her part, Maxine did not know anything about the pregnancy until Kelly was six months into it. Most everyone who saw Kelly suspected she was pregnant, but Maxine was clueless. Some speculated the mother was simply in denial. Others said she was so out of touch with her daughter that Kelly was nonexistent. How could she not notice?

When told of the impending grandchild, Larry Brookshire reconnected with his daughter. He wanted the child to bear his name.

Kelly graduated from North Gwinnett in June 1986 and two weeks later gave birth to a son. She named him Brandon Brookshire. Kelly finally had someone whom she could love unconditionally and who could love her in the same way. Her life had meaning and she doted on the boy.

A few months later, she became reacquainted
with a guy she went to high school with, Jeff Banks.
They hung around together, talked, and he got to
know Brandon. Within a few months, Jeff and
Kelly were married. Brandon was not quite a year
old. They spent a lot of time with Kelly's family, especially Larry Brookshire. One night, they were
having dinner and Larry asked Jeff to pass the
corn bread. When he didn't, Larry threw a bowl at
him. They lunged at one another and started fighting. Other family members pulled them apart.
Larry Brookshire stormed from the room.

Kelly shouted, "Run, he's gone to get his gun."

Banks fled, running down the street with Brookshire close behind brandishing a .357 Magnum.
Banks got away safely and called police. He
dropped the charge after he and Kelly split up several months later. They were married for six
months. It was 1987. Kelly Brookshire was nineteen, the mother of a fatherless toddler and living
in a trailer in north Georgia with her mother.

She went out with friends and the group was
arrested for shoplifting some cassette tapes. She
pled guilty and received one year of probation.
An argument over whether Brandon should go
to church ended with Larry Brookshire slapping
her across the face with such force, she fell over
backward in her chair. She couldn't keep a job.
She worked at Stouffers Hotel at Lake Lanier for
less than four months, then didn't work for a
time. She got a job at Intracorp for a year, then
Control Data. Coworkers thought she was imma-
ture and could not make adult decisions. Money
problems haunted her. The roller-coaster life
continued unrestrained.

Chapter 8

Before Greg Owen became Kelly Gissendaner's lover, alcohol played a starring role in his life as well. In some ways, his childhood mirrored Kelly Brookshire's. His father, Bruce, loved Budweiser more than his family. Bruce Owen grew up in Union, South Carolina. Union is like all Southern towns that are held together by a textile mill. There are those who have much and those who have little. The mill owners run the town, own the town, and the workers get what the owners decide they'll get. It is an insular place, a place with no major highway nearby. It was unknown to outsiders until a young woman named Susan Smith killed her young sons by letting her car slip into a lake.

Bruce Owen was long gone by the time that happened. In fact, he had lived in more places than a career soldier. In his case, however, he was not serving his country. He was attempting to stay a step ahead of the law and all the people to whom he owed money. Spartanburg, Clinton, back to

Spartanburg, Greenwood, Greer—Owen moved across northwestern South Carolina like a gypsy.

When he was nineteen, he married Myrtis Gregory. She was sixteen. She had lived most of her life in Spartanburg, South Carolina, in a little house not far from the town's cotton mill, where her father worked in the slasher room. In her teens, the family moved fifty miles south, to Clinton, and Myrtis was reacquainted with Owen, who had dated one of Myrtis's sisters for a time. He was independent, had a good job in a body shop, and Myrtis was ready to be on her own, away from her three sisters and five brothers. They went to a preacher's house and he and his wife stood up for Myrtis and Bruce. It was November 1967. Within months, they moved into his mother's Clinton apartment, he was drafted into the army and Myrtis was pregnant.

After training at Fort Jackson in South Carolina and Fort Benning in Georgia, Owen received his orders: Vietnam. The United States' involvement in Vietnam simmered to the boiling point in stages by the time he arrived in country. The first major skirmish between U.S. and Vietnamese forces had taken place just two years before and antiwar protests had grown to the point of fifty thousand people descending on Washington, D.C., over three days in October 1967. Bruce certainly knew of the protests, but he went willingly to serve his country. In the eighteen months he was gone, Myrtis lived with his mother and gave birth to her first child, Belinda.

When he received his discharge, he joined his family at his mother's home, a shotgun house on mill hill in Clinton. Their second child Gregory Bruce—named for his mother's maiden name and his father's first name—was born on St. Patrick's Day in 1971. The family lived for a time in Columbia when Bruce and Myrtis were hired by BFGoodrich. It did not last long.

"We just weren't plant workers," Myrtis said when they returned to Clinton. "We didn't like being confined inside."

He worked at this body shop and that body shop, drifting around as he lost one job and got another. Soon enough, he'd be laid off or fired or just not show up, and when he couldn't pay the rent, he and Myrtis would move someplace new. They went on a trip to see a friend in West Virginia in 1973 and got stranded for two weeks when the transmission in the car gave out. They had to wait until his brother could come from South Carolina with a used one and the two of them installed it. It was during that trip that Myrtis discovered she was pregnant again.

Katina was born in 1974. They were living with his mother again. Myrtis spent most of her time in the house taking care of the children while Bruce worked. One Friday night, he came home and told her to get fixed up; he was taking her to a movie. Excitedly she primped. He ran to the store. Bruce did not come home that night or the next. Myrtis heard he was at the home of a friend, so his mother drove her there. He was sitting in a car with Myrtis's best friend, a girl of barely sixteen who lived down the street from his mother.

"You believe me now, don't you!" Myrtis screamed to her mother-in-law, who had refused to believe her son was cheating on his wife. Myrtis suspected it for some time. All the anger of the deception, all the hard work of caring for three children younger than five, rushed out. Myrtis jumped from the car. She ran to the passenger-side window, leaned in and beat the girl in the face. The girl's mother arrived soon after at the Owen house and yelled at Myrtis.

"You're lucky you've got a daughter left!" Myrtis screamed back.

Not long after that, Bruce came home, his face bruised. He said he had an accident. Myrtis believed the girl's father or brother beat him up.

She took him back, thinking she could not make it on her own.

"It's over with that girl," he pled. "I was wrong. Let's work things out for the kids."

They moved into a trailer in Columbia, and the fourth child, David, was born in 1976. Jaundiced, he stayed in the hospital for two weeks. He had been home only a few days on Greg's birthday that year. Myrtis had baked Greg a cake, green as usual to honor him and St. Patrick, and he and Belinda were at the table. Katina was playing on the floor. Myrtis went into her bedroom to check David, who was lying on the bed. He was not breathing.

"Bruce, Bruce, the baby!" she screamed. Greg's blue eyes grew huge as Belinda stared at him in horror. Bruce ran to his wife and started CPR, all the way to the hospital. Push down on his tiny chest, blow into his mouth. After an autopsy, doctors told them it was sudden infant death syndrome and he was dead before they left the house.

The family gathered at the chapel in Gray Funeral Home in Clinton. Her parents' preacher performed the service. Fifty people showed up. David Owen was buried in a cemetery down the road. Sometimes it seemed he was the lucky one, for life for the Owen children only got worse.

They moved almost immediately and left everything they owned. First to a little town named Joanna and then to Spartanburg. Their frequent moves left the Owen children the perpetual new kids in school. Friendless, they clung to each other. Belinda performed her duties as eldest impeccably, especially for Greg, who was shy to the point of being withdrawn. He feared his overbearing father, who was more likely to use his fists against his son than a reassuring hand.

Myrtis had become overprotective of the children, especially two-year-old Katina. She slept with the child, not wanting her out of her sight.

Bruce Owen regularly yelled at his children and his wife. He called them names and made demeaning comments. Their father's beatings were frequent and unpredictable. And he had started getting drunk every day. Everything and nothing annoyed him. He drank Budweiser when he could afford it and whatever was on sale when he couldn't. Often he spent all the grocery money on beer.

One day, when Belinda Owen was twelve, her father had her mother up against a wall, choking her. Belinda snatched up Greg and fled next door. The neighbor called police and they all stood outside while officers tried to talk to Bruce. He had his wife in a bedroom, holding her down with a knife. Police coaxed him out and took him to detention. Myrtis vowed to leave, but as with all the other times, she stayed away only a few days. And as with all the other times, she did not pursue a charge of criminal domestic violence. Belinda did not forgive her mother for going back for quite a while.

Years later, Belinda said, "I don't know why

she went back. She couldn't make it, or she loved him."

Nothing the children owned was safe from their father's rage. He regularly went into their rooms and tore up their belongings. He smashed the model cars Greg had meticulously made. He pulled the tape out of Belinda's cassettes that she bought with the money she earned at Wendy's. When their mother would leave, he would destroy whatever the children left behind. Once, they went back to get their clothes to find he had slashed them with a knife and left them in a heap on the living-room floor.

When Belinda was fourteen and Greg twelve, she was driving the family home from a visit with their grandparents. The car was a 1972 Grand Prix. As she rounded a curve, the tire dropped off the side of the road. She overcorrected, as an inexperienced driver would, and the car bounced side to side on a bridge. Her brother and sister hit the door panel and the seats and her father hit the window. When the car finally came to a stop, Belinda looked around and saw blood spattered all over the interior of the car. Her father sat motionless. She thought she had killed him.

Everybody else got out and ran from the car. Her father remained motionless. Finally he roused up. He was not hurt. The episode, however, had a profound effect on Bruce Owen. The family started attending church, and Bruce stopped drinking. Their lives took on a calmness they had never known. Bruce and Myrtis even began teaching Sunday school at Valley Falls Freewill Baptist. They were still living in a trailer and had little, but life seemed better, much better. Bruce started his own body shop and the preacher came out one afternoon and blessed it. Bruce hired an employee.

But then one customer didn't pay, and another, and soon Bruce was out of business. Beer became his friend once more. The mean Bruce Owen returned.

One day when Greg was about fourteen, he skipped school. His father took the call. Myrtis was at work. Bruce stormed into the room Greg and Belinda shared and punched him in the face.

"You are stupid!" Bruce shouted. "You will never amount to anything!"

Greg cowered while Belinda stormed into the room in his defense.

"Stop it!" she cried. "Don't hit him. That's not what he's for."

But for Owen, his fists were all he knew when he was drunk. And Myrtis had been slapped into submission. She could not defend her children.

"He was one way or another," Belinda said years later about her father.

School offered no respite for Gregory Owen. He was always among the smallest in the class and provided an easy target for bullies. He suffered from a severe inferiority complex. His strong-willed sister watched in despair. Self-doubt permeated everything he did and said. He had always preferred to play by himself, even as a young boy, and the loner in high school is a mark for everyone.

He kept up his grades until the first semester of his eighth-grade year. He just didn't care anymore. He spoke only when spoken to, if then. He sat by himself at lunch. No friend ever came to the house, but he always had Belinda. They shared a room well into their teen years, decorated with unstacked mobile-home bunk beds and a particleboard dresser that the drawers never sat in properly. They spent hours in their room not making a sound because they didn't want to anger their dad.

Greg could count on Belinda to stand against all those who opposed him. His father, other kids. When a group of guys jumped him at school one day, Belinda returned the next and beat them all up. She was the fierce mother figure in his life. When she got her first job—working at Wendy's— she took her first paycheck and bought him some Reeboks and some pants. His pants were always too short, his shoes were tattered and cheap. They called them bo-bos. When he cried, she was the one to wrap her arms around him. When it got too bad at home, they'd leave together. They'd ride around and listen to music. She knew how he felt and she knew what it was doing to him.

She managed to hang on with the family, despite attending eighteen schools from the time she started first grade until she graduated from Spartanburg High School in Spartanburg, South Carolina.

Greg Owen's school career ended about the same time. He dropped out without making it out of the ninth grade. He went to work as a stock boy at a local grocery store. He was fourteen. By then, he started drinking a little and smoking marijuana. He stood barely five feet eight inches, with the skinny build of a boy who didn't eat enough. He decided he had been everybody's punching bag for way too long.

He and Belinda were at a pool hall near their home one afternoon. Their mother came in and the three were enjoying some time together.

Myrtis Owen said she was tired of being home and going nowhere, but Bruce Owen thought different. He showed up at the pool hall and started belittling her and the children. Greg stood between him and his mother and said, "Do not embarrass Mama. You need to get your clothes and leave."

Bruce Owen finally did. Myrtis met another man, and when Bruce Owen wanted another chance, she finally had the courage to say, "You've one-more-chanced me to death. I can't do it anymore."

They divorced in 1989. He left her owing the landlord for back rent and any number of other bills. She paid him every Friday what she could until she was paid up. No more moving.

Years later, Belinda would realize all the moves, all the violence, left a void nothing could fill. She had no pictures of her childhood. No report cards. No uniform from her dad's army service. She lacked all the belongings others have that say "look here's a family." Even in the most dysfunctional of clans, there were the holiday pictures of happy times. Christmas morning or Easter Sunday. Not for the Owens.

Chapter 9

In March 1989, Doug Gissendaner was twenty-three and still living with his parents. One evening, he went to see Teddy Beam, his childhood friend who lived with the Gissendaners for a time. Also there that evening was Kelly Brookshire, a friend of Teddy's wife, Lorraine.

Something about her was intriguing to Doug. Perhaps it was her "rescue me" nature. Doug Gissendaner was the kind of man who could not turn away from anyone who needed help. As he and Kelly spent more time together, he learned more about her and met her young son, Brandon. Doug immediately took to Brandon, then only three years old. He always liked kids and Brandon was easy to be around, a cute and fun-loving child. In Doug, Kelly saw everything her family wasn't: stable, hardworking, steady. It didn't escape her that Brandon was the same age that she was when her stepfather came into her life.

Doug's parents met Kelly at Teddy's house not long after the two started seeing each other. The elder Gissendaners had stopped by to see Teddy, already married with children. He was an electrician and had the kind of family life he had always yearned for, secure and loving. The younger Doug brought Kelly and Brandon to meet his parents. Kelly struck Sue Gissendaner as a personable and fun young woman. It didn't bother Sue that Kelly had been married before and that she had a small child. She seemed full of life, the kind of woman who could pull her reserved son out of his quiet world.

Doug and Kelly decided to get married the following September. Sue planned it and the elder Doug paid for it. A few days before the wedding, Kelly was sitting at the kitchen table in the Gissendaners' home, waiting for Doug. They had planned to go for the blood tests required for a marriage license. Doug had been driving the gray 1986 Monte Carlo he bought for Kelly. Kelly loved the car. It was the newest car she'd ever owned. Doug walked into the kitchen and sheepishly told her he had dented the bumper a bit pushing a stranger's car that had broken down on the road.

Kelly screeched. She couldn't believe Doug would do that. How could he damage her car helping someone else? What idiot does such a thing?

Sue Gissendaner said, "Why are you so mad?"

Kelly could only yell louder. Sue had never seen her act like that.

"Kelly, you need to calm down," Sue said, reaching to calm her future daughter-in-law.

Kelly jumped up and stormed outside. Sue followed her and they looked at the damage. Sue didn't think it amounted to much. Kelly got in the car, backed out swiftly and zoomed down the street.

Doug Gissendaner Sr. found out later that his

son had taken out a loan with a 27 percent interest rate to buy the car for Kelly. And the car she traded had a lien on it because she didn't pay her bills. Their credit rating was going the wrong way with every financial decision they made.

The First Baptist Church of Buford never looked lovelier when Kelly Brookshire married Douglas Gissendaner. Sue and Doug Sr. had some reservations about the match, but nothing serious. They had grown fond of Brandon, and Doug seemed to love him and Kelly deeply. There was no turning back for Doug Sr. and Sue once they learned Kelly was pregnant, due in March 1990. Shortly after the wedding, Doug and Kelly lost their jobs and they moved into the trailer with Maxine Wade. Their lives were perpetually in turmoil. Maxine yelled at Kelly, who yelled at Doug. But yelling was not Doug's nature, and when he wouldn't fight back, it annoyed Kelly even more. Once she became so enraged, she picked up a baseball bat, but before she could swing it, her brother grabbed it from her. Kelly and Doug did not know how to communicate with each other. Kelly had no model for a good marriage, and while Doug did, he did not know how to handle someone so confrontational one minute and so alluring the next.

Doug's work life seemed headed for nowhere, and with one child to feed and another on the way, he decided he needed something steady, something with benefits. He chose the U.S. Army. He enlisted in December 1989. He spent his nine weeks of basic training at Fort Knox, Kentucky, where he would also learn to be a loader on an M1A1 Abrams tank. His 5:00 A.M. to 9:30 P.M. days kept him not only busy but exhausted. He worked hard and learned the skills he needed to survive, should he be called to defend his country.

As with all new recruits, the toughest part was learning to get along with fifty strangers. But Doug was an easy enough fellow and he quickly made friends. He learned basic rifle marksmanship, including the M16A2 rifle's history, how to clean it and how to fix it. Range procedures, firing positions, safety precautions, it all figured into a long day's work.

Doug had kept his weight at his high-school level and was proud of the eight-mile march and the various training exercises in the field that tested his smarts and endurance. During one field exercise, he and the other recruits had to crawl two hundred meters under flares and simulated M60 machine-gun fire.

Doug was faithful about sending his checks back home to Kelly to pay bills, especially to make the payment on the Monte Carlo. Soon, however, Doug's parents learned Kelly was not making the payments. A bank had placed a lien on Doug Sr. and Sue's house and checking account, confusing them with their son. No one at the bank thought to look at the Social Security numbers. The Gissendaners cleared up their credit and their name, but they didn't want their son to come home to even worse credit and no car. They started making the payments themselves.

Doug tried to concentrate on his studies. He was assigned to be a loader on the M1A1 in the 1st Armored Division, commonly known as "Old Ironsides." The job required loading the main gun and the coaxial machine gun ready box and used the machine gun installed at the loader's station. The loader also searched for targets and acted as air or antitank guided missile guard. It's a job that usually went to the second most experienced crewman because the loader's job required he observe the area around the tank and monitor digital displays. He had demonstrated his competence to his superiors.

On March 28, 1990, almost exactly a year after Doug and Kelly met, Kayla Renee Gissendaner was born in Lawrenceville, Georgia. Doug was twenty-three years old. He was a proud daddy and despite his reservations about whether his wife could be a good mother, he vowed to stay with her.

He was sent to Wiesbaden, Germany, in August, home to some eighteen thousand soldiers in the Rhine Valley. Doug wanted Kelly and the children to join him, so he secured a home on the base where they would live.

They flew over the next month. As part of his training, Doug was in the field for days and weeks on end. Kelly stayed in their home on the base. Soon word got back to Doug that while he was gone, she had parties. There was talk she was seeing other men. A few times Doug was called back from maneuvers to straighten her out. She wasn't paying their bills and the company commander had to get Doug a loan so he could take care of some long-outstanding debts.

The base chaplain was called in to counsel them.

"She was an embarrassment to the command," Doug Gissendaner Sr. said years later.

In one of their meetings with the chaplain, Kelly exploded in rage. Doug sat passively. She jumped on him, smacking him on the shoulder. The chaplain had to pull her off her husband. Kelly and the children were sent back to the States.

"She's big and she's strong and she's mean," Doug Sr. said some years later.

Meanwhile, the United States was gearing up for what seemed an inevitable confrontation with Saddam Hussein over the oil in Saudi Arabia. It came to a head on the morning of August 2, 1990, when the Iraqi Republican Guard invaded Kuwait and seized control.

Operation Desert Shield was launched by the United States on August 7 to protect Saudi oil. On November 29, 1990, the United Nations Security Council issued an ultimatum: if Iraqi dictator Saddam Hussein did not remove his troops from Kuwait by January 15, 1991, a United States–led coalition was authorized to drive them out.

Two days after the deadline, coalition forces launched air attacks against Iraqi targets, followed by ground forces. On February 27, Kuwait City was liberated.

Doug Gissendaner was nearby in Turkey as a member of the 1st Armored Division. Kelly lived with her mother for a time, got mad at her and moved in with her father. That ended badly and she moved in with a friend. Doug could not be sure one day to the next where his children would be living.

On leave in July, he came home a war hero. By October, his army career was over.

Life with Kelly had not improved by the separation. Turmoil reigned. Within a month of his return to the States, Kelly had joined the army. Her work career had been spotty at best and the time she was with her husband overseas was fun. Perhaps the army would show her a road to a better life or at least a life other than Winder, Georgia.

Doug told his parents he intended to get a divorce. They feared Kelly would fall back on her tried-and-true method of holding on to their son: she'd convince him yet again she would change. She'd be a good wife, a good mother. She'd watch her spending. If all else failed, she would pull out the one threat that would work every time: she would keep Kayla from him.

"She would beat him down," Doug Sr. remembered. The elder Gissendaner did not tell his son but he believed Kelly was emotionally abusive. He knew it was unusual but Doug Sr. considered his son an abused husband.

Doug told his father, "I love my daughter. I love those kids."

"Son," his father answered. "There's something wrong. She's going to have to fix herself."

By the time she left for basic training at Fort Story on Cape Henry, near Virginia Beach, Virginia, she and Doug had decided their marriage was over. They filed for a legal separation in July 1992. It had been a long three years.

Kelly was assigned to the hovercraft program. The facility included miles of sandy beach and served as a training facility for all the branches of the armed forces. But Kelly did not want to live on the base. She learned she could get off-base housing if her family was with her. She called Doug and asked him to join her. He put her off at first, but eventually her persuasion skills proved too strong to overcome. He agreed to go. His parents were incensed. They did not understand why their son kept bailing out this woman. They saw nothing worth saving in the marriage.

But before Thanksgiving, Doug was home in Georgia. He went ahead with divorce proceedings, and in May 1993, Doug and Kelly's marriage was officially over. Doug—and his parents—thought they were through with her forever. They would have to find a way to remain part of Kayla's life. They'd do what it took, but they did not want to have any dealings with Kelly.

"Now's the time for you to start over," Doug Sr. told his son. "Get you back on track."

"Yeah, I really let her fool me into thinking she really loved me, but she didn't," his son responded.

It was one of those morning talks father and son shared over the years in the country kitchen in Buford, Georgia. They'd drink a little coffee and get their day started right. The elder Gissendaner cherished those moments. He agreed to help his son financially. Doug was welcome to live there. Eventually the parents would end up giving him thousands of dollars to get out of debt, to start anew.

Chapter 10

Army life did not suit Kelly Gissendaner. Everyone but Kelly knew it wouldn't. In fact, Doug's parents even wondered how in the world she got in. Five o'clock reveille and nine-thirty lights-out was never her lifestyle, even when she was a small child.

She made a few friends as she learned to be part of the hovercraft program, but she desperately wanted out. One way, she knew, would be if she was pregnant. She started a relationship with William Stewart, a fellow soldier.

Soon enough she was pregnant. And discharged. She never intended to stay with him, never intended for Stewart to be involved in the child's life. He was a sperm donor, in her opinion. A means to an end. He died of cancer not too long after he and Kelly were together. He was twenty-six.

In September, Kelly returned to north Georgia. Jonathan Dakota Brookshire was born in November. She called him Cody. Kelly was living with her mother in a trailer not far from the Gissendaners. It was close to Maxine Wade's job as a correctional officer at Phillips State Prison, a facility that houses inmates who have been in trouble at other facilities or who might hurt themselves or others. All levels of mental-health therapy were available.

Kelly Gissendaner worked there for a time. A short time. She was fired for improper relations with an inmate. Personnel records are sealed, so it is unknown precisely with whom Kelly was involved or what they did, but it is clear she had sexual relations with an inmate while she was a guard.

The feminist's quip "a woman needs a man like a fish needs a bicycle" would have been lost on Kelly Gissendaner. She was a woman who didn't like to be without a man. Some of her friends muttered behind her back that Kelly didn't seem capable of making decisions for herself. She went with the flow and let others guide her, for better and for worse.

She filled the time spent apart from Doug with other men. Men she worked with, men she met elsewhere, following a pattern started in her teen years. She was twenty-five.

Kelly met Belinda Leicht when she applied for a job with International Readers League of Atlanta, a magazine telemarketer. Belinda was the interviewer when Kelly came for an interview. If Kelly got the job, Belinda would be her supervisor. She started with a few simple questions about Kelly's previous work experience and what sort of job she was looking for. Kelly seemed pleasant, and Belinda liked her right off. Kelly looked around Belinda's work space and saw the family pictures Belinda had on display. One was of Greg.

"He's cute," Kelly remarked. She liked his big blue eyes and long brown hair that hung in wisps on his forehead. His goatee was sparse, but it set off the angle of his chin just right. It was a kind face, one that had obviously seen sorrow. He could only be called slight, and seemed short, shorter than Kelly. But his size did not trouble her. He was a man and he was cute.

Belinda hired Kelly in customer service and collections. The more they worked together, the more Belinda liked her. She was funny. They had a lot in common. Moving around as much as she had as a child left Belinda without a lot of lasting friendships. She and Kelly went to lunch together. Then they started going out after work, often to bars. Kelly loved to dance, even though she wasn't particularly good at it. Her large frame and lack of coordination made her look more like a man than a woman. And the more she drank, the more she liked to dance. Beer was usually her drink of choice.

Belinda knew Kelly had been married and that she was separated from her husband. Kelly never mentioned her father, but she told Belinda about her mother. She could be mean, Kelly confided. She had been married three times and didn't pay her daughter much attention. She was a corrections officer at a local prison.

Belinda spent time with Kelly and her children. She didn't like the way Kelly yelled at them. Belinda thought Kelly talked to them just like her mother talked to her, but Belinda gave Kelly room to make mistakes. She commiserated with her. Belinda's father had been equally distant and demanding. And Belinda did love Kayla. With no children of her own, Belinda grew close to the girl. Belinda didn't understand why Kelly Gissendaner wanted everyone to think she was going to church. She might have been a faithful churchgoer, but, to Belinda, Kelly's actions said otherwise. The F-word was a standard of her vocabulary, drinking a favorite pastime. Another thing she noted: Kelly still lived with her mother and, in fact, had never had her own place.

When Kelly asked to be introduced to Greg Owen, Belinda thought it would be a nice match for her brother. He had dated just three women in his life and Belinda had asked each of them out for her painfully shy brother. This was just one more fix-up. Belinda thought he could use the companionship of a fun girl. Her brother, Belinda thought, was more in love with the idea of not being alone than in love with any of the women he had dated. He just wanted companionship.

Belinda Owen considered Kelly Gissendaner to be one of her best friends. Belinda invited her to spend the weekend at her house, and she asked her brother to come over. Greg and Kelly hit it off.

Greg Owen worked all sorts of odd jobs since he quit school. Stock boy at a grocery store, furniture refinisher. He did dynamite blasting, one of his favorites.

Whenever Belinda saw her brother and Kelly, they seemed happy. However, the longer they went out, the less often Belinda Owen saw them. She never saw her brother by himself. He had lived with Belinda for a time, but he had moved out to live in a small building behind the house of a former girlfriend, Lori. Their families were tied in many ways. Greg dated Lori and was friends with her younger brother, who was a teenager. Lori was best friends with Greg's sister Katina.

Belinda started seeing troubling signs in her brother's relationship with Kelly Gissendaner. She bossed him around. Kelly went to Virginia to try to get child support for her third child and demanded Owen go with her. He did. She had

angry spells. On Greg's birthday, Kelly threw a
bottle of Jack Daniel's Belinda had given him out
the car window on their way home.

Myrtis Owen met Kelly at Belinda's house. She
seemed high-strung and wild, like a girl who liked
to party a bit too much. Not to say Greg didn't also.
Greg had a bad history with women, his mother
knew. They cheated on him. She wasn't so sure his
relationship with Kelly would last. Three children
seemed like a lot to take on, Myrtis thought.

"That's a ready-made family," she told Belinda.

One Christmas, Kelly brought her children to
Myrtis Owen's house. They seemed like sweet children, well-behaved. She thought of Kelly as a good
mother and the children acted like they were
proud of her.

Doug Gissendaner knew his ex-wife was seeing
Greg Owen. Doug met him when he went to pick
up the children one weekend and saw him a
time or two thereafter. He didn't have a feeling
about the relationship one way or another, but
he worried about Owen's influence on the children. He seemed shiftless and he heard rumors
he drank heavily and smoked pot. Doug made
no distinction between his one biological child
and Kelly's two. He loved them all, and many of
his family members were especially proud of the
way he acted as dad for all three. It would have
been easy for Doug to refuse to accept Cody as
his son, to take his mother's indiscretion while
Doug was married to her out on him, but Cody
was his own as much as Kayla and Brandon.

Finally Greg Owen and Kelly Gissendaner
broke up.

On occasion, Doug would see Kelly when he
picked Kayla up or dropped her off. Sometime

around Christmas 1994, Doug started seeing Kelly again. They spent time with the kids and started going to church.

When his parents found out about the relationship, they pled with Doug to discontinue it. Doug was working on the assembly line at Pro Shocks, doing well. He'd straightened his finances out. He was a popular employee, whom everyone considered a friend.

"Your mother and I are very upset about this, Doug," his father said. "Son, please do not go back with her."

"Dad . . . Dad," he said in the gentle tone he always used in tough situations, "I've got her going to church. She's promised she's going to take care of the kids. We're going to get a house. We're both going to work on the financial stuff."

His father was adamant.

"You and the kids are welcome anytime, but don't bring her over here."

They remarried in May 1995. The Gissendaners did not attend.

Doug served as the primary caregiver for the children. He woke them, made their breakfast and took them to school. He was the one who made sure they had lunches or lunch money and clean clothes. He loved to take them to Six Flags, an amusement park outside of Atlanta. Doug would spend hundreds of dollars on the entrance fee and all sorts of food and memorabilia during a day's trip to Six Flags. Whatever the children wanted, it was their day. Doug Gissendaner simply wanted a happy family of his own. He wanted a home. He had so much love to give and the children latched onto him like a dead bolt lock. They all called him

"Daddy." Biology did not matter. He considered them all his children.

But when Kelly found out he had spent hundreds of dollars at Six Flags, she exploded. How could he do such a thing? How could he waste money like that? She, however, would have had no trouble spending the money on herself for clothes or going out to eat with her friends or for liquor.

Most mornings, Doug would take the children to school and then stop by for coffee with his dad. They had become more like friends. They would talk about the kids, talk about work. Doug's father would try to advise him about the trouble in his marriage to Kelly. She would call Doug at work so often, it was becoming a problem for him with his supervisor.

"Please get away from her," his father told Doug. By fall, Doug Sr. thought he had finally gotten through to his son.

"Got to go to work," Doug would say after their talk. He'd stand and put his arms around his father and say, "Dad, I love you." He'd walk out the door. The elder Gissendaner was hopeful that Doug would finally be all right.

In September 1995, Doug and Kelly separated. The Gissendaners were ecstatic. But early the next year they were back together. Kelly told Doug she couldn't make it without him. She had no family. No one loved her.

They started going to Atlanta Church of Christ and met some nice couples. Kelly fit into the women's groups easily and some of the women befriended her. The Gissendaners volunteered for outreach activities, including passing out flyers about upcoming events. They even went to Sunday school.

Doug and Kelly found a house in a small subdivision in Auburn that was for sale. It was a ranch with three bedrooms and two baths, a nice-sized kitchen, living room and dining room. Doug went to his father for money. Doug Sr. refused. He remembered it as one of the hardest things he ever did.

"I will not give you any money or help you as long as you are with her," the father said. "Tigers won't change stripes."

The younger Doug went to his uncle, his father's brother, and asked him for money. He turned him down, too.

Doug managed to get a high-interest loan to buy the house. They moved in just after Christmas 1996. Doug's hopes that they would be one big, happy family flared brightly once again.

But what Doug did not know was that one evening Kelly Gissendaner called Belinda Owen and asked to meet at a local bar. They were once again working in the same place—at Rooms To Go—but Belinda had little to do with her.

Belinda got straight to the point.

"What do you want?" she asked.

"I want to talk to Greg," Kelly responded. "Here's the pager number."

And then Kelly said something that meant one thing when Belinda heard it, and another after Doug Gissendaner disappeared.

"I'm going to stay in the house long enough and then I'm going to get rid of him."

Belinda felt torn. She knew her brother cared for Kelly Gissendaner. She knew he would want the pager number. She passed Kelly's number on. Perhaps this time her brother would find happiness. Kelly could be a lot of fun and she had adorable children. It was a ready-made family.

Chapter 11

At twenty-five, Greg Owen didn't have much going for him in his life. He worked odd jobs, most recently for a longtime family friend who owned a cabinetmaking shop. He had lost his license to drive the car he so loved due to a drunken driving conviction. His relationship with his beloved sister was rocky—ever since he and Kelly became serious with one another. He lived with a much younger roommate, Ricky Lee Barrett. Kelly stood out as a bright spot. Where he was weak, she was strong. In many ways, he remained the same frightened little boy who cowered when his dad screamed, who relied on his big sister to pull him through troubled times.

Gwinnett County police officers met the afternoon of February 24 to review the Gissendaner case. They had a taped interview with Barrett in which the roommate now said Greg Owen left the night of the murders. The last Barrett saw Greg Owen that night was when he was walking down the driveway. He did not see him again until the next morning after eight. Investigators decided to reinterview Greg Owen. They picked him up at his woodshedlike home and returned to police headquarters about seven that night.

One officer took him outside for a smoke and they chatted amiably about the earlier interview with police. Shortly before eight, Greg Owen was led into the interview room, known by officers as the "Safe Room."

Doug Davis remembers it as the toughest interview he had ever done. Greg Owen simply would not speak. Davis would ask a question. Owen would look him square in the face and not answer. Finally he said he would talk about the murder of Doug Gissendaner. He squirmed and fidgeted. He said he did not tell police about his involvement in the crime because he thought they would not believe that Kelly was involved, that she was the mastermind.

"Am I going to jail if I tell you?"

He was told he would, and he was reminded he faced the death penalty if convicted. They advised him to talk. They could make a deal. He needed to tell what he knew. It was in his best interest.

Owen was read his rights and then agreed to give a statement.

One detective described Greg Owen's response: "He decided to sing like a bird." Prosecutors would agree to life with parole after twenty-five years if he would testify against Gissendaner.

"It was her idea," Owen said. She raised the subject first by asking him whether he knew anyone who could "take care of someone." Then a couple of weeks later, she said she wanted someone to take care of her husband, but she wanted to make sure they bought the house and moved into it before it was done. She wanted it to be a night when Doug and the kids were out and she could stage an alibi by going out with friends. About two weeks before the murder took place, Greg said, he agreed to kill Doug.

"Why don't you just divorce him?" Greg said he asked her.

She said he would never leave her alone.

On the night of the murder, Greg claimed, they were driving to Kelly's house and she was paged by Pamela Kogut and he was paged by his sister. They stopped at a CITGO station to make the calls from side-by-side pay phones. Kelly took him to her house. She gave him a nightstick and a hunting knife.

"It needs to look like a robbery," Greg quoted Kelly as saying before she changed her clothes and left him in the dark house. When Doug came inside about eleven that night, Owen came up behind him and pulled the survival knife across his neck. He made him drive to a secluded road outside town. Owen said he forced Doug Gissendaner to walk about one hundred yards into the woods and get down on his knees. Owen hit him in the head with the nightstick and then stabbed him repeatedly with the survival knife Kelly had given him.

He left him in the woods to bleed to death.

Owen said he rode around in Doug Gissendaner's car until Kelly paged him with their predetermined code—123. Kelly drove down Luke Edwards Road in the car her husband bought her and found Owen standing on the side of the dirt road, just at the foot of the embankment he had climbed minutes before with Doug.

"Is he dead?" she said, rolling down the window.

"Yes."

"Show me," Kelly demanded, her voice cold.

Owen said he wasn't going back into the woods. Kelly grabbed the flashlight she had given him earlier and stomped off into the moonless night to make sure her husband was dead. When she returned, she calmly showed Owen a Coke bottle full of gasoline she brought to set the car on fire. They burned the car on that secluded road, Doug's body slumped over in the dirt a mile away, rain pelting his back. No one saw anything. Kelly Gissendaner drove Greg Owen home afterward, he said, and cautioned him not to talk to each other for a while.

Prosecutors had no forensics. The car was burned beyond any crime scene tech's ability to reconstruct. The place where Doug died had been frozen and rained on for more than a week before his body was found. But now they did have a star witness. And he had a believable story. Telephone records showed Greg Owen and Kelly Gissendaner talked on the phone forty-seven times in the days leading up to Doug's murder. She had paged Owen eighteen times.

Chapter 12

With Greg Owen's confession in hand, police had but one more act to wrap up a case that had stymied them for weeks. Arrest the wife. They certainly suspected her all along. It was standard in murders. Check out the family members. Often it proves to be true. And in this case they did not seriously consider anyone else, a decision that could prove their undoing.

Davis and five officers from Gwinnett County and two from Barrow County, where Kelly Gissendaner lived, went to her house after midnight on February 25, the day after Doug's funeral, eighteen days after Doug was abducted from his living room. Kelly, clad in pajamas, answered the door. Davis told her he had a warrant for her arrest in the murder of her husband; Kelly Gissendaner started sobbing. She fell into her mother's arms. She kept repeating that she couldn't believe she was being arrested. Davis told her to get dressed. He handcuffed her and led her outside.

Three officers stayed in the house to search it. One officer drove while Davis read her her rights. They took her to police headquarters and into an interrogation room. She said she did not have anything to do with her husband's murder, but she started to recast her story. She told them she had seen Greg Owen that night. She had picked him up. He had called her, she said, and asked that she come and get him. She didn't know anything about what he had done until he told her in the car. She said he told her he had beaten her husband, and he threatened to kill her and her children if she said anything to authorities. He held a knife to her throat, she said.

Police and prosecutors didn't believe her. They felt she was the mastermind. She wanted her husband dead. Her father-in-law told them she had known immediately at the funeral home that she needed ten copies of the death certificate, as if she had checked it out, as if she knew precisely how many she needed for insurance purposes, probate court, banks and all the other places she would need to visit to get everything in her name, under her sole control. Her reactions the day after her husband disappeared seemed unnatural. Too calm. Cold, even. A police officer remarked at her unusual behavior at the funeral.

A few hours later, Kelly Gissendaner was taken to Gwinnett County Jail. Prosecutors knew Owen's testimony was key. They could get a conviction against Kelly Gissendaner. She and Greg Owen were indicted on charges of murder, felony murder and possession of a knife during the commission of a felony.

When Davis typed up his narrative of the investigation a month later, its fifty-two pages of exhaustive detail ended simply: *Case cleared arrest.*

Doug Gissendaner, the father, was barely adjusting to the fact that he would live life without his son, when police delivered another blow. Roused from sleep by a ringing phone, Doug Sr. heard the lead detective say his daughter-in-law and her lover had been charged with murdering his son.

"I knew she could be mean," Doug Sr. said of his daughter-in-law, "but I didn't think she could do that."

Junior Flanigan, the funeral home director who handled Doug's service, heard the news about Kelly Gissendaner's arrest. Like everyone else who had any involvement with the family, he was shocked, but then he remembered her steely demeanor in his parlor.

"It gives you kind of a cold feeling how anybody could do such a gruesome thing," he said. She had viewed the body in his holding room without emotion. He stood beside her as she did it. And now police said she was responsible. Such an odd feeling to know a murderer stood among you.

The longer Doug Gissendaner Sr. dwelled on what had happened, the more convinced he was that his son had been an abused husband. Doug Sr. spent long hours on the road, driving for work, thinking about what went wrong and what role he had in it all. The plight of women controlled and hurt by abusive husbands and boyfriends was well-documented. Doug knew little about men, supposedly the stronger sex, being dominated by their wives. However, he was convinced that was what happened with his son. For whatever reason, his son rose to Kelly's side whenever she called. She manipulated him and used him. And his son never saw what was coming. Doug and Sue Gissendaner Sr. had a good marriage—faithful, caring, centered on family. Their son simply wanted the same. Was there something he could have done? Did he miss a key moment? Did he fail his son? So many questions when a parent loses a child. And few answers.

He worried that Kelly would somehow get off. She always seemed to get out of the trouble she got herself into. Would it happen again? No investigation was foolproof. Defense attorneys were cagey and smart. Kelly, it seemed, had many lives.

The Trial

Chapter 13

From the moment Gissendaner was arrested, prosecutors started debating whether they should seek the death penalty. Doing so would be a bold move. No women were on Georgia's death row. In all, thirty-six states have capital punishment in America today. Approximately 3,300 inmates inhabit their death row. Fifty of them in 1998 were women. Georgia had put to death only one woman, a black housekeeper who killed her white employer in 1944. She alleged her employer, a prominent mill owner in a small town, treated her as a slave. He forced her to care for him and to have sex with him, and when she wanted to leave, he pulled a gun and threatened to kill her. She snatched the gun away and shot him.

The U.S. Supreme Court struck down the death penalty in America in 1972, ruling state's laws were "arbitrary and capricious." The majority on the court ruled the death penalty laws constituted cruel and unusual punishment and violated the Eighth Amendment to the U.S. Constitution and the due process guarantees of the Fourteenth Amendment.

Over the next five years, thirty-eight states

enacted new laws and got back into the death penalty business. Georgia's law was one of the first to be validated by the U.S. Supreme Court.

In the thirty years since then, thousands of men were sent to America's death rows (although only 1,099 were actually executed as of October 2007). Yet, women were another issue altogether. Studies showed that only one in sixty women prosecuted for murder is condemned. Even in Texas, the state with more men on death row than any other, juries simply did not impose death sentences on women. In 2004, 444 men were on Texas death row, as opposed to nine women.

Lawyers and sociologists say juries find it distasteful to sentence a woman—a life-giver—to die an unnatural death. There is something that says even in the most gruesome crime, something must have happened to a woman to make her do such a thing. The case of Susan Smith in South Carolina was such an example. She killed her two sons by strapping them in car seats and rolling her car into a murky lake one fall evening. She lied to deputies, accusing a black man of snatching her car with her children inside. In the end, she confessed, there was no man. She was the murderer. But a jury in her small town said she should be sentenced to life in prison. They could not take her life.

Phil Wiley, the assistant district attorney for Gwinnett County, knew all that, but he believed Kelly Gissendaner was as coldhearted and guilty as anyone he had ever prosecuted. He believed she deserved to die.

"She was the moving force," he argued. "Had it not been for her, Greg Owen would not have killed Doug Gissendaner."

He talked it over many times with Danny Porter,

the elected district attorney (DA). Porter and his predecessors in office aggressively sought the death penalty wherever merited. From 1981 until 1997, three district attorneys sought the death penalty fourteen times, yet juries imposed the sentence only three times. One was overturned by the Georgia Supreme Court. That did not dissuade Porter. Elected in 1992, he prosecuted some high-profile murder cases, but the respect law enforcement officers felt for him came because he reached out to them. He was known as one of the guys, standing with them on rainy days or in the searing heat of a Southern summer day as they investigated murders. When he was hired as an ADA in 1981, he often rode with officers to see what they were up against in the community.

He encouraged his assistants to go to the scene of every murder they would try. He believed that it helped paint a picture for jurors in the courtroom, but it did something much more. It helped them remember what the case was all about: people.

By the time he ran for reelection in 1996, he was so revered that he ran unopposed. He had been known to say prosecution and law enforcement were in his blood. So much so that once when Porter was sitting at a red light in Buford, he heard on his police radio that officers were searching for someone wanted for a domestic assault. Police were looking for a certain blue Malibu, which just happened to be passing Porter's car. He pursued and stayed behind the car until a police officer could pull the driver over and arrest him.

Porter felt the facts were clear: Kelly Gissendaner deserved the death penalty. But he also wanted to know Wiley's opinion. Wiley felt sure he could win a conviction against Kelly Gissendaner, but he wasn't so sure he could convince a jury to give her death. She was, after all, a mother of three children.

But Georgia has one complication in its laws that convinced Wiley to seek death. The law says a sentence of life without parole can be imposed only if prosecutors attempt—and fail—to get a death sentence.

He and Porter discussed the fact that if they did not seek the death penalty and Kelly Gissendaner was convicted, she could be out on parole in a matter of years. Unacceptable, Wiley said.

"We have to preserve life without parole," Wiley argued.

"Let's think about it," Porter responded.

Wiley had served as a lead attorney on one other death penalty case, and sat in the second chair—as the assistant to the lead attorney is known—on another case, which was tried twice. The Georgia Supreme Court had reversed that conviction, saying a female juror had too strong an opinion on the death penalty and should have been excused by the judge.

In 1997, Wiley had been practicing law for sixteen years. He graduated from Georgia State University in 1974 and worked for eight years as a parole officer. For the last three and a half years of his time working with parolees, he was in night school at the Atlanta Law School.

Wiley and Porter talked about seeking the death penalty several more times before Kelly Gissendaner's arraignment, which was the deadline for telling her whether she faced death.

When she was brought from the jail to court, she entered a plea of not guilty. Wiley announced he was going to try to send her to her death.

Chapter 14

Gwinnett County Justice and Administration Center is a huge white edifice in Lawrenceville that looks more like a corporate headquarters than a courthouse. It was built in 1988 after a superior court judge ordered the county to build a new courthouse. The old two-story brick building downtown was so old and cramped, it was a hazard. It housed all facets of county government and some agencies spilled out into other buildings.

Kelly Gissendaner went on trial there on November 2, 1998. Selecting a jury took ten days. Wiley could not have been more pleased with the outcome. Ten women made the cut and two men. He believed women would be harder on a woman than men would be.

"We have a better chance of convincing women she deserved to die," he said. Men are more apt to think of a woman as having the characteristics of their own mothers or wives. They are the care-givers, the life-givers. Women are less likely to feel sympathy. Most know, no matter how tough their lives have been, that killing is not an answer, no matter what.

The jurors reflected the community. Eleven had gone to college; eleven were white. Ten owned their homes. Ten were older than thirty-five. They worked at all sorts of jobs. There was a computer network analyst, a middle-school chorus teacher, a college student at the University of Georgia, an occupational-health nurse, a project manager for AT&T, an insurance agent and a homemaker, among others. None, though, had lived lives that mirrored that of Kelly Gissendaner, who couldn't hold a job, had not been to college and now, not even thirty, faced a fate similar to that of her husband.

Judge Homer Stark, who had been a lawyer since 1955 after he graduated from the University of Georgia School of Law, swore in the jury on Thursday afternoon, November 12. He told them to give the bailiff their cell phones and beepers, and set down the rules. They would be sequestered for the duration of the trial. Spouses and friends would be able to visit them on Sunday.

"It's kind of a restricted type of environment that you will be in for the next week or so," the judge said. "But you would . . . No, you're not going to be totally cut off from the outside world. You will be able to check on your family and find out what's going on and keep up with that—you won't have enough time to keep up with business matters, but you will have time to call and check and see if everybody's all right and give them a report on your status."

They would each have a private room, but no TV, no radio, no VCR. They would be allowed to read books and magazines, as long as they contained nothing about the trial. The bailiffs might get them some movies to watch, and an exercise room was available at the motel.

"The bailiffs are there to serve you," the judge said. A typical day would start at nine o'clock and run until five forty-five.

The jury was taken to the motel and Stark laid some ground rules for the lawyers.

He said Doug Gissendaner's father would be allowed in court after he testified and Doug Gissendaner's sister Lee, and Kelly Gissendaner's mother, Maxine Wade, would be allowed to stay in court the whole time, even though they would testify during the punishment phase, if it came to that.

Stark advised the lawyers and those in the courtroom that he would not abide facial expressions from anyone. No one related to either side could get close to the jury box. TV cameras would be allowed in the courtroom.

Three lawyers would represent the state, Phil Wiley as lead counsel and George Hutchinson and Nancy Dupree assisting. Kelly Gissendaner would be represented by Edwin Wilson and Steve Reilly. The lawyers gathered at their respective tables in the modern wood-paneled courtroom, each one wearing a dark suit.

They began shortly after nine o'clock on November 13, 1998—Friday the Thirteenth.

Kelly Gissendaner, in a skirt and a pink-and-white-striped blazer, sat expressionless at the defense table. Her hair was cut much shorter than when she was arrested. Wispy bangs framed her ample forehead. She seemed confident and composed.

Dupree began. She had worked in the DA's

office since 1982 and for years went after the parents who refused to pay child support. A graduate of Mercer School of Law, she had asked to try a fuller range of cases. She had worked a variety of them in the sixteen years since. When she addressed the jury on that November day, she was no-nonsense in her approach, explaining the circumstances, one by one, for jurors.

"Let me tell you right off, ladies and gentlemen, why we're here," she said, walking toward the jury. "On Friday February, 7, 1997, Douglas Morgan Gissendaner got off from his job at Pro Shocks in Lawrenceville. He drove to the home of his friends Kathy and Tom Nesbit, also in Lawrenceville. He had dinner with the Nesbits. He and Tom Nesbit spent several hours working on their cars together.

"Around ten or ten-thirty, Douglas Gissendaner said good-bye to the Nesbits and got in his car and headed for his home in Auburn, Georgia. It would be a long time, ladies and gentlemen, before anyone knew what happened to Douglas Gissendaner next. Anyone that is, ladies and gentlemen, except his murderers.

"Kelly Gissendaner, sitting right here, was one of them. She planned it for a long time."

Dupree said Kelly Gissendaner went to work at Rooms To Go in Suwanee, drove to Cumming to her boyfriend's house, picked him up, took him to her home in Auburn, where "she left him to lie in wait for Douglas Gissendaner while she went out partying with her girlfriends, constructing her alibi.

"Before she left him, she gave him a nightstick. It's the type of club law enforcement officials sometimes use. And she gave him a knife."

Dupree continued to describe the circumstances. She told about Kelly Gissendaner's visit with friends, their trip to a bar. At about the time Kelly was telling friends she had to go home, her husband arrived home and was ambushed by Greg Owen, who held him at knifepoint and forced him back into his car. Doug drove, according to Kelly's directions, to Luke Edwards Road. Greg Owen forced him from the car and stabbed him to death.

"Douglas Gissendaner died that night out there in the woods on Luke Edwards Road," Dupree said.

Kelly Gissendaner gave Owen a soda bottle full of kerosene, which he used to burn Doug's car, and then she took him home, Dupree said. Dupree then described the phone calls Kelly Gissendaner made the next morning and the way the elder Gissendaner drove the roads between the Nesbits' house and his son's house, "desperately searching for any sign of his son.

"Meanwhile, Kelly went on television playing the role of the distraught wife," Dupree said. "She expressed her anxiety about Doug's disappearance. We'll play you a brief videotape of that performance, ladies and gentlemen. As you watch it, please note that all along Kelley Gissendaner knew exactly where Doug was. She knew he was dead, and she knew that his body lay in the woods off of Luke Edwards Road."

Dupree told the jury that after police learned about Greg Owen, they found Doug's body. On the night Doug was buried, police talked again to Owen.

"This time, ladies and gentlemen, Greg Owen confessed to his part in the murder of Doug Gissendaner."

Hours later, police arrested Kelly Gissendaner. And from jail, she called a friend and told her she did it, Dupree said. She called again in the afternoon and said the only reason she did it was that Greg Owen threatened her and her children. Kelly Gissendaner also talked to an inmate, Dupree said, a woman by the name of Laura McDuffie. Kelly asked her to find a witness to testify she unwittingly helped Greg Owen murder Doug.

"Kelly wrote out a script for the witness and drew a floor plan of her house and gave it to Laura. Laura gave it to her lawyer, who gave it to the district attorney," Dupree said before offering jurors a brief history on Doug's life and his on-and-off relationship with his wife.

Next it was Wilson's turn. He had been a lawyer for twenty years, and worked for a year as a prosecutor. He began a general practice law firm in 1980. He went back to the prosecution table for three years and then returned to private practice as a criminal defense attorney. Wilson had been on both sides of the aisle in murder cases. He also had been lead counsel on several death penalty cases before being appointed to the Gissendaner case. He knew what he was doing and felt good about the case and especially good about saving Kelly from lethal injection, should the first part of the trial go bad.

He stood before the simple wood podium, hands resting on his notes, and began in the slow Southern drawl that made most of the folks in the courtroom want to shout, "Spit it out, Ed."

"This will be an interesting trial, I promise you," Wilson told jurors. "The evidence will show a lot of things, but it will not show that Kelly Gissendaner is guilty of murder, because Kelly Gissendaner is not guilty of murder. Kelly Gissendaner had an affair, several. Kelly Gissendaner was not always faithful to her husband."

He described their relationship, offering date after date. They met in spring 1989, moved in together, got married, Doug joined the Army, went to basic training, Kayla is born. They move to Germany, Doug goes to Turkey, home on leave, out of the army, Kelly enlists, moves to Virginia, divorced, remarried two years later.

"The state builds its case on two witnesses, both completely unbelievable," Wilson said. "Laura McDuffie and Greg Owen. Both made deals with the state. McDuffie is a thief and prostitute. Owen is a murderer. A liar."

Wilson felt confident he could show the jury that the state did not do its due diligence. They sought no one other than Kelly Gissendaner in the murder of her husband. They had no hard evidence tying her to the scene other than the word of a man who had changed his story to save himself. Greg Owen had no standing in the community. He couldn't even hold a job for very long. He didn't make a believable witness.

Wilson knew this wasn't an open-and-shut case. He knew just where the prosecution's weaknesses lay and he intended to make sure the jury saw every one.

Chapter 15

After lunch, Hutchinson called the first witness for the prosecution: Douglas Mack Gissendaner, the fifty-six-year-old father of the victim. Hutchinson wanted to hit the jury immediately with emotion. A father whose stable life was undone by loss and grief. Doug Sr., wearing a suit and tie, spelled it out simply for the jury. He had been with the same company as a district sales engineer for almost eighteen years and had been married to the same woman—now a grieving mother—for thirty-five years. He pointed out his wife for jurors. Sue Gissendaner sat with her daughters, a tissue in hand, tears already welling in her eyes. When Hutchinson asked about their children, Doug Sr. responded quietly. Three, he said, looking down. He wanted to keep his emotions in check and knew it was probably something he'd be unable to do.

He explained that he met his future daughter-in-law a few months before she married his son. He knew she had a son from a previous relationship. Kelly and Doug had been married a month

when she left him and went back home to her
mother. The next month, they got back together.

"It was a very rocky relationship," the father said.

He described the breakups and the reunions.
Doug at home with them, Kelly with her mother.

They had been separated for a year when
Doug went to Virginia to be with Kelly. Doug
took all the household goods that he and his
father bought and stayed for six weeks.

"He was back home by Thanksgiving," he said.

"What had happened?" Wiley asked.

"They had—as far as I know—they had a big
argument or something and decided that they
didn't—"

Wilson objected that the information was hearsay and Stark sustained the objection.

Doug Sr. explained that his son came back
home, filed for divorce, and spent all his time
working two jobs to pay off the debt he and Kelly
had piled up. Doug worked at a plumbing fitting
company and with his uncle in an antique refin-
ishing business.

They reunited before the divorce was final, but
problems arose quickly.

"My son said this is it and he planned to seek
another divorce for good," the father said, describing the on-and-off nature of the relationship. "Doug stopped the divorce the very day
they were supposed to go to court. They were
going to church. They wanted to start a family
and wanted to be baptized, which they were, and
they were wanting to buy a house."

They seemed happy, the senior Gissendaner
said.

"He thought everything was going to work out
fine."

He described how his son had come to him to ask for money to buy a house, but the father put his foot down. He said no to the down payment, but did buy a dishwasher and helped him paint and remodel. Church members helped, too, and life seemed finally to be stable.

"He loved those children more than anything," Doug Sr. said. "He took them to a lot of different places—for instance, Six Flags. He would take them to the Malibu Grand Prix, Putt-Putt. He treated them all just like they were his.

"He seemed to be very happy. He was always— he thought that this was what he wanted. He was basically a homebody. He wanted a family."

The last time he saw his son was the Monday before he disappeared. His son called him on Thursday of that week to ask something about the car, but Doug Sr. was out of town and did not speak with his son.

He described how he learned his son was missing and of seeing his car after it was found.

"It was burned to the ground," he said, and the place it was found was "remote, very, very remote."

He also told the jury that his son's wife took the children to the circus on the Sunday after their father disappeared and then went back to work two days later.

"Which I thought was kind of unusual," he said. "I mean, I certainly wasn't. I wouldn't have. . . . My family is the most important and I think most companies would have recognized that, too."

He also thought it was unusual that she knew how many death certificates she needed.

"She immediately came up with a given number of ten that she needed right away," Gissendaner Sr. said.

"She knew exactly how many she needed?" Hutchinson asked.

"She knew exactly how many she needed and we didn't. . . . My wife and I were saying, well, we don't know how many we need."

"Did your son have any life insurance, sir?"

"He had a life insurance policy at the company that he worked for. It was a ten-thousand-dollar life policy. I think it was pretty much a standard-type policy that the company provided."

"Who was the beneficiary?"

"Kelly."

Hutchinson showed Doug Sr. letters that Kelly Gissendaner wrote in jail when she was looking for someone to confess to the crime and asked if he had ever seen his daughter-in-law's handwriting.

"It's Kelly's handwriting," the elder Gissendaner said.

Wilson went easy on Doug Sr., asking simply what his son did in the army—a tanker in the armor corps—and then about how the license plate from Doug's car was found. Wilson took a swipe at the Gwinnett County Police Department, trying to put some doubts in the minds of jurors about how well the crime was investigated.

Doug Sr. said the tag was given to police. They didn't find it before they took the car from the scene, even though it was there, lying in the road underneath the car.

Kathy Nesbit took the stand next. She explained where she lived and that she was married and had three children.

She described Doug for the jury.

"He always had a smile on his face and he was always easygoing," she said.

She met Kelly for lunch in April 1996 at Wendy's, off Jimmy Carter Boulevard, after Kelly had visited the Atlanta Church of Christ. She met Doug the following July.

She explained about cooking dinner for her husband and Doug the night Doug disappeared and about Kelly Gissendaner calling the next morning.

"I said, 'Well, something must have happened.' I said [that] because he said he was coming straight home. I said maybe his car broke down or something. It was raining very hard that night that he left. I said maybe he was in an accident or something, and, you know, we need to, you know, something is not right."

She asked Kelly Gissendaner if she had called the police. Kelly hadn't and wanted to call Doug's parents.

Kathy Nesbit recalled Kelly saying: "Sometimes on his way home from some place he'll stop and start talking and lose track of time and he'll end up spending the night over there."

Fifteen minutes later, Kelly called back and said Doug didn't go over to his parents'. Kathy sent her husband out to look for Doug. He came back an hour later and she went to the Gissendaner home.

Wiley asked about a conversation she had that afternoon in the Gissendaners' driveway.

"Who all was present?" he asked.

"Just Kelly and I."

"No one else."

"No."

"Tell the jury that conversation."

"Well, I had seen Kelly walk out of the house, and by that time, people had started coming in.

She walked out the back door of the kitchen and so I walked out after she had walked out, then I walked out after her to talk with her and to see how she was holding up. I walked down to the end of the driveway with her, and as we started walking back, I said, 'Kelly, do you think Greg had anything to do with this?' and she stopped walking and she turned and she looked at me and she said, 'What makes you say that?' I said, 'Well, you know that he had threatened you in the past.' I said, 'Maybe he was home waiting for you to come home and Doug showed up first.' And she said she was kind of not really saying too much and I said, 'Well, if he did come home . . . the headlight he would have pulled into the driveway and his headlights would have been shining right in your neighbor's house.' I said, 'Why don't you go over and ask the neighbor if he saw anything. And she said, 'No, he wouldn't have seen anything. He'd kind of . . .' She made some kind of remark like he was odd or something."

Wiley asked what Kelly Gissendaner said to her about the police.

"She was very angry, saying, 'Who does he think he is? He's treating me like a suspect. He has no right coming in here.' And I said, 'Well, they have nowhere else to start.' I said the family is always a suspect. I said that's why he's out here. He's trying to find some clues."

She was also angry that someone found a knife and gas spout at the scene after police had already been there. The widow punched a garbage can at work because she was so angry.

Kathy Nesbit also told the jury about Kelly Gissendaner stopping to eat on the way to the cemetery after Doug's funeral.

* * *

The prosecution used Martha Lawrence, the videotape librarian at WXIA-TV, an NBC affiliate, to show an interview Kelly Gissendaner did while her husband was missing.

The jury watched as reporter Nina Jimenez said, "Kelly Gissendaner sits and waits with loved ones for a sign her husband, Doug, is all right."

"I'm just praying that he comes home safely, that they find him and he walks back through the door," Kelly Gissendaner said. "This is not like him at all. This is so out of the ordinary."

Lead investigator Davis was called to testify. He walked to the witness chair, looking every bit the former football player he was, in charge and in control. The prosecution introduced as evidence the phone records of the Gissendaners as well as the tapes of Davis's interviews with Kelly Gissendaner. Davis told the jury about the times he had met with Kelly Gissendaner before she was arrested, her demeanor and how he came to believe she had conspired to kill her husband. He was believable and businesslike.

But Wilson intended to find the burrs. Under cross-examination, Davis admitted he had no evidence to offer that an accelerant was found and no murder weapon.

"To the best of your knowledge, where is the murder weapon?" Wilson asked.

"Somewhere in the landfill in Cherokee County," Davis responded.

"When Mr. Gissendaner's body was found, was he missing any jewelry?" Wilson asked. As with any good lawyer, he knew the answer to the question before he asked it. He knew jewelry was missing, and he knew if something was missing, that raised the possibility that theft was the motive. He was looking for that moving target—reasonable doubt—and if theft from an unknown assailant was possible, that meant it wasn't a wife seeking insurance money.

"I don't remember what jewelry he had on him at the time when his body was found."

"Would you have that information in your notes?"

"I don't have it in these notes, sir," he said. "It would be in the medical examiner's report, what was on him when he was found."

"In fact, his watch was missing, wasn't it?"

Hutchinson objected. Stark sustained. But Wilson got the information before the jury. They might be told not to consider it, but they heard it.

Davis was dismissed and the prosecution moved on. Kerri Otis, Kelly Gissendaner's supervisor at Rooms To Go, was next. Dupree asked her about Kelly's relationship with her husband.

"There were times she said she wasn't sexually satisfied with Doug and that she did not want to be with him at home or spend time with him at all," Kerri answered.

"Did Ms. Gissendaner ever mention a man named Greg Owen to you?"

"Yes."

"When did she first mention him to you?"

"In the fall of '96."

"Where did that conversation take place?"

"I'm not sure of the exact place."

"What did she tell you about Greg Owen?"

"She and Greg were having a relationship. She

was in love with Greg. There was one point she was going to leave town with Greg. She loved Greg."

Otis described a weekend she spent with Kelly Gissendaner at a cabin in Cherokee, North Carolina.

"It was five females, I believe, that went. During that weekend, Kelly and another girl left the cabin and went into town. I didn't—"

"And let me just caution you—I want to make sure that you don't go into what . . . into any conversation that took place when you were not present or what someone else said."

"Okay."

"Is that where you were headed?"

"No."

"Okay. Excuse me for interrupting, go ahead."

"When they returned, they returned with a male that we did not know. The male had a knife with him."

"Let me ask you another question, Ms. Otis. What was the purpose of that trip to the mountains that weekend?"

"Just to get away."

"Was there any business purpose involved in that trip at all?"

"No."

She said the group got together on Saturday morning.

"Did there come a time later that fall when you had a further conversation with Kelly Gissendaner about her relationship with her husband, Doug?"

"Yes. During the month of December, toward the middle of December, is when her relationship with Doug took a turn and they were working out their marriage and she wanted to build her family back together."

"Was it your impression that by January of 1997, Kelly had ended her relationship with Greg Owen?"

"Yes."

Otis told the jury about the evening Doug went missing, that Kelly Gissendaner left work about four-thirty and Otis saw her again about eight, when they went dancing. Otis said she had tried to reschedule the evening, because she didn't like going out after working all day. Another friend wanted to reschedule for Saturday as well.

"Did you have a conversation with Kelly Gissendaner about rescheduling the outing?"

"Yes."

"When did that conversation take place?"

"The Wednesday or Thursday, I believe, before we went."

"What was Kelly's response?"

"Kelly did not want to reschedule. She said we couldn't reschedule. It had to be Friday night. She had made arrangements for her kids to be out of the house."

"What did Ms. Gissendaner do while she was at your apartment?"

"We had some drinks and she laid on the floor and we talked."

Otis described going to The Shack and testified they left at Kelly Gissendaner's insistence, at about eleven-thirty.

"Do you recall any specific thing Kelly Gissendaner said to you on the way back to your apartment?"

"Yes. On the way home, she stated that she had a bad . . . she had a feeling that something bad was going to happen that evening."

She said she saw Kelly the next day.

"They had called me—Pamela had called me in the morning and stated that Doug didn't come home that night before. So I went over there that afternoon to be with them."

"What did you do while you were at her house?"

"We helped with the kids and talked," Otis said. "We did a lot of talking."

She said she left the house with Pamela to look for Doug. Kelly told them the route Doug would have taken and they searched it and the dirt roads next to them. They didn't find anything. She went back to the Gissendaner home the next day. They sat around and waited.

Then a group went out to search again.

"There was a van—there was a bunch of people. I'm not even sure who some of them were."

"Did Kelly Gissendaner make any statements during that time about her efforts to find out what had happened to her husband?"

"She stated she had been to see a psychic."

"Did she say what the psychic had said?"

"On Saturday, she stated that the psychic told her that Doug was in some woods next to a tree, and that if he was not found by Sunday morning, that he would be dead."

"Did she add any additional information on Sunday?"

"On Sunday, she went back to the psychic and the psychic added that there was water nearby."

"Were you present at Ms. Gissendaner's home on Sunday when information arrived that Doug Gissendaner's car had been found?"

"Yes."

"Could you describe Kelly Gissendaner's reaction at that time?"

"She fell into the arms of some of the people

that were at the house. I don't know if—I did not see her face. I was in the other room."

"Did you ever leave the house with Kelly Gissendaner that Sunday?"

"Yes."

"Who drove?"

"I did, I believe."

"Did anyone else go with you?"

"Pamela and, I believe, Nicole was with us."

"Where did you go?"

"We went to see where the car was found."

"What did you do when you got to that area?"

"We walked around that area trying to see if there was anything else that we could find out there. We walked through the woods, walked up the dirt road farther."

"Can you describe Kelly Gissendaner's demeanor while you were at the scene?"

"Very calm," Otis said. "She was trying to find out if she could feel his presence around there. She looked at the burn spot where the car was with no emotion, just very calm."

"What did you say about his presence?"

"She was trying to find out if he was there, if she could feel him there, and I don't remember what the outcome of that was."

Otis said Kelly Gissendaner returned to work the Tuesday of that next week because she said she needed the paycheck. But Kelly told her she wasn't worried about her house payment because it would be paid off by the insurance.

"Did you observe any unusual displays of emotion by Kelly Gissendaner during the time that Douglas Gissendaner was missing?" Dupree asked.

"Yes. There was one morning that she was at her desk at work, and for some reason, she got up and ran into the bathroom, and she was beating the wall in the bathroom to where everybody in the building could hear it."

"Do you recall, approximately, when that occurred?"

"I believe it was toward the end of the second week after," Otis said, but she didn't know what caused her to become angry. Otis said she told Gwinnett County police investigators about Greg Owen after Doug's body was found.

"Did you have any conversation with Kelly Gissendaner regarding Greg Owen during this time?"

"We suggested to Kelly to inform the investigators about Greg because she had not mentioned him up to that point."

Dupree concluded her questioning by asking Otis to tell the court about Greg Owen's sister Belinda, who was referred to Rooms To Go by Kelly.

On cross-examination, Wilson asked Otis about her friendship of seven or eight months with Kelly Gissendaner. Otis said she knew about Kelly's marriage and its problems.

"And you're aware that it was an up-and-down thing?" Wilson asked.

"Yes."

"Sometimes it was good and it was real good?"

"It wasn't good until after December. At that— up until that point, it was always bad."

"And she also discussed her relationship with Greg Owen with you?"

"Yes."

"Sometimes that was good?"

"That was good."

"And sometimes that was not good?"

"Right."

"Is that a fair statement?"

"After December, he became . . . that the relationship turned bad."

Wilson asked about a man named Bill Johnson, whom Otis described as a contractor at Rooms To Go. He did deliveries for the company every day. He had a relationship with Kelly Gissendaner, as did a man named Ethan. Sean Swoope, a service tech at Rooms To Go in North Carolina, had a relationship with her, too, Otis testified.

"Do you recall at one point Greg was getting obsessive with Kelly?" Wilson asked.

"According to Kelly, yes. I did not see any of it."

"But you related that to the police?"

"That was—according to Kelly, he was getting obsessive."

"And that he was getting more serious than she wanted to be?"

"I don't recall that," Otis responded.

He asked her about her conversation with Investigator David Henry, on February 11, 1997, when she told him Owen was much more serious than Kelly.

"And that Greg was obsessive about her?" Wilson said.

"Yes."

"And that Kelly had gotten a lot of phone calls from him?"

"That he was paging her."

Wilson asked whether Kelly was a salaried employee or an hourly employee at Rooms To Go, and Otis said she was hourly. Wilson wanted the jury to know why Kelly Gissendaner went back to work so soon. He had an explanation for her actions.

"So if she didn't work, she, basically, didn't get paid?"

"Right."

When Wilson finished questioning, Dupree said she had one point of clarification to make.

"Ms. Otis, you testified that while you were in the mountains in North Carolina, Kelly and another person left, and when they came back, a man was with them. Was that a man that any of you-all had met before?"

"No."

"Is that a man from North Carolina?"

"Yes."

Otis left the stand and her coworker Pamela Kogut took her place. Pamela was dreading this day. She had heard that Kelly had made a list of people she wanted to get rid of and had actually tried to find someone to do it. She knew her name was on the list and she believed Kelly was mean enough to follow through.

"Ms. Kogut, do you and Kelly work with someone named Kim Harrison?" Wiley asked.

"Yes, sir."

"Did you, during the time that Doug Gissendaner was missing, have an occasion to tell Kelly anything about Kim that referred to Doug's disappearance?"

"Yes, sir."

"All right. I want you to tell the jury what you told Kelly."

"I told Kelly that Kim Harrison had said that, 'Don't you think it's funny how Kelly and Doug had their physicals, and then he came up missing?'"

"You told Kelly that?"

"Yes, sir."

"Was this at work?"

"Yes, sir."

"Do you remember, approximately, when this was during the time that Doug was missing?"

"It was that week that she came back to work."

"Okay. Did Kelly have any reaction to that?"

"Yes, sir."

"What was her reaction?"

"She got real angry and she went in the bathroom and she tried to tear the toilet paper holder off the wall and she kicked in the bathroom door."

"All right. Sometime after that occurred, were you in the car with Kelly when Kelly was driving and you-all saw Kim Harrison?"

"Yes, sir."

"Where was that at?"

"It was in the parking lot. We were going to lunch."

"Did Kelly say anything about Kim at that time?"

"Yes, she did."

"What did she say?"

"She said, 'I ought to run the bitch over.'"

"What did she do then?"

"She didn't slow down. She didn't swerve. She just kept on going."

"Where was Kim at that time?"

"Kim was trying to walk across the street to go in the building."

"Was that in front of where you-all were driving?"

"Yes, sir."

"Did Kim Harrison have to do anything to keep from getting hit?"

"Yes, sir. She had to run to get out of the way."

Wiley asked Kogut how she learned Kelly Gissendaner had been arrested. Kogut responded that a member of the Gissendaners' church told her. It was about two o'clock in the morning, but Kogut dressed anyway and went to the Gissendaners' house. The church member was there with Kelly's mother and brother.

Later that morning, Kelly Gissendaner, in jail, called her at home.

"Tell the jury what Kelly told you that morning, February twenty-fifth. Take your time."

"She said, 'I did it, Pamela. I did it,'" Kogut said, visibly trembling in the witness-box. She started crying. She did not look at Kelly.

"Did you say anything?" Wiley asked gently.

"I said, what? And she said, 'I did it.' And I said, 'No, you didn't. No, you didn't.'"

Kelly Gissendaner called again that afternoon. She said Greg Owen had held a knife to her and threatened to kill her and her kids if she told anybody. Three days later, Kelly called again as Kogut and her husband were getting ready to go out.

"I asked her, 'Why? Why did this have to happen?'" Kogut testified. "And she said, 'I can't talk. The phones are wired.'"

About five months later, Kelly Gissendaner, still in jail, called Kogut at home one evening.

"She said, 'You better stop calling my family. They've been through enough.' And I said I had only talked to Ms. Lottie."

"Who is Ms. Lottie?"

"I think she's Kelly's aunt."

"She was the only family member of Kelly's you had talked to?"

"Yes, sir."

"Did you consider yourself to be friends with Ms. Lottie?"

"Yes, sir."

"Is that why you would have talked to her?"

"Yes, sir."

"All right. After you told her you had only talked to Ms. Lottie, what did she say? What did Kelly say?"

"She said, 'I know you talked to Ms. Lottie and I know you've talked to the detectives. I've seen the witness list.'"

"Did you say anything else to her?"

"I asked her, 'Are you threatening me?' And she said, 'No, I'm telling you.'"

Kogut was certain Kelly would hurt her if given the chance. She was clearly uncomfortable as she testified. Even though Kelly spent most of the days in court looking down at the papers on the table in front of her, Pamela feared Kelly's cold stare.

"She said, 'No, I'm telling you,'" Wiley repeated.

"Yes, sir."

Wilson began his cross-examination by asking Kogut about her friendship with Kelly Gissendaner. She had known her for about six months and felt close to her. They confided in one another. Kelly told her intimate details of her life with her husband and her lover.

"Do I understand that in November, basically, you took her to the Jameson Inn to spend the night with Greg Owen?"

"Yes, sir."

"Then you took her car and picked her up the next morning?"

"Yes, sir."

"Did you know she was going to stay with Greg Owen that night?"

"Yes, sir, I did."

"You yourself use that expression from time to time, 'having a bad feeling,' don't you?"

"Yes, sir, I do."

"And you had used that, that very week, I believe, hadn't you, before you and Kelly and the other girls went out?"

"Yes, sir."

"When you had used that, that week, what did you mean?"

"I knew that she was going to stay with—spend the night with someone else, and I told her not to go because I had a really bad feeling."

"During your last conversation with Kelly, basically, she told you she didn't want you calling her family members?"

"Yes, sir."

"When Kelly was arrested, you felt betrayed and embarrassed, didn't you?"

"Yes, sir, I did."

Wilson reminded her she had been interviewed by two police investigators while Doug was missing and told them Kelly was crying the morning she found out her husband was missing.

"I don't recall," Kogut said.

"Do you remember having told them that she was very upset?"

"I don't remember the conversation that I had with them. I apologize."

"It's okay. Could you have said to—in response to the question from Detective Pesaresi, 'What else did she say?' Could you have said, 'That's it, I didn't give her time to say anything else because she was so upset. I immediately got dressed and drove over there'?"

"I'm sorry, sir. I don't remember the conversations that I had with them."

"Do you remember Detective Pesaresi asking what happened when you got to Kelly's house?"

"As I've stated before, sir, I apologize. I don't remember the conversations that I had with them."

"Could you have told them, 'I just sat there with her, she was upset, and she was crying, and she was on the phone calling people'?"

"I don't remember what I told them. I'm sorry."

Wilson gave her a transcript of her police interview and then asked if that refreshed her memory.

"Not really. As I stated before, sir, I'm sorry. I don't remember what I said to them. I apologize."

"That's quite all right. You knew Kelly was concerned how Greg Owen might react when she broke up with him?"

"Not really. I mean—"

"Did you not tell the officers that you were aware she was concerned about how Greg might react when she broke off with him?"

"I don't remember the conversations that I had with . . . I don't remember that conversation. I'm sorry."

He showed her more of the transcript, and again she said she didn't remember the conversation.

"Do you recall knowing that Kelly was concerned about how Greg might react when she broke up with him?"

"I don't remember whether—I know Kelly wasn't afraid of anything."

"Do you remember that Owen would regularly beep Kelly when you were with her?"

"Yes, sir. He would page her."

"Sometimes a whole lot of times in a short period?"

"Yes, sir."

Wilson had hoped Kogut would paint a picture

for the jury of Owen as a monster, a feared man who was obsessed with Kelly Gissendaner. He also hoped she would tell the jury that while Doug was missing, she saw Kelly as a wife distraught and afraid, not cold and calculating. The strategy did not work completely. But the jury did hear about some compulsive behavior from Greg Owen. He also managed to show Kogut as a woman who remembered all sorts of details about Kelly's affairs, but had no memory of what she told police about Kelly's behavior while her husband was missing.

Meanwhile, Wiley was setting the groundwork, working through the people who were around Kelly Gissendaner the most. The people she drew near while her husband was gone, while she had affairs, while she worked. Belinda Leicht testified about how she introduced her brother to Kelly. She told of the secret meetings. She also testified she asked Kelly what her intentions were with her brother.

"She said she was going to get the house and then get rid of him (Doug)."

The words meant nothing at the time. But now everything.

Wiley was ready to move into the police work that led to Kelly Gissendaner's arrest. Bell described finding the car and the body.

Then Hal Bennett, a forensic investigator with Cobb County Medical Examiner's Office, was called to the stand to talk about collecting evidence at the scene. He was newly at Cobb County, and he had spent the previous ten years in the same job in Gwinnett County.

He said his duties included going to the scene to collect the body and gather the evidence and take it back to the forensic science center for examination by the medical examiner. Bennett said he was a trauma nurse since 1972, a police officer for nine years and had specialized training at the Dade County Medical Examiner's Office, in Miami. He estimated he had been involved in one hundred death investigations.

Doug and Sue Gissendaner Sr. left the courtroom for the testimony about how their son's body looked when it was found. They could not bear to hear what they already knew, that animals had eaten their son's face.

Bennett said he was called to the woods near the Walton County line at about four-twenty on February 20. He met with several police officers, who showed him where to find the body, about seventy-five to one hundred yards up a hillside.

"Where the body was located, it was off of a dirt road, which runs off of Indian Shoals, which is a paved road. In this section of the county, it's very rural. There's no buildings. It's heavily wooded. This being in February, the majority of all the foliage of the trees had fallen and was on the ground. The trees were bare."

"Do you recall what the weather conditions were like?"

"Very similar to what we have today. It was typical February, cool weather, overcast. It had been raining the previous week, and, at that time, you know, it was not raining."

"Generally speaking, sir, when you approach a body that you're going to conduct an investigation in connection with, how is it that you approach it? What is it that you're trying to do?"

"In this particular situation, when we approach a body or find a body like this, the area around the body is marked off to prevent anybody from going in the area and disturbing any type of trace evidence that may be located around the body. The police had already done this prior to my arrival by marking it off with the yellow crime-scene tape, which extended about twenty yards beyond the body in a circle around where the body was located. At that time, what I do is I circle the area looking from outside the crime scene area itself so that I can get an overall idea of what is, you know, at the scene. After that, the police ID unit takes videos and thirty-five-millimeter photographs of the scene in order to have picture representation of what the scene was like before it was disturbed."

Hutchinson showed Bennett photos taken that day and entered them into evidence.

"These, again, are photographs of the victim at the scene. One photo was prior to being moved. The other photo, after we rolled the victim over and placed him onto a clean sheet at the scene prior to the removal from the area."

Wilson asked for a short recess and Stark agreed. When the jury left, Wilson told the judge he considered the pictures of Doug Gissendaner rolled over to expose his body, which had been mangled by animals, unduly gruesome, and asked that they not be allowed as evidence.

"They're not necessary, Your Honor," Wilson said. "They have plenty of photographs of this body and how it was found out there."

Doug Gissendaner was the kind of man who regularly stopped to help strangers. *(Photo courtesy of Doug Gissendaner, Sr.)*

Kelly Gissendaner and Greg Owen conspired to kill Kelly's husband. This is the only known picture of the two of them together, taken at an Owen family gathering not long before the murder. *(Photo courtesy of Belinda Owen)*

Doug and Sue Gissendaner met as college students and raised three children. *(Photo courtesy of Doug Gissendaner, Sr.)*

The Gissendaner family—parents Doug Sr. and Sue (seated), daughters Lee and Jennifer, and son Doug—were a close family. *(Photo courtesy of Doug Gissendaner, Sr.)*

Doug Gissendaner and his younger sisters had a
loving upbringing. *(Photo courtesy of Doug Gissendaner, Sr.)*

Family life included happy Christmases with decorations and lots
of presents. The family usually traveled to the grandparents' house
for holidays. *(Photo courtesy of Doug Gissendaner, Sr.)*

Doug Gissendaner's parents remember him as a happy young man who loved cars. *(Photo courtesy of Doug Gissendaner, Sr.)*

The extended Gissendaner family was especially close.
(Photo courtesy of Doug Gissendaner, Sr.)

Doug Gissendaner adored his daughter as well as his wife Kelly's children from other relationships. *(Photo courtesy of Doug Gissendaner, Sr.)*

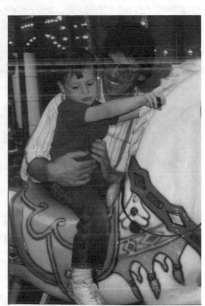

Doug enjoyed spending time with oldest son Brandon. *(Photo courtesy of Doug Gissendaner, Sr.)*

Doug grew up in this house in Buford, Georgia.
(Photo courtesy of Vickie Y. West)

The Owen family.
(Photo courtesy of Belinda Owen)

Greg Owen with his sisters long before he became involved with Kelly Gissendaner, a married woman.
(Photo courtesy of Belinda Owen)

Belinda Owen had both her siblings in her wedding.
(Photo courtesy of Belinda Owen)

Prosecutors alleged Kelly Gissendaner arranged to have her
husband murdered to get this home in Auburn, Georgia.
(Photo courtesy of Vickie Y. West)

Luke Edwards Road was the place Owen took Doug Gissendaner
to murder him. *(Photo courtesy of Vickie Y. West)*

After the murder, officials had to install a barrier to keep people from going down the road. *(Photo courtesy of Vickie Y. West)*

The area where Doug Gissendaner was murdered is a particularly lonely place. *(Photo courtesy of the Gwinnett County District Attorney's Office)*

Doug Gissendaner's car was burned to its frame. *(Photo courtesy of the Gwinnett County District Attorney's Office)*

Even the dirt road was charred from the intensity of the fire set by Owen to cover up Doug's murder. *(Photo courtesy of the Gwinnett County District Attorney's Office)*

The license plate from Doug's car was found in a foot search of the area as friends looked for any sign of him. *(Photo courtesy of the Gwinnett County District Attorney's Office)*

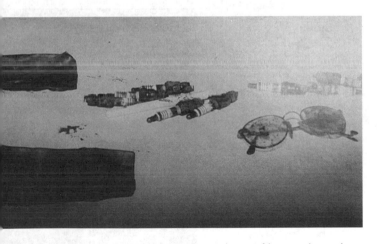

Doug's glasses and the spark plugs he took out of his car the night he died were found in his pocket covered in blood. *(Photo courtesy of the Gwinnett County District Attorney's Office)*

Kelly Gissendaner in a prison mug shot. *(Photo courtesy of the Georgia Bureau of Prisons)*

Greg Owen in his booking photo. *(Photo courtesy of the Gwinnett County District Attorney's Office)*

Phil Wiley and George Hutchinson were appointed to prosecute Kelly Gissendaner. *(Lyn Riddle photo)*

Greg Owen directed officers to the place he threw out the sweatpants he was wearing when he killed Doug Gissendaner. *(Photo courtesy of the Gwinnett County District Attorney's Office)*

Kelly Gissendaner and one of her lawyers, Ed Wilson, during opening statements of her murder trial in Judge Homer Stark's courtroom at the Gwinnett Justice & Administration Center in Lawrenceville. *(Photo by Louie Favorite/Atlanta Journal-Constitution)*

Maxine Wade, mother of convicted murderer Kelly Gissendaner, breaks down on the stand during the sentencing part of the trial, November 19, 1998. *(Photo by Richard Fowlkes/Atlanta Journal-Constitution)*

Sue and Doug Gissendaner speak out about their feelings during a support group for families and friends of homicide victims at the Gwinnett County Justice Center. *(Photo by Cathy Seith/*Atlanta Journal-Constitution*)*

Greg Owen's mother and grandmother visited him regularly in prison in south Georgia. *(Photo courtesy of Belinda Owen)*

Greg Owen's sister Belinda has never given up on her brother's innocence. (Photo courtesy of Belinda Owen)

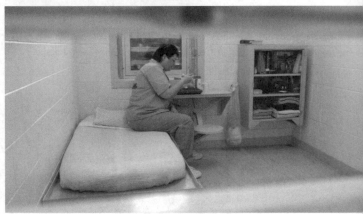

Kelly Gissendaner, the only woman on Georgia's death row, eats lunch in a 9-by-12 cell at Metro State Prison in Atlanta. The shelving unit at right holds all her possessions. She's photographed through the slot in her cell door through which guards pass Gissendaner her lunch tray and other items throughout the day. (Photo by Bita Honarvar/ Atlanta Journal-Constitution)

"Let me see the photographs," the judge said.

"Especially number twenty-seven. If I may, Your Honor, I believe that's the one—Mr. Bennett, is that the one you're talking about that was after the body was moved?"

"That's when we rolled the body over onto the clean sheet prior to removal from the scene, yes," Bennett responded.

"All right, sir," Wilson said. "So the body was not found as it is right here?"

"No. He had been moved at that photograph. Yes, sir. I moved him."

Stark asked if the prosecution had any other photographs. Hutchinson said there were none, but he did have a videotape of the crime scene.

Hutchinson said he needed the pictures because he was going to ask Bennett about the condition of the body when it was discovered.

"Mr. Gissendaner's body laid out, subject to the conditions in the woods, the animals, and, particularly, his body was subject to animal intervention," Hutchinson said. "I need this witness to be able to testify that what's depicted in these photographs is as a result of what animals and Mother Nature may have done to the body as opposed to something that's attributable to the acts of the defendant."

Stark allowed one picture but excluded the other that showed the body after he had been moved.

The jury came back in and Bennett described the crime scene.

"After the photographic documentation was made of the body in the position that it was in, I had donned protective clothing to enter the scene without contaminating the area. At that point, I was able to make a closer external examination. The victim was found to be resting upon his knees, bent at the waist, with his head and shoulders leaning forward.

"Both hands were drawn up and underneath the victim's chest and were unobserved at that time. The victim's head was leaning forward with his forehead resting upon the ground. The right side of the victim's neck and the side of his face was—the tissue was gone and a lot of this looked like it was due to what we call 'insect and animal intervention,' which wounds or open areas generally attract the scavengers of the woods more prominently to those areas. The jacket and shirt was pulled up slightly, exposing part of the back, and other than that, that's, basically, the way the victim appeared."

Hutchinson played the police videotape as jurors watched intently.

When the tape finished, Bennett described that he conducted an external examination of the victim to see if he could tell how the man died.

"With the darkness setting in of the evening, it was a little difficult to get a clear view of the whole body. So we proceeded—we removed a wallet from the victim's right hip pocket and I turned that over to the police at the scene in hopes that we would be able to get a positive ID, or identification, of who the victim was at that time."

"Did you see any identifying information inside of that wallet, sir?"

"Yes, sir, there was. There was cards, video cards, letters—or notes, driver's license, and these items that were in there was—they had been tucked way inside the wallet."

"Let me show you what's been marked for the purpose of identification, sir, as state's exhibit number thirty-five and ask if you can identify that."

"This appears to be the wallet that I removed from the victim's right hip pocket. It's black nylon with the number three on it. I guess it's Dale Earnhardt, if you're a race fan."

"Is it in substantially the same condition now as it was at the time you found it on the body of the victim?"

"Yes, sir, it is."

"Investigator Bennett, looking into the wallet, sir, whose identifying information is contained within that wallet?"

"Primarily, the key piece here was the victim's driver's license identifying him as Douglas M. Gissendaner, with the address and date of birth and a photo ID."

Hutchinson wanted the jury to hear all the grisly details of Doug's death. He wanted to drive home the point that not only was he murdered, but his body was left in the woods, exposed to the elements and to every living thing in the woods for days.

"A moment ago, sir, in describing the condition of the body at the time that you found it, you mentioned the term 'animal intervention.' What is that?" Hutchinson asked.

"When a tissue or muscle deteriorates, particularly around the site of a wound, there's fresh blood. This attracts insects and animals, such as possums, raccoons, flies, and they are attracted primarily to those points where the blood is most prominent. The protein in the blood in the neck has the most odor as the body decomposes. At these points, animals will chew or gnaw at that particular site, and oftentimes, as in this case, destroy most of the area around where they attack."

"Was there evidence of animal intervention on Mr. Gissendaner's body?"

"Yes, there was."

"How much, sir?"

"Most of the right side of the face, the neck, and part of the scalp and the hair."

"It had essentially been eaten away?"

"Been eaten away, exposing the skeletal portion of the body underneath."

"Was there any indication on or near the body that Mr. Gissendaner had been bound or fettered in any way?"

"No. When we rolled the victim over onto a clean sheet, we saw no signs of where he had been tied or bound in any way."

"Was there any weapon or anything in the vicinity that might have caused the types of wounds that you observed on the body?"

"Nothing that we were able to observe. No, sir."

"What did you do with the body, sir?"

"After we rolled the victim over onto a clean sheet, we were able to look at the front portion of the body and determine whether or not there was any obvious signs of injury or trauma, and seeing none, we continued to wrap him in that clean sheet and then we placed him in a clean disaster pouch and carried him down and placed him in the medical examiner's vehicle that I was driving. . . . I carried him back to the forensic science center, located at the Gwinnett County Police Department, and secured him in a refrigerated locker."

The autopsy was performed the next morning

by Dr. Steven Dunton, who was the medical examiner that day, Bennett said.

"In examining the body, sir, did you find a wedding ring on the body?"

"The only jewelry that we discovered on the body was a class ring, silver, with a stone in it from Buford High School, I believe."

"Was there a watch on the body?"

"I didn't see a watch, and I don't remember documenting any on the property sheet."

"The victim was obviously dressed, of course, on what we have seen in the video. What happened to the victim's clothing?"

"The victim's clothing was removed from the body and laid out on a clean field, where we were able to do a closer examination of the body. It was a black jacket that had Pro Shocks written on the front breast pocket, a gray tank top T-shirt that he was wearing underneath that, jeans and shoes. Each of these were examined in the lab itself under a controlled situation."

Bennett identified the clothing Doug was wearing that day: a black jacket and gray tank top. He moved off the stand at Hutchinson's request to show the items to the jury.

"In looking at that jacket, sir, do you see anything on that jacket that is consistent with stabbing defects?"

"When we took the jacket off in a more lighted condition, in the back, we could see up here at the collar and in the back you could see slice defects in the material. These are consistent with being cut or involved with by stabbing with a knife or a rather sharp object."

On the tank top were cuts in the shoulder strap and the neck and around the back of the shirt.

"Okay. You can sit down. Based on what you know about the evidence in this case, sir, and based on your investigation of the body, both at the crime scene and during the course of the autopsy, do you have any opinion as to whether or not the person that would have been responsible for causing these wounds to the victim would have had significant amounts of blood on him as a result of participating in this attack?"

"In the way the victim was found on his knees and leaning forward, the blood that we found on the shirt and on the front of the victim was more consistent with blood having been drained out of the body. I would not expect to see a large amount of blood spatter in any direction as a result of these wounds."

"So based on that, would you expect there to be significant amounts of blood on the attacker?"

"No, sir, I would not."

Wilson moved to try to undo the damage.

"Mr. Bennett, do I understand from the examination of the clothing you're telling us the attacker had no blood on him?"

"No. I didn't say he had no blood on him. I said I would not expect to find a large amount of blood on the victim—or on the perpetrator."

"What do you consider a large amount of blood, sir?"

"A large amount for me would be a pint or more, similar to what you would have if a person donated blood, something that would spatter or cover a large area."

"How many times was this individual stabbed?"

"We do not know exactly how many times he

was stabbed, because a lot of the area that was missing from the neck and the side of the face was gone. From looking at the back of the jacket, we can tell he was stabbed four or five times in that area."

"Minimum?"

"Minimum."

"Possibly more in the jugular there, right?"

"In the jugular vein he could have, yes, sir."

"If you stab him in the jugular, that jugular is going to spurt blood all over the place, isn't it?"

"No, sir, not the jugular vein. You would have to hit an arterial vein—arterial artery in the throat to cause a spurting. The artery is the only vessel that spurts blood. The jugular vein drains."

"You work in close conjunction—your office does in close conjunction with the state crime lab, don't you, sir?"

"Yes, sir, and we send evidence to them for analysis."

"All right, sir. Some of these things have been to the crime lab, haven't they?"

"I would imagine so. Yes, sir."

"The crime lab has the ability to ascertain whether or not items of clothing have blood in them, don't they?"

"Yes, sir, they do."

"They routinely do that, don't they, sir?"

"Yes, sir."

"They do that in conjunction with your office, don't they?"

"Yes, sir, upon request."

"They also do DNA analysis to determine whose blood is in the clothing, don't they?"

"Yes, sir, if requested."

"It's frequently requested in murder cases, isn't it?"

"Yes, sir."

"Did anyone ever show you a pair of sweatpants?"

"No, sir."

"Mr. Bennett, when you first observed this body, it was about seventy-five yards off the road?"

"Yes, sir, up a slight incline in the wooded area."

"All right. I believe you said a thirty-degree incline?"

"About a thirty-degree incline up the hill, yes, sir."

"And that's from the roadway, right?"

"Yes, sir."

"All right. And that was a dirt road?"

"That was a dirt road. Yes, sir."

"Is it an easy-to-travel dirt road?"

"Yes, sir."

"Is it graded?"

"The grade was suitable to travel, in that a normal passenger car or vehicle could have driven it. Yes, sir."

Wilson hoped to show the area was not as remote as it had been described, that many people knew about it and traveled there. A thief would have taken a victim there as easily as anyone.

"Is that a heavily wooded area?"

"Yes, sir, it is."

"Did you go back to that area the next day with the crime scene technicians?"

"No, sir, I did not."

"You were not present when a projectile was found?"

"No, sir, I wasn't."

"When you examined the area out there, did you see any targets?"

"No, sir, I didn't."

"Did you see any shell casings?"

"Not to my recollection, sir."

Steven Frank Dunton, a medical doctor and medical examiner, took the stand. He had been with Gwinnett County since 1993 and a medical examiner for nine years. He earned a Bachelor of Science degree at Emory University and attended medical school at the University of Texas. He did residencies in pediatric oncology and then pathology at Emory. He told the court he had performed about 2,500 autopsies.

Dunton said Doug Gissendaner's hands were wrinkled, as if he had been in a pool. The cause of death was a stab wound to his neck. He couldn't tell the precise injury that caused the death, because the right side of the neck, the skin and much of the soft tissue, including the muscles underneath, were devoured by animals after his death.

"One of the structures that is missing because of these animals is the jugular vein on the right side," Dunton said. "It's one of the largest veins in the body. And I could not assess the jugular vein to see which of it had been severed by the thrust of the knife that began a little bit to the right of center in the back. The wound track came forward through the skin and then disappeared into this open area. The carotid artery on this side was not involved, but there was a lot of blood in the area and I think it's very likely that that jugular vein had been severed."

Other stab wounds didn't strike major vessels, he said.

"There were no stab wounds to an exposed area when the knife went in?"

"That's correct," Dunton answered. "The exception would be if there's a very superficial cut of the finger. I don't really consider that a stab wound because it's very superficial. All the stab wounds to the back of the neck and shoulder area, you can actually see the perforations through the jacket that he wore over that area."

"All right. If someone was stabbed through clothing, would that affect whether or not there is any blood spatter?"

"It may very well."

"All right. Do you have an opinion based on your examination of the victim in this case as to whether the person who attacked Mr. Gissendaner would have a significant—or how much amount of blood that person would have on him from this attack?"

"Of course, much of this is going to depend on how the attack occurred and what sort of contact there is between the victim and the assailant. For instance, if there is a violent struggle going on, where there's a lot of activity between the two and a lot of changing of positions while wounds are being inflicted and blood is flowing from them, you would probably expect a fair degree of blood transfer from the victim to the assailant. However, if the victim is not resisting in any particular fashion and the stab wounds are inflicted from such a direction that the blood is likely to be caught by the clothing or otherwise absorbed, there may be little, if any, blood transferred from the victim to the assailant."

Dunton said he doubted a lot of blood was

transferred from Doug to the assailant. He also said no major artery was severed in the attack.

"The arteries were all there," Dunton said. "Even the carotid arteries on the right side of the neck were still there. They're a little bit deeper, and they were not injured in any way."

"You mentioned earlier that you felt the jugular vein on one side possibly was the cause of death, because it possibly had been severed," Wiley said. "If the jugular vein is severed, would you have spurting of blood to any significant extent?"

"No. It wouldn't spurt. The blood spurts from the arteries with each pump of the heart. Arteries carry the blood from the heart to the rest of the body. So it's under a certain amount of pressure with each pumping of the heart. The veins bring the blood back from the body to the heart, and it's a much lower pressure system. When a vein is severed, even a large one, the blood wells up and flows out of it, but it does not spurt in an arterial cascade because the heartbeat has very little effect on it."

Wiley said he was finished questioning the medical examiner, and Wilson rose for cross-examination.

He began mildly asking about Dunton's experience and how many autopsies he had performed. Dunton said perhaps as many as 2,500.

"All right, sir. In connection with your duties, you and the rest of the folks at the medical examiner's office work closely with the Georgia State Crime Lab, don't you?"

"Yes."

"And you routinely send things down there for analysis, don't you?"

"Yes."

"And then, in particular, as between you and the crime lab, which one would have the responsibility for determining whether an item of clothing has blood on it?"

"As far as identifying the substance as blood for certain, the crime lab does that."

"All right, sir. As for identifying whose blood that is, who would do that?"

"The crime lab."

"And if a pair of pants had Mr. Gissendaner's blood on it, who would determine that?"

"The crime lab."

"And let me ask you this. Prior to receipt, you had a good analysis of the health of this individual prior to his receiving these wounds, or did you? Were you able to determine that?"

"You mean his general physical state?"

"Yes, sir."

"From performing the autopsy, yes."

"Notwithstanding the decomposition and animal activity, you were able to determine whether or not he was in general good health?"

"Yes. As I said, he was fairly well-preserved internally."

"All right, sir. So was he or was he not in good health?"

"He appeared to be."

"As best you could determine, was he capable of defending himself?"

"As far as I can determine, yes."

"And what is a defensive wound, Doctor?"

"In general, a defensive wound is received somewhere in the hands, forearms, upper arms, sometimes legs or feet areas, clearly, when someone is trying to ward off an attack of some type."

"And what defensive wounds did you find here?"

"He did have one very superficial cut on the tip of his index finger that may or may not be a defensive wound during this particular assault. Other than that, that was the only injury of note on the extremities."

"None of the real typical ones on the arms that you would find?"

"Correct."

Wilson asked whether Dunton knew a .22-caliber projectile was found near the body and whether he examined the body with that in mind. Dunton said he did, but he couldn't rule out that a gun was used on Doug Gissendaner because of the animal damage to his neck.

Wilson asked what Dunton meant in the autopsy report when he wrote, *The scalp is reflected to reveal absence of subgaleal hemorrhage.*

"The galea overlies the skull," Dunton said. "It's a very thin tissue. If a significant blow is received, sometimes it will be deep enough to where there will be like a bruise on the outer surface of the skull."

"Did you report the absence of scalp contusions?"

"Yes."

"What is a scalp contusion, sir?"

"That would be a scalp bruise."

"And how are they typically received?"

"By a blunt impact of some type, whether it be a blow or a fall, generally."

"Did you report, sir, 'underlying skull fractures are not discovered'?"

"Yes."

"Tell us what that means, please."

"He had no evidence of skull fracture."

Dunton also testified that Doug did not have any hemorrhaging inside his brain.

"Would that be typical, for instance, if someone was struck on the head with a nightstick?" Wilson asked.

"It can happen."

He also asked about swelling in the brain.

"Certain areas of the brain that under pressure may get forced under a membrane or some sort of dividing structure and they would, actually, herniate from the place they're supposed to be to somewhere else. Essentially, the absence of these things confirms that his brain was not terrifically swollen," Dunton said.

"All right, sir. And it typically would be if someone were knocked unconscious with a nightstick or some other blunt-force instrument?"

"No. That really doesn't happen too often. You have to have sustained swelling of the brain over a period of time, so much so that the brain has no other place to go except to force itself in areas where it doesn't really belong. Unconsciousness can reflect purely concussion, and concussion shows no evidence of injury on exam. I didn't say that very well. By definition, a concussion is when you lose consciousness, but you can't see any evidence of injury on the brain, just the lights have gone out and they usually come back on."

Dunton said he found no significant injury to the brain.

"So you reported no evidence of blunt-force trauma to the head?" Wilson asked.

"Correct."

Wilson said he was finished with the witness.

* * *

Wiley, believing he needed to clear up some possible confusion with the jury, asked, "Dr. Dunton, did the absence of any evidence of blunt-force trauma mean that the victim in this particular case was not struck in the back of the head?"

"No. It does not mean that."

"Did you find any evidence from your examination of this body during the autopsy that this victim was shot?"

"No."

"No evidence whatsoever?"

"No."

"Dr. Dunton, if Douglas Gissendaner was struck in the back of his head while he was on his knees, and he fell forward on the ground face-first, and he was stabbed in the areas that you have noted from your autopsy report, is that scenario consistent with the results of your examination of him?"

"Yes."

"Thank you," Wiley said. "That's all the questions I have."

"Just briefly, if I may, Your Honor," Wilson said.

"Dr. Dunton, if a suspect in this case had the victim's blood on his pants, on sweatpants, would that be consistent with what your findings are here?"

"Potentially, yes."

"Quite likely, he would have blood on him?"

"He may very well have blood on him. He may not."

Chapter 16

He'd been billed as the star witness, the man who loved a woman enough to kill for her . . . but not enough to go to death row. Owen had agreed to testify against Kelly Gissendaner in exchange for a life sentence with the possibility of parole. He pled guilty to murder three days before Christmas in 1997.

Wiley got straight to the point.

"Whose idea was it to kill Doug Gissendaner?" he asked.

"Kelly's."

"Kelly Gissendaner?"

"Right."

"Where were you when you and Kelly first talked about this?"

"It was over the phone."

"Do you remember approximately when this was?" Wiley asked.

"I would say the first of November of 1996."

"Approximately three months or so before you actually killed Doug?"

"Right."

"Tell the jury what the conversation was about. What did Kelly say?"

"She just asked if I knew a way to get rid of him."

"Was that the word that she used?"

"Right."

"And what did you say?"

"I told her to divorce him."

"Did you-all discuss it any further at that time?"

"No, sir."

"Did she have any reaction to your saying just 'divorce him'?"

"She just said that it wouldn't work, that he wouldn't leave her alone by just divorcing him."

"She said what?" Wiley asked, hoping to drive home the point with the jury.

"That he wouldn't leave her alone if she just divorced him."

"Now, was that the only time that y'all talked about it?"

"No, sir."

"Approximately how many times did you and Kelly talk about doing that before you agreed to do something?"

"Four or five times."

"Who brought it up when you-all talked about it on those occasions?"

"Kelly."

"Did you ever bring it up yourself?"

"No, sir."

"At some point, did you-all agree on how to do it?"

"Yeah."

"And how did you-all decide on how to do it?"

"Well, she would pick me up and take me to their house and then leave, and I would wait on

Doug to get home, and then I would take him out in the woods and kill him."

"Was that discussed between you and Kelly?"

"Yes."

"And you agreed to do that?"

"Yes."

"How was the date of February 7, 1997, arrived at?"

"She planned to go out with friends that night and he was supposed to be somewhere, some friends' house that night too."

"That's the only way you knew—that's the only reason."

"Right."

Wiley asked Owen about his plea and whether he had been promised or coerced to testify. Owen said no.

He described his relationship with Kelly. He met her in September 1995 and had sex with her the first night they met. Many people had testified to Kelly's on-again, off-again relationships with men, but when Owen described it, he seemed bothered. He was with Kelly until April 1996 and they got back together in October. They were together until he went to jail in February 1997, he said.

Wiley led him into the night of the murder. Doug and Sue Gissendaner Sr. sat in the audience. It was the first time they had seen Greg Owen in person. Prosecutors asked them to keep their emotions in check, but as Owen testified, it became harder and harder.

"So you walked up behind him and what did [you] do with the knife?"

"I put it to his neck," Owen said.

"What did you say to him?"

"I told him to finish closing the door."

"You told him to do what?"

"I told him to finish closing the door, because he tried to open the door back up when I walked up behind him."

Wiley asked whether Owen touched Doug with the knife blade. He said he did.

"Did he say anything?"

"He asked me what I wanted."

"He asked what?"

"He asked me what I wanted."

"Did you respond to that?"

"I just told him we're—I need to go for a ride somewhere."

"But you told him to close—to go on and close the door?"

"Yes."

"If you-all were going for a ride, why did [you] tell him to close the door?"

"He already had the door closed one time, and when I walked up behind him, he seen me and he tried to open the door to go back out. I just told him to shut the door."

"After he—did he shut the door?"

"Yes."

Owen said they stood there for a few minutes and then he told Doug to get in the car. Owen said he didn't know whether Doug knew who he was.

"Did he put up a fight, struggle, anything like that?"

"No."

"He never did?"

"No."

When Owen told him to get in the car, Doug

walked out the door and got in the car. He didn't say anything, just got in the driver's seat.

"Did you walk him around to get him in the car? Did you walk all the way around to the driver's door with him?"

"Yes."

"After he got in the car, what did you do?"

"I walked around the car and got in on the passenger side."

It was Doug's Chevrolet. He did as Owen told him. He pulled out of the driveway and drove to Luke Edwards Road. Owen testified it was Kelly who told him of the place and to take Doug there. He had never been there before—not even in the daytime—and was not sure whether Kelly had, either.

"How did she describe it to you so you would know where to go to?"

"See, my mom was living not too far from there at the time. She just gave me directions from my mom's house how to get there."

"And you remembered those directions?"

"Yes."

"When, about when, did she give you those directions in . . . I mean, how much before the night of the seventh did she give you those directions?"

"That morning. I think it was."

"That morning?"

"Yes."

"When you got out to Luke Edwards Road, did you tell Doug where to stop the car?"

"Yes."

Doug didn't say anything on the drive there.

"How were you holding the knife when you-all were—when Doug was driving out there?" Wiley asked.

"I had it in my lap."

"Where was the blade at?"

"It was pointing up."

"Could he see the knife?"

"Yes."

Owen had the nightstick Kelly gave him in the back of his pants. He had not shown it to Doug. He also had a flashlight.

It was dark, Owen testified, no streetlights, no illumination of any kind, no moon. He told Doug to stop the car and Owen reached over and turned it off. Doug turned off the lights. They sat in the car about five minutes. Owen said he was nervous. He didn't want to get out right away. It was about midnight, and it was raining.

Finally Owen told Doug to get out. And Doug did. Owen got out of the passenger side.

"When he got out of the car on the driver's side, and you got out of the car on the passenger side, who went where?" Wiley asked.

"He got out and shut his door and stood there and I walked around the car."

"Back or front of the car?"

"The front."

"Where was the knife?"

"It was in my hand."

"And was the nightstick still in your back pants—upper pants?"

"Yes, sir."

"After you got around to him, what did you do?"

"I got behind him and kind of gave him a push and told him to walk up in the woods."

"Did he say anything?"

"He asked me why."

"Did you answer?"

"I told him, just walk up in the woods."

"Did he say anything else?"

"No."

"Now, when you-all, you say, walked up in the woods, was this an uphill walk?"

"Yes, sir."

"And where you go up that hill before you get up there—as you go up the hill, there's maybe a three- or four-foot embankment there, is there not?"

"Right."

"How did you get him across that embankment?"

"He walked it."

"He just jumped up there?"

"Yeah."

"And, again, he didn't take off or try to run?"

"No, he didn't."

"Now, how close were you to him when you-all were walking up in the woods?"

"Maybe a foot."

"You were right behind him?"

"Yeah."

Owen said he had the knife in his hand beside him. It wasn't touching Doug. They walked perhaps five hundred feet and he told him to stop.

"Did you then take anything from Doug?"

"I took his watch and his ring."

"What kind of ring?"

"I think his wedding band."

"His wedding band?"

"Yes."

"Why did you take his watch and wedding band?"

"So it would look like he had been robbed, I guess."

"Whose idea was that?"

"Kelly's."

"Did she tell you to do that?"

"Before she left her house, she told me to make sure I got his jewelry, yeah."

Doug turned over the jewelry without protest. Owen put it in his pocket. He asked Doug if he had any money. Doug said he didn't and took out his wallet to show him. Doug put the wallet back in his pocket and Owen turned off the flashlight.

"I told him to get down on his knees," Owen said. And Doug complied without saying a word. Owen grasped the knife in his left hand and took the nightstick out with his right. He was standing beside Doug.

"I hit him with the nightstick in the back of his head. He fell forward. Facedown."

"Did he say anything or make any sound after you hit him with the nightstick?"

"No."

"No?"

"No."

"What did you then do?"

"Well, I put the nightstick back in my pants—in the back of my pants."

"Where you had it previously?"

"Yes, sir."

"Then what?"

"I took the knife and I stabbed him."

"Where did you stab him?"

"In his neck."

"How many times did you stab him, Greg?"

"I'm not sure exactly, but maybe eight or ten."

"Did Doug say anything after you stabbed him in any one of those occasions, or did he make any sound?"

"No."

"No sound at all?"

"No."

"Even after you hit him with the nightstick, he didn't make any sound?"

"No, sir."

"He didn't say anything to you?"

"No."

"After you stabbed him, you said—you thought eight to ten times, is that correct?"

"Yes."

"Did you believe he was dead at that time?"

"Yes, sir."

"Did you do anything to his body to try to make sure he was dead?"

"No."

"You didn't touch his body at all after you stabbed him?"

"No."

Owen said after he stabbed him, he put the knife back in its sheath in his pants and walked down the hill to Kelly's car. She arrived about the time he was killing Doug. He heard her car and knew she was there, even though her headlights were off. She stayed in the car.

"Did you say anything to Kelly, or did she say anything to you when you got there?"

"She asked me if he was dead."

"What did you say?"

"I think so."

"Did she do anything then?"

"She took the flashlight, and I guess she went to make sure if he was dead or not."

"You said you guess. Did you watch her go somewhere with the flashlight?"

"She walked off and walked around his car."

"Did you see if she walked up into the woods?"

"That's the direction she was heading, but I didn't watch her go. No."

Greg Owen then told the jury about a detail that he had initially withheld from police and prosecutors. He did not tell them until not long before the trial that at about the time he and Doug were getting out of the car, his beeper went off. The message displayed: *one, two, three,* a signal to him that Kelly was on her way out there.

After Kelly walked into the woods, Owen got in Doug's car and waited for her.

"When she got back, she got in her car and we turned around and drove back out to Indian Shoals Road."

Wiley handed him a picture of Doug's body in the woods.

"Is that how you left Doug Gissendaner out in the woods that night?"

"Yes, sir."

"Who drove whose car when you-all left that area?"

"Kelly drove her car, and I drove Doug's."

"Had you taken the keys out of the ignition and kept them when you walked up in the woods with Doug?"

"When I reached over to turn the car off when we first got there, I took the keys out then."

"All right. When you and Kelly drove—you driving Doug's car and she's driving her car—where did you-all go?"

"Back out to where Indian Shoals Road meets Luke Edwards Road."

"Did you stop somewhere?"

"Right there we did."

"About how far is that from where you had been down—where you stopped at with Doug?"

"I'm not sure."

"Approximately?"

"Three-quarters of a mile to a mile maybe."

"All right. You-all stopped at that location?"

"Yes."

"For what purpose?"

"Well, I got out and got the kerosene that Kelly had in her car."

"You got kerosene out of Kelly's car?"

"Well, when she was on her way down there, when she passed that intersection, she threw it out the window of her car and I got out and got it off the ground."

"What did you do with the kerosene after you got it off the ground?"

"I got back in Doug's car and turned around and went back down Luke Edwards Road and I stopped and got out of the car and poured kerosene in the car."

"What kind of bottle or what kind of container was the kerosene in?"

"It was a Coke bottle."

"A Coke bottle?"

"Yes."

"Did you pour it all out inside Doug's car?"

"Yes, I did."

"Did you then light it?"

"Yes."

"Where was Kelly at this time?"

"She was, I guess, driving down Indian Shoals Road."

"She wasn't there with you when you did this?"

"No."

"Okay. How did you start the car on fire?"

"With my cigarette lighter."

"Now, whose idea was it to burn the car?"

"It was just both of ours, I guess."

"Had you and Kelly talked about it—"

"Yeah."

"—prior to doing it?"

Greg Owen nodded his head yes. He said he set fire to the driver's seat, which was covered in plastic, first, closed the door and walked off. Kelly came back and he got in the car with her.

"And when you got in the car with Kelly, was anything said?"

"No."

Kelly drove him to his house. She left and he took off his clothes and put the knife, nightstick and jewelry in a garbage bag. One or two nights later, he put the garbage bag and the clothes he was wearing—black jeans, black sweatshirt, black long-sleeved shirt, pair of black gloves and a pair of hiking boots—in a Dumpster at a convenience store near his house. He kept the sweatpants he was wearing underneath the jeans.

"Did you talk to Kelly any further that night?"

"No."

"Greg, whose idea was it to kill Doug Gissendaner?"

"Kelly's."

"Would you have done it if not for that?"

"No."

"Did Kelly ever tell you why she wanted you to kill Doug?"

"Well, because if she divorced him, he wouldn't leave her alone and that she wanted him out of her way. If something happened to him, her house would be paid for."

"Did she tell you that?"

"Yeah."

Wiley asked Greg Owen if he knew Kelly

Gissendaner was seeing other men at the same time she was seeing him. He said he had a feeling she was, but he went along with her plan to get rid of her husband.

Kelly told him they should not see each other for a while after the murder. But he did talk to her four times while Doug was missing.

"We was just asking one another how we were doing. She would ask me if anybody tried to contact me, the police or anybody. I told her no. And then one time, she called me and told me the police were wanting to talk to me, and for me to make sure I have an alibi when they did."

"Was anyone else involved in the death of Doug Gissendaner?"

"No, sir."

Wiley asked why Owen did not tell police when he was arrested that Kelly Gissendaner was at the scene that night.

"I didn't want to," Owen replied.

"Was Kelly out there that night, Greg?"

"Yes, she was."

"You say that, knowing that you're under oath to tell the truth?"

"Yes, sir."

"That's all the questions I have, Judge," Wiley said.

Wilson asked the prosecution to turn over all the interviews they taped of Greg Owen. Wiley said he had two tapes in court, but he was not sure if it was all the state had.

Wilson began cross-examination by getting Owen to tell about himself. He was almost twenty-six, five feet nine inches and weighed 130 pounds in February 1997. He said he was living in a house behind the house of a friend at that time. And the friend told police that Greg Owen was with him the night of the murder. He was drinking Jack Daniels'—his regular drink—that night.

"Kelly didn't like you drinking, did she?"

"No."

"She got onto you on the fifth about it, didn't she?"

"Yeah."

"Were you smoking marijuana on the seventh?"

"Yes."

"Is that a regular thing?"

"Yes."

"Do you recall Detective Davis making a statement to you that Kelly is having relationships with other men?"

"I recall somebody saying it, yeah. I don't think it was Davis."

"Do you remember who Davis is?"

"Yes."

"Detective Davis?"

"Yes."

"He's the first one that said it, wasn't he?"

"I can't remember."

"You had a discussion with Detective King later on about all that, didn't you?"

"Yeah."

"You-all shared some cigarettes and talked about Kelly and her boyfriends, didn't you?"

"Yeah."

"Was that right before you decided to confess and say that Kelly was a part of this, right?"

"Right."

"It was your idea for Kelly to toss out some kerosene somewhere?"

"Yes."

"You've never been out to that area before?"

"No."

"Your mama lives how far from there?"

"Two or three miles."

Owen testified he did not tell his friend who lived in the other house, Ricky Lee Barrett, where he was going the night Doug was murdered. Barrett was in the living room watching television when Owen left.

"Did you tell him not to ask any questions where you were going?"

"Yes, I did."

Kelly picked him up at the end of the driveway, he said.

Wilson asked about his interviews with police.

"Do you remember telling Detective King you wanted to talk to him, but you were afraid he wouldn't believe you?"

"Yeah, I remember that."

"Do you remember asking him if Kelly took part in her husband's murder, would she go to jail?"

"Yeah."

"Did Detective King ask you whether somebody else was involved in this?"

"Yes, he did."

"What did you tell him?"

"I told him no."

"Did you tell him repeatedly that Kelly never came out to where you were killing Doug until after he was dead?"

"Yeah."

"At some point, did you take the detectives out to Luke Edwards Road?"

"Yes."

"And did you point out an area where you burned the car?"

"Yes, I did."

"Did you point out an area where you killed Doug Gissendaner?"

"Yes."

"Did you point out an area where you claimed to have thrown Doug's keys?"

"Yes."

"Did you point out an area where you hid in the woods while you were waiting on Kelly to come out there after you killed Doug?"

"Yes."

"Do I understand it was dark out there?"

"Yes, it was."

"Do I understand it was raining?"

"Yes, it was."

"Other than your flashlight, there was no source of lights around there?"

"No."

"Do you recall having told the detectives that on the way to your house after Kelly picked you up, you stopped and threw away some items?"

"I don't remember telling them—when we left on the way to my house, I threw the bottle that had the kerosene in it. I threw that out the window then."

"Where did you throw it out?"

"I don't remember the name of the road, but it was near where I burned the car at."

"Did you point that location out to the police?"

"Yes, I did."

"Why did you throw away your clothes?"

"In case they had blood on them."

"In fact, they had blood on them, didn't they?"

"I didn't check."

"You knew the pants had blood on them, didn't you?"

"No."

"What did you do with the sweatpants?"

"I kept the sweatpants."

"Were you aware that your sweatpants had Douglas Gissendaner's blood on them?"

"I didn't know until the police got them and they said they did. I don't know."

"The DNA report came back?"

"Right."

"So you know your pants had Doug Gissendaner's blood on them?"

"Yeah."

"But you already knew that. That's why you threw away the clothes, right?"

"I didn't know. I never checked."

"You didn't look at yourself to see if you had blood on you?"

"No."

"Do I understand you and Kelly didn't talk on the way to your house that night?"

"No."

"Do you recall having been in court on December 22, 1997?"

"Yes."

"Do you recall having been in front of Judge Stark that day?"

"Yes, I do."

"Your lawyers, Ronnie Batchelor and Keith Davidson, were with you, weren't they?"

"Yes, sir."

"What did you do that day?"

"I pled guilty."

"To what?"

"Murder."

"Why did you do that?"

"Because I was guilty."

"Is that the only reason?"

"Well, if I hadn't pled guilty and went to a jury trial, I could have ended up getting the death penalty."

"So as a result of your agreement and your guilty plea with the state, you got a life sentence?"

"Yes, sir."

"A life-imprisonment sentence?"

"Yes, sir."

"Now, at that plea hearing, were you sworn in? Did you give sworn testimony?"

"I think so."

"Do you remember being sworn? Do you swear to tell the truth, the whole truth, and nothing but the truth?"

"Yeah."

"Mr. Wiley swore you in, didn't he?"

"I think so, yeah."

"Now, during that proceeding, Mr. Wiley told the court the basic facts of the case, right?"

"Yes."

"And Mr. Wiley told the court that you alone took Doug Gissendaner at knifepoint out to the woods, had him get out of the car, had him walk up a hill, had him kneel down, hit him with a nightstick and then stabbed him to death, right?"

"Right."

"And Mr. Wiley subsequently then in that proceeding asked you if those facts were true and correct, didn't he?"

"Yes."

"And you said they were, didn't you?"

"Yes."

"At no time during that proceeding did you

say that Kelly Gissendaner was out at the scene after that murder, did you?"

"No."

"So you lied in that proceeding, didn't you?"

"I don't remember being asked if Kelly was there."

"You affirmed the facts that Mr. Wiley told the court, didn't you, sir?"

"Yeah."

"Mr. Wiley didn't tell the court anything about Kelly being out there, did he?"

"No."

Wilson kept at Owen. He wanted the jury to hear that Greg Owen had not implicated Kelly Gissendaner in the murder when he pled guilty. Wilson counted on the jury not knowing that in such a proceeding, a co-conspirator is not discussed. In a plea hearing, only the information pertaining to the defendant is necessary and admissible.

"That was because you had never told anybody, right?"

"Right."

Wilson wanted to throw Owen off-guard, to make him appear a liar. He looked at Owen and slowly sputtered, "So when you told the court that the facts Mr. Wiley told the court were true and correct, you were wrong, weren't you?"

"No."

"Within that plea hearing when Mr. Wiley explained your agreement and the recommendation in your case to a life sentence, he explained the contract not to ask for parole, right?"

"Right."

"He also explained that you were agreeing to testify against Kelly Gissendaner, correct?"

"Right."

"All right. Mr. Wiley did not say you were agreeing to testify truthfully and accurately, did he?"

"I don't think so."

"So your deal is, to get your life sentence, you have to testify against Kelly Gissendaner, don't you?"

"Yeah."

"Now you still have another charge pending in Barrow County, don't you, sir?"

"Yes."

"You're charged in Barrow County with the kidnapping of Douglas Gissendaner, aren't you?"

"Yes."

"All right. You understand you could get a potential life sentence over there?"

"Yes."

"Life in prison?"

Owen nodded.

Wilson wanted the jury to come away with one thought: Greg Owen changed his story time and again to save himself from lethal injection. His statements to police were nothing but self-serving. It was an essential point in Kelly's defense. Wilson asked about his contact with police. Somewhat reluctantly, although not unexpected, Owen admitted that two or three weeks after the guilty plea, he talked again with investigators. He told them what happened that night, but he did not say Kelly Gissendaner was there before he killed Doug Gissendaner. It was October 1998 before he told authorities she was there.

"Did you ever serve in the military?" Wilson asked.

"No, sir."

"Have you ever killed a man with a knife before?"

"No, sir."

"Have you ever studied how to kill people?"

"No."

"How did you know how to do it?"

"Common sense, I guess."

Wilson asked about the area where the Gissendaner house was. Owen said it was a subdivision that had been there for a while, not fancy, just average. Houses were perhaps one hundred feet apart on either side of the Gissendaners'. He arrived there about seven o'clock the night of the murder and walked into the house unarmed. Kelly Gissendaner went to her car and got the knife and nightstick out of her trunk and gave them to him, Owen testified.

Then Wilson changed subjects. He wanted to know what Owen had told investigators about the possibility that someone else was there that night, someone other than himself and Kelly. Wilson asked him whether he said he wouldn't tell investigators if someone else had been there. Again he wanted the jury to see a liar, not a helpless love-struck puppy.

"Would you tell this jury?"

"Yes."

"You would?" Wilson asked incredulously.

"Yes."

"You just wouldn't—you didn't like that investigator?" Wilson mocked him.

"Yeah. Well, there was nobody out there while I was killing Doug. Kelly didn't get out there until I was getting finished killing Doug. He was already dead when she got there." Greg Owen did not want to let Wilson get to him.

"Douglas Gissendaner never struggled?"

"No."

"He never attempted to get away?"

"No."

"He never said, 'Drop that knife or I'll hurt you'?"

"No."

"Prior to going out to the woods, did you cut him a little bit?"

"No."

"You never told him anything about his wife or kids, right?"

"No."

"And when you told him to go out to the car, you-all went and he walked around to the driver's side, right?"

"The driver's side was facing the house."

"Okay. He goes to the driver's side?"

"Right."

"And then you told investigators he reached over and unlocked the passenger door?"

"Yes."

"Douglas Gissendaner, who had just been taken out of his home at knifepoint and told to get in the car, reaches over and unlocks the door for you to get in the passenger side?"

"Yes, sir, he did."

"You had not shown him the nightstick?"

"No."

"You didn't have a gun?"

"No."

"You never said you had a gun?"

"No."

"Did you pass other cars along the way as you were going out in the woods?"

"Yes."

"There were other people out that time of night?"

"Right."

"Houses have lights on them, some of them?"

"Yes."

"Did you pass any police cars?"

"If we did, I didn't notice."

"Did you go past a Waffle House?"

"Yes."

"Which one? Do you remember specifically?"

"Highway 316 and I think it's Harbins Road."

"Across 316?"

"Yes."

"When you got out to the intersection of Indian Shoals and Luke Edwards Road, did you tell Mr. Gissendaner to go down that dirt road?"

"I told him to turn left."

"Did he say anything about going down a dirt road?"

"No."

"He didn't say anything?" Wilson wanted the jury to see how improbable Owen's story was— that Doug, a trained soldier, would simply get in a car with a stranger and walk off into the woods to his death when the assailant had no serious weapon and was smaller in height and stature.

"No."

"He turned left down the dirt road?"

Owen shook his head yes as Wilson took him through the story of sitting in the car, of getting out.

"So for some period of time, Mr. Gissendaner is standing outside the automobile along a dirt road in the middle of the night on a dark rainy night. Is that correct, sir?"

"Yeah."

"With you on the opposite side of that automobile?"

"Right."

"—with a knife?"

Greg Owen nodded and explained he told
Doug to walk into the woods because he was worried someone would drive down the road and
see them. He was in the woods perhaps twenty
minutes. He said he carried a small flashlight,
five inches long.

"Did you run into any trees or anything walking up through there?" Wilson asked.

"No."

"Who went ahead?"

"Doug did."

Wilson shifted the questioning again. He wanted
to keep Owen off-guard.

"Why did you kill this man?"

"Because Kelly wanted him killed."

"Kelly wanted you to kill him?"

"Yeah."

"How long have you known Kelly?"

"At the time, a little over a year."

"You had been dating off and on?"

"Yes."

"Fall of '95 was pretty much on, is that right?"

"From September of '95."

"During the fall—"

"Yes."

"—it was pretty much on, right?"

"Right."

"Spring of '96 it was pretty much off?"

"In April, yeah."

"And did you all mess around a little again in
the fall of '97—excuse me—'96?"

"Right."

Dates, times . . . Wilson kept the tempo going in
his questioning. He hoped Owen would stammer.

"Did you have a real burning passion for her?"

"I guess so, yeah."

"Well, describe it to us. How did you feel about Kelly?"

"I loved her."

"Well, is that it?"

"Yeah."

"You loved her, she said kill my husband, so he's dead, is that it?" Wilson made the story sound laughable, but he was zeroing in for the kill.

"Basically, yeah."

"You thought with Doug out of the way you would have Kelly all to yourself, didn't you?"

"That's what she said, yeah."

"That's what you thought, wasn't it?"

"Yeah."

"You believed that, didn't you?"

"Yeah."

"No longer would you have to worry about whether she was getting back with Doug next week or not—you would have her all to yourself?"

"Yeah."

Wilson asked about his interview with police in January 1998, after he had pled guilty. Greg Owen told them he stopped at the Dumpster on the way home.

"And that was a lie?" Wilson asked.

"Yes," Owen answered.

"That was false?"

"Yeah."

Success. Owen had admitted on the stand he was a liar. It was a pivotal moment for Kelly's defense.

"All right, sir. And you told investigators that lie after you had done your guilty plea?"

Owen nodded.

"Mr. Owen, after you killed Mr. Gissendaner, was there a period of time where you drove around while you were waiting on Kelly or waiting on a beep from her?"

"No."

"In your first two statements with the police, you told them there was such a period of time, didn't you?"

"Yes."

Another lie exposed to a jury listening intently twenty feet away. All eyes were on the thin man in a prison uniform who had once again admitted to being a liar. It was an essential point for the defense as it attempted to prove to the jury any story the man told was suspect. He could not be trusted. Wilson wanted to put a point on it when he asked, "In the course of this investigation, you've told a lot of lies, haven't you?"

"Yes, I have," Owen said.

"How did you get Douglas Gissendaner to allow you to kill him?"

"What do you mean?"

"I mean, how did you get him to allow you to kill him?"

"I don't understand what you're saying."

"Did you tie him up?"

"No."

"Did you slit him at the ankles so he couldn't run?"

"No."

"Did you cuff his ankles?"

"No."

"So he just casually knelt down and allowed you to kill him, sir?"

"Well, when he got on his knees, I hit him on

the head with the stick and he fell forward, and when he did, I stabbed him."

Owen said he was facing him, standing at his right shoulder. He didn't say anything before he hit Doug with the stick, swinging backhand.

Wilson asked Owen to stand up and demonstrate, which he did, indicating that he hit Doug in the back.

"Did he scream?"

"No."

"Did he say, 'Don't do that anymore'?"

"No."

"What did he do?"

"He fell forward on his face."

"When did you decide that you were going to kill this man?"

"That night."

"When that night?"

"That afternoon before Kelly picked me up."

"Well, did you psych yourself up?"

"Not really. I just decided if I get in that car and leave with her, I've got to kill him. If I don't, I don't—"

"You decided that before you left the house that day?"

"Yes."

"Did you anticipate he might resist?"

"Yeah."

"Did you anticipate that he might take that knife away from you and use it on you?"

"It's possible, yeah."

Wilson wondered about Owen's choice of weapon. The story of Doug getting into the car without resistance would have been more believable if Owen had had a gun. A gun was the equalizer between a big man and his smaller assailant. If the story didn't make sense, it could raise reasonable doubt in the mind of a juror. And one was all Wilson needed.

"Why did you go on—why did you go without a gun?"

"I didn't have a gun."

"You could have gotten one if you wanted one?"

"If I tried hard enough, yeah, probably."

"Did that go through your mind?"

"Yeah."

"But you decided to go ahead?"

Owen nodded.

"When you left that day, you didn't have a weapon?"

"No."

"When you decided that day you were going to kill this man and you left the house to go do it, you had no weapon?"

"No."

"Did you think you would do it with your bare hands?"

"I knew she had the knife in her car waiting for me."

"So you planned to abduct a man, take him out to the woods and kill him all with a single knife?"

"Yes."

"A man that's bigger than you?"

"Yes."

"A man with recent combat experience?"

"Yes."

"Did it ever cross your mind to take reinforcement with you?"

"No."

Owen said he met Doug three or four times, but

never talked with him on the phone. He denied calling Doug at work and threatening him.

"What goes through your mind while you're killing a man, Mr. Owen?"

"Nothing."

"Nothing?"

Owen shook his head no.

"Did it feel good?"

Wiley stood up. "Your Honor, I'm going to object to that question. He's badgering the witness."

"I'll sustain the objection," Stark said.

"Nothing went through your mind?" Wilson said.

"No."

Wilson asked that Greg Owen be subject to possible recall for further cross-examination and sat down. He had shown Owen a liar. He had shown him cold. He believed he had given the jury some reason to doubt the truthfulness of what they had heard.

Wiley had a few more questions.

He asked where Greg Owen was working the day Doug was murdered. Owen said it was near the Gwinnett Place Mall. He called Kelly around four-thirty that afternoon at work from a pay phone at a Texaco station.

He also asked about his interview with Investigator King.

"During that time, did Investigator King say anything to you about other people that Kelly might have been seeing?"

"He could have, but I don't remember if he did or not."

"You don't really remember that?"

"No."

"Would that have had anything to do with your statement implicating Kelly Gissendaner in this case?"

"No."

"Now, when you entered your plea last December in this court, the sentence you got was a life sentence with an agreement not to seek parole for how many years?"

"Twenty-five years."

"Now, when you killed Doug Gissendaner, was it your plan to take up residence with Kelly Gissendaner and her kids?"

"I guess, yeah."

"Is that what you wanted to do?"

"Yeah."

"Whose idea was it to kill him?"

"Kelly's."

Wiley wanted that to be the last word jurors heard from Owen. Kelly. Without her, Doug Gissendaner would be alive today. Doug Sr. sat back and watched Owen leave the stand. All he could think about was how cold he seemed. To Doug Sr., Greg Owen seemed like he was recollecting a day when nothing eventful happened. His detachment was chilling.

It had been a long day. Stark recessed until Monday, giving jurors Sunday off to be with family members.

Chapter 17

When court reconvened on Monday morning, Wiley called Laura McDuffie, who was no stranger to small-time crime. She was in jail for stealing two cars. Her cellmate at Gwinnett County Jail for two months had been Kelly Gissendaner.

"We talked a lot," she said.

In their late-night and daytime talks, Kelly told Laura about her husband's murder. She said she was mad because Owen had been sentenced to life in prison with the possibility of parole after twenty-five years and she was facing the death penalty.

"She said he wasn't going to make it out of the prison system because her mother was a security guard there," McDuffie testified.

The day Owen was sentenced, Kelly Gissendaner wrote McDuffie a letter. She asked McDuffie to find someone to take the blame for Doug's murder and thereby absolve her of the crime. In childlike handwriting, Kelly outlined in painstaking detail a story to be told by whomever McDuffie found. Kelly offered $10,000 to the person— a woman—who would take the fall for her.

The letter started with a description of Owen—five feet ten inches, blue eyes and dark brown hair.

Teeth are all messed up (black). He's a little guy, Gissendaner wrote.

She wrote out Owen's home number and her address (seventh house on the right, yellow). She told McDuffie what time Doug got home the night he disappeared and what Owen wore.

Then she wrote out the story for the accomplice to tell. The accomplice was to say that she had known Greg for a couple of months at the time of the murder. On the day of the murder, Greg and an unnamed friend picked up the accomplice and they all drove around smoking pot and drinking Jack Daniel's. Greg's friend dropped Greg and the accomplice off at Kelly's house. No one was home. Greg broke into the house using his driver's license, according to Kelly's story. In the letter, Kelly said the accomplice was to say Doug came home and Greg forced him into the car while the accomplice stayed in the house to wait for Kelly to come home.

Kelly's story went even further. The accomplice was to say that when Kelly walked in the door, the accomplice came out of the bathroom and put a gun to Kelly's head. She forced Kelly to page Greg with the one-two-three code.

Kelly spelled out the specific language the accomplice was to tell police. "This would let Greg know we were on our way to pick him up," the paid accomplice was supposed to say. "I made sure I stayed behind Kelly so she could not get a good look at me. I was also wearing a black ski mask."

Kelly embellished her story with all sorts of details, such as the accomplice held the gun to her as she walked down the hall and into the living room. Her keys were on the bookshelf in the living room on the left near the hallway.

"I told her to pick up her keys because we were going for a little ride," the accomplice was to confess to police. "We went through the kitchen and out the back door into the garage. She opened the car door. I made Kelly look away from me so I could get in the backseat of the car."

The car was a white Cavalier Z-24 with bucket seats.

"I held the gun to the back of her head the whole time." They drove to Luke Edwards Road and Owen came out of the woods, wet. Owen got in the car and told Kelly Gissendaner to go back down Luke Edwards Road. He held a knife to Kelly's throat. He told her not to tell anyone about what he did or he would kill her children, one by one while she watched, and then he would kill her.

Greg and Kelly, according to the story, dropped the accomplice off at a convenience store, where her car was parked. Greg paid her $100 for her help. The script filled four pages. It included such details as Greg taking the nightstick from the hall closet and that the fictitious accomplice met Greg at a bar called Cruise's in Cumming, Georgia, two months before the murder. It also said when she met him, he had long hair and two weeks later cut it short.

Then Kelly drew a diagram of her house for the woman who would give her an alibi. It showed the bedrooms where her sons and daughter lived, the bed where she slept with her husband and the nightstand beside it on which the phone rested. It showed the kitchen sink and where the glass door was located in the dining area. TV, chair, bookshelf—all labeled. McDuffie testified that she was astonished at Kelly Gissendaner's story and what she had asked her to do.

"I thought someone should know about it," McDuffie testified.

But that was not all Kelly Gissendaner wanted, McDuffie said. Kelly also had another chore for someone to do. She wanted someone to kill her friends Pamela Kogut and Kerri Otis and a woman she knew from church who "has money." All had talked to the police and Kelly wanted them out of the way.

Instead of finding someone to provide an alibi or to kill Kelly Gissendaner's friends, McDuffie said, she gave the letter and diagram to her lawyer.

The news startled the jury. Kelly sat at the defense table without expression. The prosecution led McDuffie through the tale in a simple and effective way. But the drawing that showed with such precision the location of everything in the room was most shocking.

While Wilson knew the evidence was damning, he also knew he stood a good chance of showing the jury just why Laura McDuffie could not be believed. At thirty years of age, McDuffie was a woman who had known trouble. Of average height and slim build, brown hair and brown eyes, she looked like a woman defeated. It was obvious to anyone looking at her that her life had been hard. She had spent more than a few years around people used to being on the wrong side of the law.

Wilson got her to tell about her past charges,

her past convictions. Mostly theft. But she knew people who had done much worse. Wilson was counting on the jurors, especially the women, to look at McDuffie and see someone unlike anyone they knew or had met. He especially wanted them to see someone who would lie to save herself from more time in prison.

It was a break for the jury when Nicole Bennett walked to the witness-box and sat down. No more prison talk. No more criminal history. She was a woman who held a job and supported herself. She worked at Rooms To Go with Kelly Gissendaner and was with Kelly the night Doug disappeared. She testified about a conversation at the Gissendaner home while Doug was missing.

"We were standing outside after she had done the interviews with the television crews and we were smoking cigarettes, and just our conversation was I asked her if she thought that maybe Greg had done something," Nicole said. "I said maybe he had something to do with this situation and maybe she needed to tell the police about him and she said no."

Nicole also testified she went with Kelly Gissendaner to the area where Doug's car was found. There was a deputy there, she said, and they were looking around to see where the car had been.

"It was muddy and it was just this black outline of—just black burned dirt. We were standing there, looking around. Kelly was looking around the car and kicking the dirt and that was just about it, really."

The prosecution was trying to show Kelly's lack of emotion in being at the scene where the car was burned. She kicked around the dirt, even though this could have been the place where her husband had lost his life.

"Did she make any statements about her husband or about anyone else at that time?" Dupree asked.

"The only statement that she made that I remember was that he wasn't there. She said he wasn't there, 'I couldn't, I can't feel his presence here, he's not here.'"

Nicole testified she spoke with Investigator Henry on Tuesday, February 11, 1997, when he came to Rooms To Go. She told him about a man named Greg.

Dupree asked about Kelly Gissendaner's emotional condition during the time Doug was missing.

"The only two occasions that I noticed was when she was doing the TV interviews with the news stations and at the funeral," Nicole said.

As she had during all the days of jury selection and testimony—by then almost two weeks—Kelly Gissendaner sat stoically between Wilson and Reilly.

"Thank you," Dupree told Nicole. "I have no other questions."

Wilson began with familiar territory, taking Nicole Bennett again through the facts of her friendship with Kelly Gissendaner. They'd known each other for about five months and shared confidences. She knew she and Doug had good and bad times, and she knew about Kelly's relationship with Greg Owen.

"And you knew it was on-again and even off-again, too, right?" Wilson asked.

"At the time that it was on-again is when I knew her," Nicole answered.

"But you knew her over the course of some time that it had been on and off?"

"Not really. She had only mentioned that she had been with him before, and then when I met her in October, she had mentioned him again in November, and that's when she saw him again."

He asked if she knew that Greg Owen had threatened to harm Doug.

"Like I stated before, she had mentioned to me that Greg had threatened her and her children, but that was not during the time that I knew her," Nicole said. "That was before I knew her."

"But you knew that Greg had made threats to harm Doug?"

"Not to harm Doug. She never mentioned that Greg had made threats to harm Doug. She mentioned to me that Greg had made threats to her that if she did not leave her husband that he would hurt her and her kids, not Doug. Doug's name was never mentioned in that."

He showed her a transcript of the interview she had with Henry and asked him to review it.

"Based on having viewed that, does that refresh your recollection some as to your discussion with Investigator Henry?"

"Some of it. Yes, it does."

"And did you, in fact, relate to the investigator that Kelly had told you about Greg threatening to do harm to Doug?"

"I guess then I do. It's been two years. It's hard to remember everything that you exactly say when you're talking to a bunch of people. I probably did say this. I don't recollect it now. What I remember now is her saying something to me about threatening the kids and her. So I'm sorry, I apologize."

Dupree had one question.

"Ms. Bennett, at the time you met Kelly Gissendaner in October and November of 1996, did she express any fear whatsoever of the man named Greg?"

"No, she did not."

A forensic document examiner with the Georgia Bureau of Investigation (GBI) testified that the letter to McDuffie was written by Kelly Gissendaner.

Wiley was winding up his case. He called the owner of the property on which Doug's body was found, who said he had seen the burned car. Another man testified he had seen it as well.

Various crime scene investigators and arson investigators testified that there was virtually nothing left of the inside of the car.

And then Wiley announced the prosecution had completed its case.

Chapter 18

The defense had a formidable task. Kelly Gissen-daner was not getting any sympathy points from the jury. She sat expressionless and emotionless through the trial so far. Seeing the photographs and videotape of her dead husband did not cause a stir. The lonely place he died evoked no reaction. She had already decided she would not testify and her attorneys concurred. She could not help them. The testimony that Kelly Gissendaner traipsed into the woods to be sure her husband was dead seemed to hover through the courtroom. As did the information that she stopped at Cracker Barrel on her way to her husband's grave site and the trip to the circus.

Their only hope was to show that Greg Owen had threatened Doug Gissendaner before, and that he had made good on the threat. Owen wanted Kelly to himself, without the possibility of her leaving him again to go back to her husband. They knew they had to show Greg Owen was a liar, and they believed they had done an ade-quate job of that on cross-examination. They also scored points, they believed, with the testimony of Laura McDuffie, the cellmate. Their strategy was to show them as not credible witnesses and to raise doubt in the minds of jurors as to Kelly's involvement. As any law school graduate knows, reasonable doubt does not mean no doubt. It means doubt that an objective and reasonable person might feel.

Steve Reilly, the second chair on the defense team, was working his first death penalty case. He graduated from the University of Georgia School of Law in 1985 and served four years in the U.S. Army Judge Advocate General's (JAG) Corps before going into private practice in Gwinnett County in 1990. He called as his first witness Bill Etheridge, a coworker of Doug's at Pro Shocks.

"You had indicated, if I recall, that you had had some conversations with Douglas Gissendaner, while the two of you were coworkers, about his relationship with his wife, Kelly, is that accurate?"

"Yes, it is."

"And did he speak with you—he being Douglas Gissendaner. Did he speak with you about difficulties in his relationship with his wife, Kelly?"

"Yes, he did."

"And did you have more than one such conversation with Douglas Gissendaner?"

"Yes, I did."

"And do you recall speaking with our investigator, Dennis Miller, about these certain conversations that you had with Douglas Gissendaner about his relationship with his wife?"

"Yes."

"Now, you indicated to Mr. Miller that you weren't particularly comfortable coming and testifying for the defense in this case, is that right?"

"That's right."

"Okay. And after Douglas Gissendaner's death, you were yourself interviewed by Detective Doug Davis, of the Gwinnett County Police Department?"

Wiley stood and said, "Your Honor, I'm going to object to leading this witness. He's got him on direct examination."

"Yes," Stark said. "I'll sustain the objection."

Reilly said, "Yes, certainly. Did you have any conversations with any detectives after the death of Douglas Gissendaner?"

"Yes, I did."

"And do you recall who that detective was?"

"Doug Davis."

"Of the Gwinnett County Police Department?"

"Yes."

"And did Detective Davis ask you specifically about what Doug Gissendaner had said to you regarding Kelly Gissendaner's boyfriend?"

"Yes."

"Was that the same subject that you later discussed with our investigator, Dennis Miller?"

"Yes, it was."

"When was it that you and Mr. Gissendaner had these conversations?"

"Late '95, early '96."

"And, approximately, what months in 1996 would the conversations have occurred?"

"January, February."

"And where did the conversations occur?"

"At work, at Pro Shocks and at lunch."

Stark interjected, "The only conversation I'm allowing is the one dealing with the telephone call, Counsel."

"The telephone call? Thank you, Your Honor.

Do you recall Douglas Gissendaner speaking with you about a telephone call he received?"

"Yes."

"Can you relate to the jury what Douglas Gissendaner said to you about that?"

"He said that he had just got a phone call. He was very—he looked jolted and all when he got the phone call. He told me—he said, 'I need to talk to you.' I said, 'Okay.'"

"And this was at Pro Shocks?"

"This was at Pro Shocks," Etheridge replied.

"Okay."

"So we went to the back of the warehouse to a cubbyhole and he told me—he said, 'I just had a phone call from a boyfriend of Kelly's and he just threatened to kill me.'"

"What else did Douglas Gissendaner say to you during that conversation?"

"He said he—I said to him—I said, 'You need to go to the cops, Gwinnett County.' He said, 'No. I'm okay. I'll be all right.' He said, 'I was in the army. I can take care of myself.'"

"Thank you, Mr. Etheridge. That's all I have."

On cross-examination, Wiley asked if that was the entire conversation.

Etheridge said it was all he could remember. Doug didn't tell him the man's name.

"I don't even know if he knew the name," he said.

"The defense would call Debra Lowery to the witness stand, please," Reilly said. Lowery worked with Doug Gissendaner at Pro Shocks for about a year and a half, until Doug died. She worked in the street rod building set up for street rod cars and saw Doug every day. She considered him a friend, but did not know his wife.

She said they talked about their personal lives, including his problems with his wife.

"When were the last of these conversations?"

"We talked up until he left on Friday and didn't come back."

"So then you had such conversations with Doug Gissendaner during the week of his death, is that right?"

She responded that she didn't talk to Doug about problems in his marriage that week.

"They seemed to be doing fine then," she said.

"Did you-all have discussions nonetheless about his relationship with his wife during that week?"

"No."

"Did Doug Gissendaner say anything to you during that week about a boyfriend of Kelly Gissendaner's?"

"I asked him was the guy still in the picture, and he said he had talked to him on the phone."

"Let me stop you there."

Reilly turned to the judge and said, "Your Honor, I believe we set our proper foundation, if I might be permitted to ask Ms. Lowery to state further the nature of the conversation."

"I'll allow her to testify as to Mr. Gissendaner's statements to her concerning the phone call. Is that what it's about, a phone call that he received?" Stark asked.

"Uh-huh," Lowery said.

"Was that during this period of time or was it earlier or when?" Stark asked.

"Doug had talked to the guy a week before or the week of his death. I don't really remember now."

"So it was sometime within two weeks of his death?"

"Right."

"He related to you something that was told to him in a phone call or related to a telephone conversation?" Stark asked.

"Yes. He talked to a guy named Harley."

"Okay."

Reilly asked, "May I be permitted to question her about that conversation?"

Stark said he would allow it.

"What, Ms. Lowery, did Douglas Gissendaner say to you about this boyfriend of Kelly's?"

"He just said he had talked to him on the phone and told him if he wanted some of him to come and get it."

"He said this—he being Doug Gissendaner—to the boyfriend?"

"Right."

"Did Douglas Gissendaner say anything specifically to you about any threats from the boyfriend?"

"No."

Reilly sat down and Wiley stood.

"Ms. Lowery, do you know who is Harley?"

"I assumed it was Greg Owen."

"But do you know that yourself?"

"No."

"You don't know who he is, do you?"

"No."

Reilly then called Jody Elizabeth Price, who lived at Parris Island, South Carolina, where her husband worked as a drill instructor at the Marine Corps base. She said she knew Kelly Gissendaner from her service at Fort Story, Virginia. They met in 1992, when both were serving in the army.

In mid-January 1997, while Price was living in the barracks at Fort Eustis, the home of the U.S. Army Transportation Corps, in Virginia, she saw Kelly again.

Reilly asked if Kelly Gissendaner was with Greg Owen when Kelly visited her at Fort Eustis. Stevens said he was not and that Kelly gave her no idea that she was traveling with anyone. She came about six o'clock in the evening and stayed three or four hours.

Reilly wanted to show it was possible that Greg Owen did not accompany Kelly Gissendaner, who appeared in no hurry to leave, even though her visit began at dinnertime and lasted several hours.

On cross-examination, Price told Wiley that she and Kelly Gissendaner spent the entire time in her room in the barracks and they did not go anywhere else.

"You didn't ride up to Virginia with her from Georgia, did you?"

"No, sir."

"And you didn't ride back from Virginia to Georgia with her, did you?"

"No, sir."

Wiley wanted to be sure the jury knew that Jody Elizabeth had no idea whether Kelly rode to Virginia alone or with Greg Owen.

"The defense rests, Your Honor," Reilly said.

Chapter 19

Judge Stark called a short recess, and once the jury was out of the courtroom, he turned to Kelly Gissendaner and said, *"Before we get into rebuttal, there's a few remarks that I need to address directly to you. The defense has rested in the case, which means that the defense will not put up any additional evidence at this point. Of course, you have the right to take the stand, to be sworn and testify under oath.*

"In any criminal proceeding, the defendant has the right to remain silent or to take the stand and be sworn and testify under oath and be subject to cross-examination. Before making a decision as to whether to take the stand and testify, the defendant should discuss that matter very carefully with your counsel and listen very carefully to their recommendation and suggestions to you in regard to that very important matter, but the ultimate decision rests upon the defendant as to whether the defendant would take the stand and testify or not.

"It's not a decision that's made by counsel. It's a decision that's made by the defendant after consulting with counsel and having the opportunity to discuss the ramifications of the case and make that very important

decision. Have you discussed this issue with your counsel?"

Stark read the prepared statement with ease. He had done it many times before and did not stray from remarks he knew would keep him out of trouble on appeal.

"Yes, I have, Your Honor," Kelly Gissendaner said.

"Have you personally then decided that you do not wish to take the stand and testify in this case after consultation with your attorneys?"

"No, I do not."

"You do not wish to testify?"

"No, sir."

"That's fine. I just wanted to make sure," Stark said. "These are matters that the court is required to inquire about. This has nothing to do with any matters other than we want to be sure that you understand your rights and that you have had an opportunity to talk to counsel and understand the situation. So as I understand it, you do not wish to testify and you have consulted with your attorneys about this matter?"

"Yes, I have, Your Honor."

These sixteen words were all the audience would hear from Kelly Gissendaner. The jury would hear none.

Wiley told Stark the prosecution had some rebuttal evidence. The jury came back into the courtroom.

Hutchinson called Keith Goff, who worked in the division of forensic sciences, also known as the Georgia Bureau of Investigation Crime Lab. He was a forensic serologist and a DNA analyst who received Bachelor of Science and Master of Science degrees in biology from Middle Tennessee State University. He also completed six months of training in the field of forensic serology and six months of training in the field of DNA analysis.

He had worked in the crime lab for just over twelve years.

"Mr. Goff, as part of the investigation in this case that we're here on today, were you asked to test a pair of blue sweatpants?"

"Yes, sir, I was."

"Did you bring those here with you today, sir?"

"Yes, sir."

"Mr. Goff, let me show you what's been marked for the purposes of identification as state's exhibit number forty-four and ask if you can identify what's contained therein, sir."

"Yes, sir. These were the sweatpants that I examined for the presence of blood, and the bag has the crime lab number, the item number and my initials on it."

"What was the purpose—or what tests was it that you were asked to perform on those particular pants, sir?"

"When the pants were brought into the lab, I was asked to examine them and determine if there was any blood present on them."

"And were you able to find any blood, sir?"

"Yes, sir, I found three areas that had blood on it."

"Okay. If you would, please describe for the ladies and gentlemen of the jury how it is that you would examine an article of clothing such as this to see if there's blood present."

"Generally, the first thing you will look for is a

reddish brown stain. A bloodstain usually looks reddish brown. However, it can look other ways according to just how much blood there is. You look at each stain. Any that appear to be reddish brown, you would conduct a chemical test on those, and if those are negative, then you go on to any other stains that are visible and appear to possibly be blood, and also conduct a chemical test on those. If you get a positive chemical test, that would indicate that you have blood in that stain."

"Did you find any blood on these particular—this particular item of clothing, sir?"

"Yes, sir."

"Where was that blood located?"

"I found three areas of blood. One of them was from what I call the waistband and there were two other areas on a drawstring or the string that you use to pull the pants tight."

"Did you find blood anywhere else on this article of clothing, sir?"

"No, sir. I did not find blood anywhere else."

"How large or small are these spots of blood that you found, sir?"

"The stain on the waistband did not really appear to be that much reddish brown material. There was just a little. It was a fairly diluted stain or fairly difficult to find. On the drawstring, there was only a very small amount of reddish brown stain. It was a very small stain."

"Would it be fair to say that these are approaching the point where they're not visible to the human eye?"

"They were very difficult to find."

"When you . . . well, what is it that you do to, actually, preserve and take those samples from the clothing?"

"Once you found a bloodstain on an item of clothing, you will cut that stain out and you will staple it to an index card and put the case number and the item number and your initials on that card. Then you file that away in a freezer."

Hutchinson asked Goff to step down from the witness stand and show the sweatpants to the jury. Goff first showed them the front, then the back, and then pointed out where the bloodstains were. One was on the waistband, which he cut out to test. He also found a stain on the section of the drawstring where it ran the bloody waistband.

There were no other stains on the pants, he said.

"You would have tested anything that appeared to be blood, is that right?" Hutchinson asked.

"Yes. Anything that looks like it could be blood, [we] would normally conduct a chemical test on."

Hutchinson told him to return to the witness stand and asked Goff what tests he performed on the blood samples.

"I used two chemicals. One is called TMB and the other one is called phenyl ethylene and what you do is you take a cotton-tipped applicator and moisten it and rub it across an area that you suspect may be blood so you can pick up some of that material that's in that stain. You'll apply one of the chemicals to one swab and the other chemical to the other one and then you'll apply what's called hydrogen peroxide. If the stain is, in fact, blood, one swab will turn green and the other one will turn pink or a reddish—actually, it's a pink color. And if both swabs change colors to those— the green and the pink, that indicates you have blood."

"Were you also supplied with certain known

blood samples of the people involved in this case, sir?"

"Yes, sir. I was supplied with three known blood samples."

"And taking those blood spots that you found off the pants, did you perform any comparisons?"

"Yes, sir, I did."

"And what did you do, sir?"

"I analyzed the blood that was present on the pants and then compared the DNA profiles that I got from the blood on the pants from those three areas to the profiles that I got from the known blood samples."

"And with what results, sir?"

"Okay. In area number one, which was from the waistband, I found DNA profiles from at least three people. One of the profiles matches up to Douglas Gissendaner. The other profile will match up to Gregory Owen, and the other DNA samples or DNA types that were present I could not conclusively assign to any particular person. On area three, which is one of the drawstrings, again I found DNA from at least three people. One of the patterns matched up to Douglas Gissendaner. The other pattern matched up to Gregory Owen, and, then again, I had other DNA types which I did not conclusively assign to any person. On area number two, I only found DNA from two people, and area two is also from the drawstring. One of the profiles matched up to Douglas Gissendaner, and the other profile matched up to Gregory Owen."

"So the third blood material that you found in those tests, do you know who that would be?"

"I can't conclusively say who it actually is."

* * *

Goff said his tests showed the blood was consistent with Doug's blood, but he could not rule out everyone else and say for certain it was his blood.

"What is your degree of certainty?"

"I can give you a frequency that I calculated when I compared the blood from the pants."

"Please do so."

"In the African-American population, about one in every four hundred billion individuals would have a pattern that's consistent with what I found on the sweatpants, and in the Caucasian population, about one in every one billion people would have a pattern that's consistent with what I got from the sweatpants."

"So you believe there's one in one billion chance this is not Douglas Gissendaner's blood?"

"Well, that's not really how we state it. What I would say is that if you took the pattern that I got on the sweatpants and you just compared that to everyone you could get a blood sample from in the world, about one in every billion people that you compared it to would match that profile."

"In your professional opinion, is Douglas Gissendaner's blood on those pants?"

"It matches Mr. Gissendaner."

"Is Greg Owen's blood on those pants?"

"It is consistent with Greg Owen's—it's consistent with Greg Owen's DNA. It could be blood. It might not be from blood, but it is consistent with his DNA."

After a recess, the jury came back into the courtroom and George Hutchinson began to sum up the state's case. He read the indictment against Kelly Gissendaner.

"That indictment, ladies and gentlemen, forms the issues which you're going to have to decide here in the next little while after the judge gives you an opportunity to hear the applicable law in this case. The judge permits me and permits an attorney—I don't know which one, but one of the attorneys representing the defendant, to give a closing argument or summation of the evidence to point out to you, ladies and gentlemen, what we believe the evidence has shown in this case.

"It also gives us an opportunity to discuss with you for a few minutes some of those points of law that the judge is going to charge you in a little while. It's not my job to tell you the law. It's not the defense attorney's job to tell you the law. Listen to what the judge charges you in connection with the law. There are a couple of principles that I do want to spend a couple of minutes talking with you about.

"The first is the concept of parties to the crime. Now, it's obvious based on the evidence that's been presented in this case that Kelly Gissendaner is not the actual killer of the victim in this case. The evidence in this case, ladies and gentlemen, is that Kelly Gissendaner is a party to the crime of murder."

He said the classic example of this principle is a bank robbery. One person goes into a bank, points the gun at the tellers and takes the money. The person that's providing the getaway vehicle helped plan. Both are guilty under Georgia law, he said.

"The judge is going to charge you that every party to a crime can be charged and convicted of the commission of that crime and among the things that the judge is going to tell you is that a person is a party to a crime when that person intentionally helps in the commission of the crime, or that person intentionally advises, encourages, hires, counsels or procures another to commit the crime.

"Now, ladies and gentlemen, I submit to you that all the evidence that you've heard during the period of time that you have been jurors in this case points to the defendant's guilt as the person that arranged the killing of her husband."

He said both sides agree on a number of points. Douglas Gissendaner is dead. Douglas Morgan Gissendaner died in the woods off Luke Edwards Road on his knees as a result of being stabbed repeatedly through the back and through the neck with a knife. Mr. Gissendaner died in Gwinnett County.

"What's left for you to decide, ladies and gentlemen, isn't whether or not Greg Owen is guilty of the crime, but whether or not the defendant on trial here today is a party to that crime. The real question that you have to answer when you go back into that jury room to begin deliberating this case, ladies and gentlemen, is did Kelly Gissendaner help in the commission of this crime, or did she intentionally advise, encourage, hire, counsel or procure another to commit that crime?"

He said the jury would have to decide whether Kelly Gissendaner intended to kill her husband.

"There's no question about the intent in this case, ladies and gentlemen. Nobody slipped and fell on top of Mr. Gissendaner with a knife. Mr. Gissendaner was intentionally murdered, and all the evidence points to the defendant's intentional involvement in the death of her husband."

He said he also wanted to talk to the jury

about alternative charges. Kelly Gissendaner was charged with two different types of murder.

"Only one person has died—Mr. Gissendaner— but under Georgia law, there's more than one way to commit a murder. The first way that she's charged with murder in count one of the indict- ment is commonly referred to as malice murder. Malice murder is the intentional killing of another person. That's all it is. It's fairly straightforward. Malice is sometimes confusing to jurors. Malice doesn't necessarily mean planning. It doesn't mean forethought. It doesn't mean premeditation or anything like that, because premeditation is not an element of the crime. It's not necessary to prove for the crime of murder under Georgia law. Malice really just means nothing more than mean- ing to do it. Malice can be formed in an instant. Of course, the evidence in this case is that there was premeditation and planning, but you're going to hear the judge charge about malice and that there's no need for any sort of premeditation in connection with murder or for the conviction of the defendant for malice murder.

"It's the state's contention, ladies and gentle- men, that this is a malice murder. There's no question about that in our minds, ladies and gen- tlemen, and all the evidence points to that. All the evidence points to a premeditated, planned- out, thought-out and ultimately executed plan to kill Douglas Morgan Gissendaner."

He said the other type of murder is felony murder.

"Felony murder deals with the following con- cept. Going back to our friend the armed robber that we discussed a little bit ago, the person goes in to commit the armed robbery. There's the guy waiting outside and knows that he's participating in an armed robbery, okay. He's planned it ahead of time, given the guy the gun that goes in to rob the bank with, and he's waiting outside to provide him a getaway.

"The person that actually goes in the bank doesn't actually plan on killing anybody when he goes in there. His point is just to get the money. But what ends up happening is somebody unexpectedly resists and he shoots and kills them. That's felony murder, ladies and gentlemen. A person who while in the commission of a felony causes the death of another person, whether they set about to do that in the first place or not, is guilty of felony murder. Likewise, the person waiting for him out in the car is equally guilty of that crime because he knowingly participated in the armed robbery that caused that poor innocent person's death.

"Now, why is that charged in this particular case? Of course, the evidence is that it's malice murder, and in that charge of felony murder, you heard that the underlying felony that the defendant and her accomplice, Mr. Owen, were in the commission of was kidnapping."

Hutchinson explained that Kelly Gissendaner was not charged with kidnapping because her husband was taken from his home in another county. Such charges were still pending against Greg Owen.

"I don't know what Mr. Wilson is going to argue or Mr. Reilly, but in the event that they attempt to persuade you that the defendant only wanted to go along with some small part of this plan and didn't intend for it to result in the

death of her husband, the defendant is still guilty
of felony murder."

Hutchinson also told the jury the judge would
talk to them about coercion. He reminded them
of Pam Kogut's testimony that Kelly Gissendaner
called her and confessed.

"That's a confession, ladies and gentlemen, to
the crime of murder, but the reason you're going
to be charged about coercion in this case is because there was a second phone call from the defendant to her friend Pam Kogut," Hutchinson
said. "In that second phone call, the defendant,
apparently having had an opportunity to think it
over some more, said, 'I did it, but Greg forced
me to do it. He made threats against me.'"

Hutchinson thanked the jury for its attention
and talked in a folksy way about how lawyers like
to ramble on.

"I know you're eager to get to the part of this
trial where you will have your opportunity to
begin deliberating the evidence," he said.

He said he'd have another opportunity to talk
to them before they deliberated, but added, in
the end, it was all about one thing: he would ask
them to find Kelly Gissendaner guilty of murder.

Chapter 20

Edwin Wilson, the man with the Deep South drawl, rose and began his closing statement by saying simply that he felt a heavy responsibility. He knew it was the last time he would talk with the jury about his client. He wanted it to count. He wanted what he said to be remembered once the jury went to its room to deliberate. He was Kelly's voice.

"Kelly has asked me to thank you for your close attention to the evidence in the case," he said, trying to make her more human. "It's been obvious that you-all were paying close attention during the evidence by the way you're taking notes and the way you nod your heads and the way you watched the witnesses. We appreciate it. We all do."

He reminded the jury that the evidence was what they heard and saw from the witness stand and what was in the various exhibits. The indictment was not evidence. As all defense attorneys do in capital cases, Wilson described for the jury the concept of reasonable doubt and the state's responsibility to prove guilt. The prosecution does not prove innocence.

"The defendant need prove nothing," he said. "Now, we believe we have proved certain things in this case, but we didn't have to. The burden of proof rests right here at the state's table. They're the ones that brought these charges. They're the ones that have got to convince you, each one of you, beyond a reasonable doubt that Kelly Gissendaner is guilty of something."

Reasonable doubt, Wilson said, doesn't mean no doubt. It is a doubt of a fair-minded and impartial juror honestly seeking the truth.

"That's all we ask," he said. "We ask that you be fair-minded back in that jury room, that you be impartial, and that you honestly seek the truth. I think Judge Stark will tell you that a reasonable doubt is the doubt that you have [when] applying your common sense and reason."

Doubt can come from lack of evidence or conflicts in evidence, he said.

"Judge Stark will tell you that if your minds are wavering, unsettled, and unsatisfied back there in the jury room, then that is a doubt of the law," Wilson said. "He'll further tell you if you individually do not believe the state has proved Kelly's guilt beyond a reasonable doubt, it is your duty to acquit her and return a verdict that says she is not guilty."

He asked them to be circumspect in deciding which of the witnesses were most credible. Think about Greg Owen, Laura McDuffie and Pamela Kogut, he said. Think about how they testified, what they said, how they presented themselves. He told them in the law such a concept is called impeachment.

"We're not talking about President Clinton or Ms. Lewinsky or any of that," he said, describing impeachment as proving that a witness is unworthy of belief. In the law, this can be accomplished by disproving the facts to which a witness has testified, by showing the witness has bad character.

He said Greg Owen's statements were not factual and McDuffie was shown to be of general bad character.

"Judge Stark will also tell you that a witness may be impeached or unworthy of belief if it is proved that the witness has been convicted of crimes involving moral turpitude," he said. That ruled McDuffie's testimony out, Wilson said.

"His Honor, Judge Stark, will tell you that theft by taking and theft by receiving are, in fact, crimes of moral turpitude. I ask you to consider whether Mr. Owen has been convicted—excuse me—has been impeached by the demonstration of a crime involving moral turpitude. As he told you, he's pled guilty to the offense of murder. I would suggest to you, both of those witnesses have been proved unworthy of belief by the demonstration of the convictions of crimes involving moral turpitude."

A witness may also be impeached if it is proven they made contradictory statements, which he believed both Owen and Kogut did.

If the defense has shown that, the jury may disregard the statement.

"We have a special type of witness in this case. We've had a lot of witnesses, but there's a special rule of law regarding what we call accomplice testimony. The state alleges that Ms. Gissendaner was involved or a party to a crime with Mr. Owen. So when Mr. Owen testified in here, he's testifying as an alleged accomplice under the law and would be defined as an accomplice. Accomplice testimony is different. His Honor, Judge Stark, will give you that law. I believe he'll tell you that in general—generally, in trials, testimony of a single witness, if believed, would be sufficient to establish—"

Hutchinson rose. "Your Honor, I have to object. The closing argument is an opportunity to argue the law, not to read it to the jury. It's the judge's responsibility. Mr. Wilson is just reading the charge to them. I don't think that is appropriate."

Stark responded that the defense can refer to the charge that he expects the court to charge.

Wilson continued: "Thank you, Your Honor."

He went on to say that in most cases a single witness can establish a fact, but an accomplice cannot. It's not sufficient evidence to convict. There must be corroborating evidence, supporting evidence, of the alleged accomplice.

"I think Judge Stark will tell you that that corroboration has got to be more than just a crime happened. It's got to be sufficient to connect the accused with the criminal act, and it's got to be more than casting a grave suspicion. So there has to be a large degree of corroboration. I suggest to you that the state's alleged accomplice cannot be corroborated. He cannot be corroborated in significant detail. He cannot be corroborated in connection of Ms. Gissendaner with criminal acts."

The judge, Wilson said, will tell the jury about witnesses who might be testifying to further their own interest or who might be testifying after they have been granted immunity or leniency.

"I would ask you to consider that regarding Owen and I would ask you to consider that regarding McDuffie," he said. "Mr. Owen is in here testifying pursuant to a deal. The state made a deal with the Devil. Mr. Owen's deal is he gets a life-imprisonment sentence and does not run the risk of the death penalty sentence."

Wilson wanted the jury to be sure to understand that Greg Owen made a deal to testify against Kelly in return for a sentence of life imprisonment. He wasn't agreeing to testify truthfully, the lawyer said. Only to testify against Kelly. Not only that, Wilson said, but Owen could be charged with kidnapping in Barrow County, where he abducted Doug. Owen could have been made to plead guilty to that charge. Owen pled guilty to the Gwinnett County charges on December 22, 1997, and that admission could have been admitted into court in Barrow County. Prosecutors could have threatened him with a consecutive sentence, which would have ensured that Owen would have been imprisoned for the rest of his life. But eleven months after Doug was murdered, no additional charges had been filed. No consecutive sentence had been handed down. And prosecutors had not told Owen specifically that they wanted the truth.

"Is that a reason for you to question Mr. Owen's believability?" Wilson asked.

"And McDuffie—she testified about her case and I'm not certain what she said about the deal she has. She had one and she didn't have one and she pled guilty and the state agreed for her to get out of jail that day, but then she was supposed to come back to be sentenced at a later date, and she was supposed to live at her parents' house and she couldn't. So she ended up back in jail, but she didn't have a deal. When we pressed her, it seems as though she kept—well, in her letter to Judge Jackson, she says she did sort of have a deal. She said Investigator Perez promised her she's going to come into court and give her time served.

"Is that a deal? Is that a reason to question that Ms. McDuffie's testimony might be slanted in such a way as to further her own interest?"

He moved on to talk about the evidence and what he believed the state failed to prove.

"Obviously, the state's central key witness is Owen. Now, Owen is, first of all, a murderer. Mr. Owen is someone who, to hear him tell it, would take a man from his home, take him out in the woods and kill him with a knife. So Mr. Owen is also a liar. He lied in here, but he lied repeatedly throughout the course of the investigation and—actually—admitted it. I guess he had to. There's too many lies. Mr. Owen is a liar and a murderer.

"The state starts out with a deal with the Devil and brings him in here to testify. And I will suggest to you that if Mr. Owen were a credible witness, his story doesn't hold water, and you have to start out with a believable chain of events. You've got to start out with something that makes general sense. You've got to start out with something you can believe."

Wilson recounted the story, mocking it as he went. Owen said it was planned by Kelly Gissendaner for months. She spoke about it in October, November, December and January. For four months, she planned a kidnapping, abduction and murder.

"If two people are together to plan a murder, can't they do a whole lot better job than was done here? To plan to take a man out of his home by having one single person accost the man in his home and do so with a knife.

"Now, would someone planning a kidnapping and a murder for a number of months end up with that plan? Is that a reason to have a doubt about the state's case? Mr. Owen tells us he was at the Gissendaner home and that he confronted Mr. Gissendaner with a knife and said let's go."

Wilson said the jury had learned a lot about Doug Gissendaner in the days since the trial began. He was healthy. He was strong.

"We know he outweighed Mr. Owen," Wilson said. "We know he was tall, we know he worked as a mechanic and we know that Doug Gissendaner had recently served in the United States Army. We know that in the United States Army he went through basic combat training. We know that he was trained in combat arms. He was combat arms–qualified. We know he was a tanker in the Army Corps. We know that he served in a combat theater in Desert Storm. And, therefore, we know that he had escape and evasion training."

Hutchinson objected, saying the facts were not in evidence.

Stark sustained the objection. Stark told the jury to remember this was counsel commenting on the evidence. It was not evidence per se. But Wilson scored in getting the words out in the open.

"I would suggest to you as a reasonable inference from his service in the army and from his having served in a combat theater he was trained in how to defend himself in the woods," Wilson told the judge.

Hutchinson objected again, and again Stark sustained.

"Owen says that he had Mr. Gissendaner leave his home at knifepoint," Wilson continued. "Owen says that he had Mr. Gissendaner go out and get in his car. Owen says that he walked Mr. Gissendaner to his side of the car, the driver's side, and then Owen walked around the car to the passenger side, and he tells us that Mr. Gissendaner reached over and unlocked the door.

"I would suggest to you there are several things wrong with that. Now, Owen also says that they then drove out of the neighborhood. There are in evidence a number of pictures of the house, a number of pictures of the neighborhood. Take a look at them.

"Douglas Gissendaner would not have left his home without a struggle. If Owen confronted Douglas Gissendaner in his home with a knife, that house would have been all torn up.

"Douglas Gissendaner would not have simply gone out that door with Owen. Had Douglas Gissendaner gone out that door with Owen, he wouldn't have gotten in that car. There's too many neighbors' houses too close.

"Had Douglas Gissendaner gotten in the car, I suggest there ain't no way in this world he would have leaned over and unlocked the door for a man with a knife to get in the car. There are too many options at this point."

It seemed obvious that had the situation played out the way Owen said it did, that Doug could have simply refused to unlock the door and then locked his door.

"In which case, someone with a knife will just be standing on the outside of his car," Wilson said. "With a little assistance from the horn, neighbors could be alerted very easily.

"Additionally, Douglas Gissendaner would probably have driven off leaving Owen standing there with his knife. That doesn't work. Mr. Owen told us there was nobody else with him. He did not have a gun. He didn't tell Mr. Gissendaner, 'I've got your kids tied up' or anything else like that.

"That story don't work. There had to have been other people, at least one, with Greg Owen. There had—there may have been or could have been—and probably was—at least one firearm involved.

"The story would make sense, had someone been in the floorboard behind Douglas Gissendaner when he got in the car. Other than that, there's no way in the world Douglas Gissendaner would have let Owen in the automobile. No way.

"Owen's story goes on to tell us about driving out of the neighborhood. Douglas Gissendaner would not have driven out of the neighborhood. There's too many options there. He could drive into a neighbor's house or drive over Greg Owen before he got in.

"If Douglas Gissendaner drove out of the neighborhood, there's no way he's going to drive out in the woods—no way—with a man seated in the passenger side with a knife. There's no way Douglas Gissendaner is going to drive way out in the woods. There's too many options.

"There are other cars driving on the road. They passed a Waffle House. Douglas Gissendaner would have driven into that Waffle House, maybe driven slap into the front door and jumped out of the car or driven into another automobile or jumped out of the car and left the car running, leave the car going with Owen in it.

"There's no way Douglas Gissendaner would

have driven out into the woods with Greg Owen. If Douglas Gissendaner had gone to the woods with Owen, there's no way he's going down a dirt road. Once he gets down the dirt road, there's no way Owen's story is true.

"Owen tells us that after he left the paved road, they drove down the dirt road and came to a rest, but he sat in the car for about five minutes, and then he says—then he says Doug Gissendaner got out the driver's side and I got out the passenger side. Now, I've got to mention the area out there a minute.

"You can't have the full flavor of this place if you personally haven't been there, and during the defense's presentation, we asked that you be allowed to go out there and see this place for yourself. That's why Sergeant Parr was dispatched out there, and he told you about it being too wet and too dangerous for you to go out there.

"We tried to give you a feel for the place in as much detail as we could. The state didn't tell you a whole lot about it. We tried to pull out of their witnesses and we gave you a whole lot of pictures and a video of as much of that area as we could. We've got aerial photographs as defense exhibits.

"We've got as many photographs as we could get to help you get a feel for that area out there. The area is important. The conditions and the nature of that area is very important. I suggest this is not—well, it's wooded. It's brushy. It's what we call difficult terrain.

"It's deer-hunting country. It's the closest thing we have left in Gwinnett County to wilderness, and there's rickety old dirt road going through it, Luke Edwards Road. On the night in question, by Owen's testimony, it's got to be after midnight or thereabouts. It's in the middle of the night. It's dark. It's raining.

"Ladies and gentlemen, there is no way Douglas Gissendaner would have gotten out of that vehicle on that dirt road out in this remote area and waited for Mr. Owen to come around the car. There's no way. No way. He would have been gone. This was a healthy, strong male.

"If he wasn't gone, he would have been finding something with which to defend himself out there, a stick, a branch, a rock, something. He would not have been sitting there waiting for Mr. Owen with his knife to come around the car. There's no way. There's absolutely no way."

Owen then claimed they walked into the woods and climbed over an embankment, Wilson said. They walked up a hill through difficult terrain.

"And I believe the distance he testified to was somewhere between three hundred and four hundred feet up there, one hundred yards or better. It was far enough off the road that nobody found the body during all these searches for a week or ten days or so.

"It was a wooded enough area that in all their searches, for days and days and days, nobody found the body seven-tenths of a mile from where the burned car was. Owen would have you believe that Mr. Gissendaner just casually walked up this hill with him out into the woods at knifepoint and that he never attempted to run. Douglas Gissendaner would have run.

"Had Mr. Gissendaner gone up that hill with Mr. Owen, Mr. Gissendaner would have defended himself. Mr. Owen says that he was standing to his side and he told him get down on his knees and he did. Nope. No way

"Doug Gissendaner ain't going to kneel for Greg Owen. No. Huh-uh."

Wilson reminded the jury of testimony from two of Doug's coworkers who said they knew Greg had threatened Doug, but he replied he could take care of himself.

"'If he wants a piece of me, let him come on.' Is that the kind of statement from somebody who would meekly submit to Owen? Owen tells us then that standing to his side he knocks him in the head with a nightstick and there was no defense at all. Now, that didn't happen like that, either. Doug Gissendaner is not going to allow Greg Owen to slap him on the head with a nightstick without defending himself."

Hutchinson stood. "Your Honor, I have to object again. I think I have been patient with what Mr. Wilson is doing, but, unfortunately, as far as I know, he can't read minds and there's been no evidence as to what Mr. Gissendaner would or wouldn't have done. We're not in a position to get to know any of that, of course, because he's dead. I, therefore, object that this is not evidence in the case."

"I'll overrule the objection. Counsel has certain leeway in making arguments and drawing inferences from the sworn testimony and from the evidence presented. You will recall what the evidence was in the case. As I say, the statements of counsel do not constitute evidence, but they're given leeway in their argument. You may proceed."

Wilson continued. "We do know a lot about Doug Gissendaner. We do know a lot about Greg Owen. We have heard Greg Owen's testimony of how these events occurred. I suggest to you there's no way Douglas Gissendaner would have allowed Greg Owen to hit him with a nightstick without defending himself.

"The medical examiner testified no defensive wounds. That's when you put your arms up, basically. That is an instinctive reaction as well as something people in the United States Army are taught. That's an instinctive reaction.

"If Greg Owen is standing on the side of Doug Gissendaner and he raised a nightstick or raised his arm back in any way, Doug Gissendaner would have defended himself. Owen would have had to knock his arms out of the way to get to his head. There's just no way. No way.

"We know that Mr. Gissendaner was last seen alive by friends at about ten o'clock that night. He was not drinking. He was not doing drugs. He was not debilitated in any way. Greg Owen did not tell you—actually, he told you he did not tie him up. He didn't do anything else to keep him from offering resistance other than waving his knife at him.

"Greg Owen's story goes on further, ladies and gentlemen, to the effect that he killed Mr. Gissendaner by stabbing him. In his testimony and in his October [1998] statement, he added this part about Kelly arriving at the scene as he's finishing up, and he testified she drove in with her lights off.

"I want you to consider whether that's reasonable from what you know about this area, from what you know about this rickety old dirt road that when it rains, it becomes impassible and too dangerous for us to go there and take a view of it.

"Mr. Owen says Kelly drove out there with her lights off as he is finishing up killing Mr. Gissendaner. Is that plausible? Mr. Owen tells us further that after he killed—after he stabbed Mr. Gissendaner, he says he didn't know if he was dead and didn't check.

"Well, excuse me, but if you plan for months to kill someone and you kidnap him and take him out in the woods and stab him a bunch of times, are you not going to check and see if he's dead?"

He said even though the area is remote, other people go there. They go because it is remote. People ride four-wheelers. They hunt. They go out there to drink.

"So Mr. Owen wants you to believe that he's off three hundred or four hundred feet in the woods killing a man and a car drives up with the lights off and he calmly and coolly walks out to it. Now, I suggest to you that makes no sense at all.

"If you're in the process of killing a man and a car drives up with the lights off—through the woods you can't see to the dirt road. You don't know who's in the car. Is that Sergeant Bell, the local DNR man? Is that Hughel Harrison, who owned the property? Who is in that car? I don't think you would just go running out to it. Is that a reason to doubt the state's case?"

Wilson mocked the idea that Kelly asked if Doug was dead, and when Owen said he didn't know, she walked up into the woods to check. Kelly would have known the general direction Owen came from, but how could she find the body in the dark?

"Take a look at these photographs," Wilson said, holding them up. "Remember the videos you have seen and try and figure out how someone could find this body off that way in the middle of the woods on a rainy, dark night to go check and see if he's dead, and just goes and checks and comes right back. Is that plausible? Is that probable? Is it possible? I suggest not.

"That's what Greg Owen has told you. Greg Owen has told you he has never even been out there before, never ever ever. According to him, right after that, he went and burned the car. We talked about kerosene or gasoline or some kind of accelerant, and Greg Owen told us—he said, 'I had told Kelly where to toss out some kerosene so I could find it after we killed him, and we took the cars back up, and I went to that place and I got the kerosene and I burned the car.'

"Now, excuse me, but how would Mr. Owen— never having been to this area—tell Kelly ahead of time where to toss out some kerosene where he could find it, and then how does he just kind of go back in that general location and immediately find it to burn the car?

"This location is important. The scene and the area out there is real important." He reiterated his question. He wanted the jury to remember the point. It was important. It further proved how unbelievable the testimony was. It was a story. Not fact.

"How can Mr. Owen have told her where to toss out an accelerant where he could find it if he had never been there before?" Wilson said, his voice rising. "How could that be? It can't be. No way. There's no way.

"About that kerosene, too, and the plausibility of that. Why—why would—why would it have been thrown out of the car anyway? If Mr. Owen wanted something to burn the car with, why would he tell Kelly to toss it out? Why wouldn't it have just been with her? What's the plausibility of the story of tossing out kerosene at all? Most of us don't go tossing kerosene and gasoline around. That's not a very smart thing to do. And then again—Mr. Owen has told different tales, has added to or taken away from and contradicting.

"On this witness stand, he told you about Kelly coming out there to the crime scene while he was killing Mr. Gissendaner, or as he was finishing or immediately after. Now—and he had to admit that he never told that before October of 1998 when he first told that to the prosecutor.

"And when asked why, he said, 'I didn't want to.' Now, is that an explanation for withholding evidence? Is that an explanation for having lied to the police repeatedly? Is that an explanation for having told them originally after he killed Doug, he rode around—drove around on the road, waiting for a beeper call?

"That was his original story. So when asked why he changed it to Kelly being out there, he says, 'Why, I just didn't want to tell them that before.' Well, excuse me, but at some point, he decided he was going to tell the police things that incriminated Kelly Gissendaner. He decided that during his interrogation."

The fact was, Wilson claimed, Greg was obsessed with Kelly.

"He loved her and had this off and on-again relationship for some time, and he really had it for her. Sometimes he had his sister intervene. Belinda Leicht questioned Kelly back in December, 'What are your intentions about my brother that I introduced you to?' Did she tell us anything?

"On the night Doug disappeared, Owen hoped he would go out with Kelly, but she was going out with her girlfriends. He didn't like it. He insisted she come and meet him and talk with him. She met with him. Then she went out with her girl-friends.

"Now, the state is going to argue hard she must have been involved because she met with him. No. All that means is that she met with him. The state is going to argue hard Kelly beeped Owen's number after midnight. Okay. That proves she beeped that number after midnight. It proves no direct connection of Kelly with any criminal acts."

Wilson was building to one of his main points. Greg Owen decided on his own, on the spur of the moment, to abduct Doug Gissendaner.

"There was no plan by Kelly, no direction from Kelly. He took it on himself to go confront a man. He probably had reinforcements, at least one, and/or a firearm, probably both. There's no way, otherwise, he would have gotten Doug Gissen-daner out into those woods, much less have been able to overcome him and kill him with a knife."

Wilson knew he had to talk to the jury about Kelly's indiscretions. He wanted to confront them head-on. She's human. She makes mistakes. He called her relationship with Greg an open secret, but, Wilson claimed, she was embarrassed by it.

"She knew Greg to have made some threats along the way at the time she had broken up with him. That's in the evidence. These various people told us about Kelly relating that, and Doug's coworkers told us about the threats he got at various times. I think one was a year before Doug went missing and one was shortly before."

Kelly told one of her friends the same thing.

"Now, that was Ms. Kogut. Now, Ms. Kogut, bless her heart, was a bit nervous in this courtroom, and she told us that she felt she and Kelly were close. She told us she was close enough she took Kelly over to spend the night in a motel with Owen back in November of '96.

"And I asked Ms. Kogut about her police interview. Before then, she had told us she was embarrassed and felt betrayed when Kelly was arrested for murder, as I suppose a good friend would. She didn't remember telling the police that Kelly was upset and Kelly was crying right after her husband was missing, even when confronted with the transcript of her interview with the police, where she had said that she didn't seem to remember it.

"But she did relate to you conversations she had with Kelly and her remembrance of that. Perhaps her memory is off a little bit in the exact nature of that conversation as well as she can't remember an interview with the police when presented with the transcript.

"I would suggest to you that Kelly probably said something like, 'I never thought Greg would actually kill him. I never thought he would harm him. I know he's made threats in the past. I know he's said things. He's threatened me. He's threatened the kids.'

"'He's threatened Doug at various times, but I never felt he would harm him.' Now, the state wants you to take something like that and tell you it's a confession. I suggest to you that it's nowhere near that."

Rather, Wilson said, Kelly probably felt responsible at that time for her husband's disappearance or death, because she was the one who brought Owen into their lives.

"I'm sure she's thinking, 'If I hadn't done that, I wouldn't be here today,'" Wilson said. "I'm sure she was feeling at that time some personal responsibility for . . . running around on her husband and for having had a relationship with Mr. Owen. And she probably shared that with her close friend Ms. Kogut.

"Ms. Kogut also told us about something with Kim Harrison, and how Kim had said something Kelly didn't like, and in the parking lot leaving [or] going somewhere one day, Kelly said, 'I ought to just run the bitch over.' And the state wants you to make some kind of admission out of that. But, ladies and gentlemen, had there been anything to that, Kelly would have been arrested for aggravated assault with a vehicle or some other crime."

Wilson asked rhetorically, where is Ms. Harrison?

"She's not been here before you. Had someone tried to run over Ms. Harrison, Ms. Harrison would have come in here and told you about it. Why didn't the state bring her in here? Now, the state doesn't have to prove motive in a murder case, but motive or lack thereof is always a consideration that you might consider."

He asked the jury to consider motive. What reason did Kelly have to want her husband dead? There was no sizeable insurance policy—a few dollars were left after burial expenses. The house was not paid off and was, in fact, in foreclosure.

"Kelly and Doug were in the process of an application for another insurance policy, but she told Doug Davis it wasn't going to be in effect for four weeks or more. She knew it wasn't in effect.

"Now, if you're planning a murder over a number of months, wouldn't it be planned to occur after a substantial insurance policy is in effect rather than four weeks prior?"

Owen claimed that Kelly's motive was that she couldn't get rid of Doug if she divorced him; he wouldn't leave her alone.

"There were times where she had been left alone by Doug," Wilson said. "Doug left her and divorced her and almost divorced her a second time. So, does that make sense? Had they gotten divorced, if there was any equity in the house, Kelly would have gotten an equal division of that, surely."

Greg Owen was the one with the motive, Wilson claimed. Greg loved Kelly. He wanted her to himself. He thought she would get some insurance if he killed her husband.

"Now, the state also brought Laura McDuffie in here, and they want you to believe her story. Laura McDuffie—her certified convictions are in evidence. She testified to some of them. She is a prostitute. For a living, she sells herself, she steals cars and she robs people. She robs her prostitution customers and she carjacks people, and sometimes you have to hurt them is what she said up there.

"Look closely at these certified convictions. She told you about she couldn't stay at her parents' home after she got out of jail on the state's deal. She pleads guilty and she gets to go home that day. One of these convictions is for stealing from her dad, Malcolm McDuffie. This woman steals from her daddy.

"She also told you about narcotics and a deal she got with the narcs. She set up her boyfriend. Is this a woman to be believed? She actually had—she actually said when I asked her, 'Could you get into

Kelly's bin under her bed and take documents out of there?' She said, 'If I was that sort of person.'

"Okay. Take her—take that at face value, please. Now, she talked about four thousand dollars. She talked about ten thousand dollars. She said Kelly wanted her to get somebody, because she knew people who robbed people. She wanted her—her story is that Kelly wanted McDuffie to get someone to come in and say, 'I was a part of this murder. I was the person they're looking for. I was the third person involved and I helped Greg Owen.'

"Okay. Well, at that time, the state is seeking the death penalty on people. Okay. So where are you going to find that big of an idiot to take a few dollars to come in and be a defendant in a death penalty murder case?

"Only someone with terminal cancer can sign up for this program. This is not a plausible story, even if it came from a plausible source."

Kelly had no money, Wilson said. She couldn't even hire a lawyer. He was appointed by the court to represent her on an indigent basis.

Hutchinson was on his feet. "Objection, Your Honor. These are, again, facts not in evidence before this jury. This is a persistent habit with Mr. Wilson, and I would ask the court to admonish him."

"I'll ask counsel to stick to the facts of the case and reasonable inferences."

Wilson was summing up.

"We brought in Lieutenant Walters. Bless his heart, he's probably in trouble with his boss over there now, but he came in here. Lieutenant Walters took a moment and paused when I asked him,

'Would you believe that woman under oath?' He had to tell you no."

Wilson went back over some of the evidence presented. Owen testified he poured accelerant in the car and burned it. He said he took the Coke bottle that held the accelerant and threw it in the woods. He showed investigators where he threw it. They searched for it. They did not find it.

"What does that mean? That doesn't prove that he didn't use an accelerant, but it proves the state cannot corroborate Mr. Owen's story. Had they found an accelerant bottle, that would be corroboration. If he said it would be over here and it was there, that would corroborate it. No. It's not there.

"Mr. Owen also told the police I took Doug Gissendaner's keys and I threw them over here. They go search. They've got metal detectors. They've got the works over there at the police department. They go search. They never found the keys. Is that important?

"Does that prove Owen didn't kill anybody? No. It's fails to corroborate Mr. Owen. The state cannot corroborate him. That's another noncorroborating piece of evidence. They don't have the keys. Where are they? Mr. Owen says they are there. Let's corroborate his little story. Let's go get them. Where are they? They don't have them."

He said another failure of the state's case was that Greg Owen testified he stabbed Doug Gissendaner multiple times. He asked the jurors to use their common sense and decide whether Owen would have gotten blood on himself.

"The state wants you to believe you do all that and not have much blood on you. Okay. That's why there's not any blood in Ms. Gissendaner's automobile. He didn't get much on him, but he claims to have just after killing the man got enough blood to get some on his sweatpants underneath his jeans, but he didn't get enough to leave any in Ms. Gissendaner's automobile. Okay. But if he has some blood there, it would corroborate him a little bit. There isn't any there. Another noncorroboration."

But what does it say about Owen's story that he got blood on the sweatpants? Wilson asked. Doug's blood was on the pants. Owen's blood was on the pants. A third person's blood is on the pants.

"They don't know who in the world it is," Wilson said. "Does that corroborate Owen's story about he alone took Douglas Gissendaner to the woods and killed him and Doug did not resist?

"Well, Mr. Owen never told the police anything about receiving any injury. He said there was no assistance. He didn't tell the police about bleeding. The sweatpants got a stain mixed with Owen's blood and Gissendaner's blood. Now, how does that jibe with Mr. Owen's story of how this event happened? Can you resolve that? Is that a reason to have a doubt about the state's case?

"Additionally, there's a third person's blood on these sweatpants along with the other two. It's obviously not Kelly's, or they would have told you that. So whose blood is it? Why is it on Mr. Owen's sweatpants?

"But Owen said there was no one else. Owen said nothing about somebody else bleeding.

"Ladies and gentlemen, if there, in fact, was some sort of a scuffle, if there was a point in which Doug Gissendaner resisted Greg Owen and someone else—it may have been down the street from Doug Owen's [sic] house.

"It may have been out in the woods. It may have

been goodness knows where. But at some point, Owen and a third person and Mr. Gissendaner bled on those sweatpants. Now, that's irrefutable evidence. That's scientific evidence brought to you by the state crime lab."

Wilson charged ahead, building steam. The state did not bring in the crime lab experts to testify. Had the defense not brought forward witnesses, the jury would never have heard from the state crime lab staff.

"You would not have heard from the crime scene technicians that processed Kelly's car. You would not have heard from the people that analyzed the evidence taken from Doug Gissendaner's automobile and determined there was no accelerant found within it.

"None of those people would you have heard from. And especially not Keith Goff, Keith Goff who found the blood on the sweatpants and determined that to be Douglas Gissendaner's blood, Greg Owen's blood and a third person's blood."

Wilson said that the prosecution should explain this inconsistency. The jury should know why the person who found the blood on the sweatpants did not testify.

Wilson moved on to the testimony of Ricky Lee Barrett, Owen's roommate of eight years, his best friend. He lied to the police, but the state did not find out what Barrett was doing on February 7, 1997. So many lies. So many liars. To Wilson's way of thinking, so much reasonable doubt.

Kelly Gissendaner did not kill her husband. The state had not proven its case. Wilson implored the jury to find her not guilty.

Chapter 21

.

George Hutchinson, who had been with the DA's office just six years, could barely contain himself. By the time he rose to make his final comments to the jury in the most important case he had worked to date, he was angry. And he intended to tell the jury so.

"The purpose of a criminal trial, ladies and gentlemen, is to seek truth," he began. "It's the ultimate reason why we're all here."

He said the judge would tell them so in a few minutes. Then Hutchinson looked at the jurors and said, "So forgive me a moment if it seems I'm a little angry right now, because what you have just heard from Mr. Wilson has done a tremendous violence to the truth in this case. What you have heard from Mr. Wilson are his hopes, his desires, his dreams, at best his speculations, and at worst his outright inclusion of evidence before you that wasn't actually presented in this case."

He called Wilson's closing argument an insult to the truth. Wilson objected and the judge did not rule, but simply said, "You may proceed, Counsel."

Hutchinson used it to his advantage.

"I'm not surprised he doesn't want to hear this, because now we're going to start talking about the truth."

He said what was most annoying was Wilson's attempt to tell the jury what Doug Gissendaner would do when faced with an armed attacker.

"None of us know what Doug Gissendaner would or wouldn't do when faced with an armed attacker in his home. We might speculate or guess about what our reactions are or could be, but we don't know and Mr. Wilson doesn't know what Mr. Gissendaner's reaction would be. That's not evidence in this case, ladies and gentlemen. It's an effort to mislead and distract you from what the evidence is in this case.

"I didn't know Doug Gissendaner. None of you did, either, and neither did Mr. Wilson. And at this point, ladies and gentlemen, no one else is ever going to get the chance to know him better because that woman seated right there"—Hutchinson turned and pointed to Kelly—"the one you spent the last several days with—set in motion a series of events that led to this." Hutchinson pointed at a picture of Doug lying in the woods. "It put that man in that position on his hands and knees in the woods alone. Nobody knows what Mr. Gissendaner would have done, and, frankly, it doesn't matter."

He said the defense attorney talked at length about the fact that Doug could have gotten away, that he could have defended himself, he could have protected himself.

"We don't know what's going through his mind," Hutchinson said. "Maybe up until the very last moment, Doug thought he could talk his way out of it or that the person that had the knife on him would only want his money. We have the benefit of hindsight."

Hutchinson asked whether the reason Doug was in the woods mattered when they determined Kelly's guilt.

"No, it doesn't. The fact is regardless of how he got him out there, regardless of what the chain of events put Mr. Gissendaner at the point of the knife, the fact is that Mr. Gissendaner is dead."

Kelly sat expressionless beside her lawyer. Sue Gissendaner wept. Her husband and her daughters did, too.

Hutchinson accused Wilson of reinventing and mischaracterizing the evidence, specifically his comments about Kelly's confession to her friend Pam. Hutchinson said Wilson concluded that Pam did not hear Kelly properly when she said, "I did it."

Hutchinson stated, "The evidence in this case was [she] did it, followed by another phone call trying to come up with some explanation for her best friend as to why she did it. There's no misunderstanding of that, ladies and gentlemen. It's not the kind of thing that people misunderstand. It's not the kind of thing that you forget. It's the kind of thing that's burned into your mind."

Hutchinson told the jury it was a simple lawyer trick: a strategy of misdirection. It's a smoke screen. An effort to divert attention from what the evidence really showed. He said one of the lawyers in his office thinks of the state's case as a diamond with a few flaws.

"It's not perfect. It doesn't have to be."

He explained how the state puts the diamond out, and the defense comes along and smashes a plate glass window on it. The shards may look a little like the diamond and the defense hopes the diamond gets lost among the thousands of pieces of glass.

Hutchinson then talked to the jury about reasonable doubt. He said it means simply that the jury must base its decision on facts. It's like putting together a puzzle. You start on the outside straight edge and work your way inside. That's what jurors do with a trial. You know what the picture is before all the pieces are there.

Step by step, Hutchinson led the jury through the evidence. The blood did not gush and Greg Owen was not covered with blood. The bullet found near Doug's body was not from his murder. The car tag mattered not. Doug's missing keys mattered not. Flammable liquid never found? "Another piece of broken glass," Hutchinson said.

He also ridiculed the witnesses the defense brought it. No drugs in Doug's body, no fingerprints on a knife, the crime lab technician who testified to putting four drops of blood on filter paper.

"It was a smoke screen."

He asked the jurors to think of the courtroom as a pool.

"What you saw with that stream of witnesses coming in is what it would look like when somebody is drowning, grasping at straws trying to present anything that they can to divert you from the real evidence."

He said the prosecution did not have to prove motive, but there was motive shown: the two $10,000 life insurance policies and the home.

"Not much of a home by some standards, but apparently enough to be willing to kill somebody for. We know the house is in foreclosure now, but at the time of the killing, at the time the murder took place, ladies and gentlemen, do you remember the conversation Kelly Gissendaner had with her friends? Kelly Gissendaner said if her husband died, the house would be paid off. Right or wrong, that's what Kelly believed would happen in the event of the death of her husband. That wouldn't have happened if they were divorced. He needed to be dead."

Hutchinson also addressed Wilson's comments about the credibility of the state's witnesses.

"We don't get to pick those people. We don't have casting calls for witnesses."

He said the defendant is the one who selects the witnesses, it was she who chose to befriend them.

"If you don't like Greg Owen and you don't think he's much of a person, that's the person she chose as a lover. That's the person she chose to kill her husband."

Likewise, McDuffie.

"You don't meet people without prior criminal records in the jail. That's the kind of people you meet in the jail. That's who hangs out in there."

He said he found both people believable, but the jury did not need to rely solely on their word. The forensic evidence backed up Owen. Blood saturated his sweatpants. The phone records. The letter Kelly Gissendaner wrote in jail that a handwriting expert testified was hers. The map of the inside of the house.

"Laura McDuffie has never been inside of Kelly Gissendaner's home. She couldn't have drawn that map. So who did? The defendant did. And why did she write that letter? Because she wanted to avoid responsibility for what she had done. She wanted to avoid responsibility for her actions, and the reason that you're going to see that letter, and the reason why it's evidence in this case, is because it's evidence of her guilty knowledge, her participation in this crime. An innocent woman doesn't need to hire people to testify for her. She doesn't need to ask to have the state's witnesses beat up and robbed. Those are the actions of a guilty person that is attempting to get away with it."

The idea that Greg Owen got a sweetheart deal was a lie, too. Owen was told to tell the truth. And he would be prosecuted on other pending charges by a different district attorney's office. Likewise, no promise was made to Laura McDuffie.

The defense claim that other suspects existed was without substance. Kelly Gissendaner herself told police there were no suspects other than Owen.

"The defendant in this case is proved to be a desperate, evil woman. Look at her. You've spent the last several days with her. That's what evil looks like. It's not like it is on TV. There's no way to tell otherwise by background music or the way they're dressed. That's what evil looks like. She set in motion a plan to kill her husband for the house, for the insurance, and just planned to have him out of the way, and then she tried to avoid responsibility for her actions by hiring somebody to testify in her favor and to get the state's witnesses beat up and robbed. She uses people, ladies and gentlemen, that's supported by the evidence in this case. She used Pam Kogut and the rest of her friends. She used them as an alibi the night her husband was being murdered."

She used the Nesbits, McDuffie, Owen and Doug.

"She used him for his credit, she used him to get a house, and then, ladies and gentlemen, she got rid of him."

Hutchinson began to show the kind of man Doug Gissendaner was. He wanted a family, a home, work. He wanted to live out his life. He worked every day. He bought a house. He thought he had sorted out the troubles that stood in the way of him and Kelly living together happily.

"Little did he realize he was being used."

Little did he know his wife had renewed contact with Owen, whom Kelly picked out "as any assassin would pick a weapon out of a closet." She began having sex with him again, and over time, she convinced him to do what he had said he would not do. She talked of marriage to Owen, who, like Doug, wanted a family; he wanted stability.

She picked the place, the weapon, the night. She picked up Owen. They are driving back to the Gissendaner home when Greg is paged by his sister, Kelly by Pam. They stop at the CITGO on Highway 20 and return the calls at the same time. But Kelly told police she had not seen Greg since November. The phone records prove otherwise. They go to the house; Kelly gives Greg the weapons and he waits. She parties with friends, knowing there is a man at her house waiting to kill her husband.

Hutchinson recounted the murder: the knife to Doug's throat, the drive to the woods, Kelly's signal to Greg after she got home at twenty-eight minutes after midnight. Kelly drove to the scene.

"She went up into the woods to check on Greg Owen's handiwork, to make sure that what she asked had been carried out. And it wouldn't be hard to find the body, ladies and gentlemen, when you knew where to look. The white of his skin, the blue of his pants, would show up very well by the light of a flashlight. She went up to make sure that what she, in effect, contracted for had been carried out, and then she went along with the rest of the plan."

Kelly drove her car, Owen Doug's. They burned Doug's car and "then they went on their way." Gissendaner took Owen home and they resolved to avoid contact. But before that night, they talked every day, sometimes for long periods. That's corroboration, he said.

"If nothing happened between these two people, if they just hadn't conspired and carried out the murder of Doug Gissendaner, why would that pattern of activity suddenly stop?"

Then Kelly Gissendaner set in motion the rest of her plan: grieving widow. And she used more people: friends, family, her church, police who searched for Doug, the press. Hutchinson told the jury to listen for an emotionless Kelly as she talked for the first time with Investigator Davis about her husband being missing.

Then the police found out about Greg Owen and then Kelly Gissendaner told police about him. But she had broken it off with him, she said.

"Why would she mislead the police? You would mislead the police if you're guilty."

He called her demeanor a "disturbing lack of emotion."

Hutchinson continued with the chronology: Greg Owen's confession, guilty plea, Kelly Gissendaner's desperate attempt to shut up the state's witnesses. He read her script for the person she wanted McDuffie to find to take responsibility for the crime, the person she would pay $10,000.

"I told you, ladies and gentlemen, that that's the look of evil over there and the evidence supports that. There's no emotion, ladies and gentlemen. No emotion at all. No pity. No concern. No remorse. Evil hides in dark places, ladies and gentlemen, and it fears exposure. That's why real evil uses others. That's why she used Greg Owen to carry out this plan. I said before she picked her weapon, Greg Owen. Greg Owen has been held accountable for his actions, ladies and gentlemen. Now it's time that the defendant be held accountable for hers. She picked Greg Owen. She trained Greg Owen. She recruited Greg Owen, and she set loose an attack dog. And that person, ladies and gentlemen, that set the animal loose on another human being has a greater level of responsibility for the results than the animal itself.

"Ladies and gentlemen, the defendant attempted to avoid being held responsible for her actions. Despite what you heard from the defense, all of the evidence supports the defendant's guilt. The evidence is independently corroborated. The evidence supports the crimes charged in this indictment. One of the witnesses told you that Kelly Gissendaner wasn't afraid of anything. She's afraid of one thing, ladies and gentlemen. She's afraid of being held accountable for her actions.

"I ask you, ladies and gentlemen, to return a verdict that speaks the truth in this case. I ask you to return a verdict of guilty against the defendant for both counts in this indictment, because that speaks the truth. Thank you."

* * *

The court took a lunch break before Judge Stark explained the law and gave his instructions to the jury. It was time to deliberate. They went to the jury room, and within a short period, they asked the judge to hear one of Kelly Gissendaner's interviews with Davis.

Two hours after they entered the jury room, they sent a message to the judge that they had reached a verdict.

Charles Haines, the foreman, turned the slip of paper over to the court. Stark asked Phil Wiley to read the verdict, as is the custom in Georgia. Wiley looked at the verdict and told the judge it was in correct form.

He read the verdict: "*Guilty.*" Kelly Gissendaner looked straight ahead as her in-laws smiled knowingly, tears welling in their eyes. A step away from the death penalty. But it was a good, long step. No woman sat on death row in Georgia. Less than one hundred sat on death rows in other states. Condemning a woman, especially a mother, to death was like stepping on the flag and ransacking a sanctuary. Most everyone agreed the state had some work to do. Most juries wanted to send a woman home to her children.

Chapter 22

Just as he had started the trial, Doug Gissendaner Sr. started the penalty phase, which began the next morning. He told the jury about his son, about what a good man he was, a good family man. He worked hard and he took care of his children, even those who were not biologically related to him. Doug came home to see his parents often, Kelly rarely came with him. He didn't tell the court, but the truth was Kelly was not welcome in their home, not since she and Doug got back together for what seemed to the parents like the hundredth time. They had begged their son not to reunite with his then–ex-wife.

"Mr. Gissendaner, I'm going to ask you at this time to describe for the court what the impact of your son's death has had on you personally," Phil Wiley said.

"That's a very difficult question to answer," Doug Sr. began. "I love him so very much and I have to look back and know we—I believe very strongly in a loving family, and we always—as a parent we wanted to leave a legacy of someone that we can be proud of and children to carry on the family name.

"In 1966, when Doug was born, we were so proud because he was a son that could carry on this legacy, and for the next ten, eighteen, twenty years, I guess we tried to protect him, as we did his sisters, from the harms and evils of the world until they get grown-up. He had become a very, very fine young man."

Doug's father described his son's service of about a year and a half to two years. He called it serving his country. Doug served in the Desert Storm campaign, the United States' successful effort to defend Kuwait after Saddam Hussein invaded the country in 1990.

"He came back and worked very hard," Gissendaner said of his son. "His main objective in life, I guess, was he wanted to have a family and children, too. He and I became very, very close friends. It was just really more than a father/son relationship, and we had planned on doing so many things, you know.

"We always liked to work on cars together. We did different things together, worked around the house on different projects. We had talked about some of his friends were playing golf at his work and I was going to teach him to play golf. We were planning on being able to go with his friends and everything. There was just so many things that we had planned to do, and it's just like all of this is— all of this has just been taken away. It's been stolen from me.

"He was a very, very strong person. He was a giving person, a very loving person, and he always tried to help anybody he could. And I just—it has just been a tremendous, tremendous impact and a loss to us. Holidays—the holidays are coming up. It's always a little sad because we know that he's not going to be there to share it with us, and we just miss him so very, very much."

Doug Sr. testified he last saw his son the day before he died. Doug came by the house after taking the kids to school and they sat down at the kitchen table to have coffee together. It was commonplace for them.

"He would ask advice," Gissendaner Sr. said.

The defense had no questions.

The prosecution called Doug's sister, Lee Gissendaner Culhane, who lived in Birmingham, Alabama, with her husband, Andy, since June 1998. They had been married since March.

Brother Doug was four years older than Lee. He was her protector. He fixed her old car when it broke down.

"He'd always come to our rescue," she said.

"Lee, would you tell the jury in your own words what impact Doug's death had on you?"

"There's always been five of us in our family. To sit here and tell you how much I have missed him—I don't know how to do that. It's like a— it's just like there's an empty space. It's like there's a gaping hole there that I know he's not coming back. It's very hard for me to accept. My family—our family has always been very close. We would go to my grandmother's on Sundays. We all would meet down there and Doug would bring the children."

"Did Kelly ever come any of those times?"

"Very rarely, very rarely."

"She did come on some occasions?"

"Just a few times that I can remember over the eight years they were together."

She said he was a great dad, who introduced all the children as his own.

Again the defense had no questions.

Wiley told the court he wanted to enter into evidence all the material from the guilt-and-innocence phase. And the prosecution rested.

Chapter 23

Edwin Wilson and Steve Reilly did not believe the jury would sentence their client to die. She was a woman, but most important, she was a mother of three. They knew they had to personalize her to the jurors. That indeed was a challenge. Kelly Gissendaner had sat through the proceedings so far like a coma patient.

Julie Kay Parker, a church friend of Kelly's, was chosen as the defense's first witness. She was the mother of three children and lived in Cumming, Georgia. She met Kelly at a woman's group the church sponsored on Thursdays.

"I was just drawn to her," she said.

She described Kelly Gissendaner as a good mother. Her children were well-mannered and clean. They seemed happy.

"I remember the first time I met Kelly. I could see how much she had a love for life. You know, I could just feel that she was compassionate, always laughing. Every time we were together, she was always in a good mood, positive, just somebody that I wanted to be close with."

She told the jury she didn't think her friend deserved the death penalty.

"She has three children that don't have a father. If I had a choice, I would want her to have life," she said.

Prosecutor Wiley set out to show Parker didn't truly know Gissendaner. He asked whether Parker knew about Kelly's other men. No, she did not. And she acknowledged that Kelly Gissendaner did not seem especially upset when her husband was missing. They bathed the Gissendaners' Dalmatian, and she seemed "normal," Parker said.

Jody Elizabeth Price, the woman Kelly Gissendaner had befriended in the army, was called to the stand again.

She described Kelly as a very close friend, upbeat, a people person and a hard worker.

"She has always been a wonderful person. The way she was described—there's no one in this room by the name of Kelly Gissendaner that even resembles the remarks that were made about her at all. She's totally opposite of those remarks."

Kelly Gissendaner was an outstanding solider. No one ever made negative statements about her. She was a joy to work with.

"Knowing the person that I know, I'm not one to judge. I believe there's only one man that can judge Kelly from this point on. Kelly is a wonderful person, and my feelings will not change about Kelly—no matter what anybody else says about her. She has three wonderful children and she's been a wonderful mom.

"And I've gotten to experience her as a mother and as a friend. Her children are always first in her life. . . . If you knew Kelly, you knew her kids. I don't think they need to suffer anymore. They don't need to be put through this. They've been put through enough. And I think Kelly has been put through enough."

Price called the death penalty outrageous and said life was punishment enough.

Wiley again asked about the other men. Price did not know about them and was not around Kelly Gissendaner while Doug was missing.

With every witness, he drove home the point: Kelly Gissendaner was an adulterer who did not show sorrow or worry while her husband was missing.

The defense began calling a series of close family friends and family members to the stand. They needed a diagram to understand the relationships, from stepsisters to aunts.

Kelly Gissendaner's stepsister Cheryl Headly, of Flowery Branch, Georgia, testified Kelly was a good person. Always had been a good person.

"We've got along great," she said. "We have done things together. We went out together. We went shopping. I have never—Kelly, to me, has always been a good, nice person, a very loving, caring person always and always to my child."

Kelly was a good mother.

"What effect, Ms. Headly, do you think it would have on Kelly's children if Kelly were sentenced to death?" Reilly asked.

"I really think it would have a lot of effect on them. I've spent a lot of time with Brandon, the oldest one, at my house. We took him to Disney World this summer. I'll go up and hug him a lot and he hugs me back and he'll talk to me. The other ones, when I'm around them, they come up to me and hug me. I just think it would be really devastating for those kids if anything like that happened to her. I mean, they're very close to her."

She testified the oldest son, Brandon, could be suicidal if his mother was sentenced to die.

On cross-examination, Wiley wanted to know about Greg Owen.

Headly said Kelly Gissendaner had taken him to a family Christmas function.

Delphi Kemp, also of Flowery Branch, and Kelly Gissendaner's stepgrandmother, described her as the perfect granddaughter.

"Anything I asked her to do for me, she done it. She never said a sass word to me when she was little, and anything I asked her to do, she done it. She was just a sweet granddaughter."

Kelly was also a wonderful mother.

"Well, I don't want them to take her life, on account of the kids are already hurting. They would be hurt worse, and I think if it's anywhere they can go see her, because they've lost their daddy and they don't need to lose their mother, too."

Wiley had no questions.

Mabel Davenport, who lived in Jerry Log, Georgia, said she worked with Maxine Wade, Kelly Gissendaner's mother, at Phillips State Prison and lived in a room in Maxine's house during the workweek. It was a long commute from her home to work, she said. She had been there for about three weeks when Doug died.

"After the funeral, Cody came into my bedroom one day. There was a picture of Doug and Kelly sitting on the dresser. He picked it up and he said, 'My daddy has gone to heaven to be with Jesus, but I need my mama real, real bad.'

"And then there was another time that I had just made up my bed and he came through the door. This bedroom suite belonged to Doug and Kelly that I used and he climbed up on the bed and I turned and looked at him, and I said, 'Don't get on my bed I just made it up.' He said, 'This is my mama and daddy's bed.' And I must have looked at him real funny or had a shocked look on my face. He reached up and put his arms around me and said, 'But that's okay, you can share it until my mama comes home.'"

She told the jury she wished they would consider life imprisonment, not the death penalty and not life without parole.

"Maybe someday, someday she might could come back to her children and her mother," Davenport said.

Darlene Bearden, Kelly Gissendaner's aunt who lived in Glencoe, Alabama, said she lived with Kelly and her family when Kelly was a teenager.

"She was a real sweet person," Bearden said.

She said the Gissendaner children were having trouble because of their father's death.

"That has just about devastated them," she said. "They loved him, and now that they're losing their mother, I don't know what will happen to them. I don't know how much more they can handle. I just beg you not to give her the electric chair. Just give her life, so she could still communicate with her children as she's doing now."

Shane Brookshire, Kelly Gissendaner's brother, described his sister as outgoing and likeable. She had many friends and he considered her popular in school.

"She was good to her kids and me and Mama, real protective mother. Brandon doesn't express himself much. He's keeping everything bottled in. It really worries me and everybody else."

Maxine Wade, Kelly Gissendaner's mother, took the stand to plead for her daughter's life. Her daughter's attorney showed her some letters and asked her to tell the jury about them. She looked at one and said it was from Kayla and Brandon, her daughter's children. Another was from Brandon. These were letters they sent to their mom while she was in jail.

She said she watched her grandchildren write them, and then she took them and mailed them to Kelly.

Phil Wiley objected to the letters being admitted as evidence, and Stark agreed the letter would be hearsay, because the children were not available for cross-examination.

Steve Reilly picked up some pictures and showed them to Wade.

"Are those photographs of the children?" he asked.

"Of the children and my mother and Kelly," Wade answered as she began to weep.

Reilly admitted sixteen pictures into evidence. One showed Kelly and Brandon when Brandon was about two years old. He took the picture from Wade and handed it to the juror closest to him. They passed the picture, one to the next.

Various times, holidays. Birthdays, Easter. Kayla, with her doll collection, Brandon and a dog. Easter Sunday hunting Easter eggs. Kayla when she graduated from kindergarten.

Reilly showed Maxine some papers. Kelly Gissendaner's honorable discharge from the army, her certificate for the watercraft operation course, certificate for a course from the army for transportation school. Kelly Gissendaner's life on paper. A certificate for the achievement of transportation, certificate of investiture, certificate as a militia specialist, certificate of training, certificate to serve as a seaman, certificate of appreciation. He handed them to the jury.

Then he picked up a frame holding a number of small pictures of the children and Maxine Wade identified them.

"Ms. Wade, I'm going to show you defense— what's marked as defense exhibit one twenty-three for identification. Can you tell us what that is?"

"That is a movie that was made of Brandon and Kayla and Cody in October," she said.

"Was that video footage filmed at your house?"

"Yes."

"And were you present when it was filmed?"

"Yes, I was."

"Is there also some additional footage on there?"

"Yes, of Kelly on Cody's first birthday. It's—"

"Were you present—I'm sorry."

"It consists of Kelly and the kids on Cody's first birthday."

"Were you present when that was filmed, all of it?"

"Yes, I was."

"Have you viewed this videotape yourself?"

"Yes, I have."

"And are the images in it true and accurate?"

"They sure are."

"Your Honor, at this time, we would tender defense exhibit one twenty-three and ask that we be permitted to play it for the jurors at this time."

"No objection, Judge," Wiley said.

The courtroom lights were dimmed and the tape began. Spilling across the screen was videotape of the Gissendaner children, laughing, enjoying life. Just a regular day. There were pictures of Kelly holding her children as she sat on the couch, two of them in her lap. Her daughter played with her dolls in one segment, a son with the dog. Kayla held Cody, and then the two boys were working on a project together, playing outside, holding Easter baskets. There was kindergarten graduation.

The defense had wanted to enter into evidence a letter written by one of the children: *Dear Mom, I miss you a lot. I wish you were here sometime so bad . . . I don't know what to do. I wish I could give you a big kiss.*

The judge ruled the jury would not see the letter.

Kelly Gissendaner had remained stoic through the trial, even as she was convicted of murder. But sitting now in the courtroom, looking at her past life, she began to cry. She grasped a tissue and dabbed at her eyes.

When the lights came on, Reilly said, "Ms.

Wade, what effect would it have on these kids if their mother got the death penalty?"

"I don't want to even think about what kind of effect it would have, because all this has just been devastating to them. Like I said, the problems we're having with Brandon—last night when I went home and I talked to him, he just turned and walked off. He's holding so much inside. Even though I've had him in therapy, it hasn't helped."

"Ms. Wade, you have been here throughout the entire trial and you've heard all the evidence. You know what the verdict is. What would you say to the jurors regarding their decision about [the] sentence for Kelly?"

"I beg all of you, and I pray to God, don't give her the death sentence," Wade said, crying hard. "Don't give her life without parole. Give her life. Maybe these babies can have a mother one day. I know it's going to be after they're grown. I think the death sentence would just destroy them. That's my baby sitting there, too. I've had to be strong through all of this for her and for those babies. I put it in your hands and pray to God that you make the right decision."

"Thank you, Ms. Wade."

"Your Honor, do we need to take a break to let her compose herself?" Wiley asked.

"We can give her a minute here," Stark responded.

"I'm okay," Wade said.

Prosecutor Wiley asked her about the tape. She said it was made by the defense attorneys and she decided what to put on it.

"Did that tape undergo any type of professional editing?" Wiley asked.

"None whatsoever."

"How did the names of the children get on the end of the tape?"

"That, I don't know."

"You weren't present when that occurred?"

"No, not when they done that."

"Okay. Ms. Wade, you have had time during the months and years that Kelly and Doug were together to observe them together, haven't you?"

"Yes."

"Tell the jury how Kelly treated Doug."

"Well, like all marriages, off and on, they had their problems, but Kelly loved Doug."

"They were divorced at one time, right?"

"Yes."

"And then they remarried sometime after that?"

"Yes."

"Is it your opinion that Kayla and Brandon and Cody were all close to Doug?"

"They worshiped the ground he walked on. Cody thought there wasn't nothing like his father. So did the other two."

"He thought Doug was his father?"

"Yeah. Well, Brandon called him 'Daddy,' too."

"Doug treated them as his children, didn't he?"

"Yes, he did. Doug never mistreated those children. He loved them."

"Tell the jury what effect his death has had on those children."

"It has devastated them."

"They're devastated?"

Maxine Wade nodded and added, "They have been in therapy."

"Now, you testified earlier, I believe, that you

have the children—you have custody of them. Is that correct?"

"Yes."

"But you let them visit Doug's parents, don't you?"

"Anytime they want her or anytime she wants to go. Most of the time, they just get Kayla."

"Has Kelly ever been a sworn law enforcement officer?"

"Yes, she has."

"When was that just approximately?"

"'94, '95."

"Where did she work?"

"She was a correctional officer at Phillips."

"The same place you work?"

"Yes."

"How long have you worked there, Ms. Wade?"

"Fifteen and a half years."

"And you have been a correctional officer that entire time?"

"Yes."

"Kelly is no longer a sworn law enforcement officer, is she?"

"No."

"She doesn't have her certification at this time?"

"No. After a year, if you don't—if you're not in corrections, then your certification expires. It's one year or two years. I'm sorry. I don't recall, but hers is no longer any good."

"When did she leave working at Phillips?"

"She didn't work there long, about seven or eight months because they had put her on third shift, and with me on first shift, we was having problems with someone keeping the children, because, you know, she couldn't get any rest because everyone being in the house."

"But she only worked there several months?"

"Yes."

Wiley wanted the jury to hear from her mother about Kelly's improper relations with an inmate that forced Kelly from the job, but Wade had another reason for her daughter leaving.

"Ms. Wade, I want to call your attention to the date of Friday, November 8, 1996. I want to ask you, do you remember where the three kids were that night? Do you know?"

"What date?"

"Friday, November 8, 1996."

"November the eighth?"

"Yes, ma'am. It was, approximately, two—a little over two months, three months, before Doug disappeared."

"I don't recall. They could have been with me. I don't know, because I work six days and off three, and on my off days, I tried to spend some time with them."

"What I'm getting at, Ms. Wade, is the night that Kelly was spending the night with Greg Owen in Winder at a hotel, do you have any idea—"

"The weekend that she was—"

"Went to North Carolina?"

"The kids was with me."

"They were?"

"They was with me or Doug. I think they spent part of the time with me and part of the time with their daddy."

"Okay. Ms. Wade, did Kelly—Kelly never told you she had anything to do with Doug's death, did she?"

"No."

"When did you learn of the existence of a man named Greg Owen?"

"Kelly and Doug was separated. I guess it was the latter part of '95 is when I met him. The exact date, I don't know. I think it was the latter part of '95."

"Did you know that after Kelly remarried Doug, that at some point after that she and Greg resumed their relationship?"

"No."

"Did you know that she and Greg were having a sexual relationship while she was still married to Doug?"

"No."

"Do you know when Doug Gissendaner's birthday was?" Wiley asked, hoping to show a distance between the families.

"December the fourteenth."

"December?"

"The fourteenth."

Wiley sat down and defense attorney Reilly asked Wade whether anything she heard during the trial had changed her mind about asking the jury to spare her daughter's life.

She forcefully answered no.

The jury was given a five-minute break and Reilly told the judge he had only one more witness, Dennis Miller, the investigator for the defense. He wanted the jury to know that the film of the children was heartfelt and unscripted.

"You actually filmed that video that we saw a few moments ago, didn't you, sir?"

"Yes, I did," Miller said.

"During the filming of that video, did we—and I was there with you. Is that correct, sir?"

"Right."

"Did we attempt to tell the children what to say?"

"No."

"And did you film that video there at Ms. Wade's residence?"

"Yes, I did."

"Did you thereafter do the editing that was part of the video?"

"Yes, I did."

"And did that include editing in the portion with Kelly Gissendaner and her younger child?"

"Yes."

"Did you do that at the behest or request of Ms. Wade?"

"Yes," Miller said. The defense wanted the jury to know Kelly did not direct or play a part in anything about the film. They wanted the jury to see a woman whose children loved her and missed her. They wanted the jury to see how much she loved them and how easy their relationship was. Hers was a life worth sparing. That was what the defense attorneys hoped the jury would conclude.

Stark asked if there were any further witnesses.

Reilly answered, "No, Your Honor. We rest at this time."

Kelly Gissendaner would not take the stand in her own defense. She would not address the jury. The courtroom was packed.

Kelly Gissendaner's plea for her life was over. It was in the hands of the jury.

Stark told the jury they had two hours for lunch.

The jury left and the judge addressed Kelly Gissendaner. He told her he was required to ask the same questions he had asked before.

Two hours later, on Thursday, November 19,

the jury returned its verdict. It was Gissendaner's youngest son's fifth birthday. Again she faced the jury stoically. She wore a beige-and-white-plaid suit. Her black hair, cropped short, was combed straight back. She wore wire-rimmed glasses.

Wiley was asked by the judge to review the verdict and to read if it was in proper form: *The state of Georgia* versus *Kelly Renee Gissendaner, verdict as to sentencing, we the jury find beyond a reasonable doubt that statutory aggravating circumstances do exist in this case. We the jury fix the sentence of death. Charles E. Haines. 11/19/98.*

The circumstances they found were the murder was committed while in the commission of kidnapping with bodily injury, and the defendant caused or directed another to commit murder. That made the death penalty a proper punishment.

The defense was asked if it had any comment. It did not.

Judge Stark said, "Ms. Gissendaner, I'll ask that you stand at this time. The court will impose sentence. The jury has returned a verdict of guilty in count one of indictment number 97-B-1356-2 of guilty of the offense of malice murder. The same jury in the sentencing phase has returned a verdict, and in paragraph two, the jury states, 'We the jury fix the sentence of death.' The court therefore has a mandatory sentence to impose in this case."

Kelly Gissendaner would be the only woman on Georgia's death row.

Doug Gissendaner Sr. issued a statement.

"Unfortunately, no one is a winner in this situation," he said. "Everyone has experienced a loss."

Legal experts surmised that the jury went against conventional wisdom and condemned a woman largely because the jury was overwhelmingly female. Women are harder on women, they said. And the fact that Kelly Gissendaner was not the actual killer had little bearing on the decision. Quite often, on America's death rows, the condemned women were more apt to have arranged the murder than to have performed it. What stunned legal observers more was that Kelly Gissendaner was condemned even though she was a mother of three children and had no history of committing a violent crime. All of her children were underage. All would grow up without her. And without their dad.

Doug Gissendaner Sr. acknowledged the jury's work. He called them courageous and hoped that perhaps his family would find some peace in the verdict.

One of the jurors called the decision agonizing and horrendous. He said the prosecution and defense performed well, but in the end, the jury believed Kelly Gissendaner deserved to die.

"Justice was served," he said.

Pamela Kogut—who had thought of Kelly as a friend, but ended up on Kelly's list of people she wanted to harm—said she was ecstatic that Kelly Gissendaner got death.

"She got what she deserved," Pamela said.

Phil Wiley and the other prosecutors went out to face the press after the sentence was rendered.

"I know a lot of people doubted this case, didn't think we had enough, but the jury spoke volumes today." The *Atlanta Journal-Constitution* quoted the lead prosecutor, Wiley.

They were asked if there were any major problems getting the death penalty.

"Kelly made it easier because of her lack of emotion," Wiley said. "They didn't feel like anything was done to humanize her. She was very cold during the whole thing."

Years later, Phil Wiley would remember Kelly Gissendaner as the coldest female defendant he had ever seen.

Appeal

Chapter 24

Kelly Gissendaner passed her first night as a convicted murderer at Gwinnett County Detention Center under constant watch. She arrived at Metro State Prison, a woman's facility on the southern side of Atlanta, the next morning, November 20, 1998. She was one of about seven hundred at the maximum-security prison, but the only one under sentence of death. She would be treated not like the other women at the prison but like the 119 men waiting at Jackson State Prison for their death sentence to be carried out. That left her alone in a cell for twenty-three hours of every day. One hour out for recreation and shower. Alone to think about her life.

"She will have no interaction with the general population," a prison spokeswoman told the press.

Kelly Gissendaner spent her first few weeks being evaluated, as all inmates are upon going into the custody of the Georgia Department of Corrections. She was allowed no phone calls, mail or visitors.

As with all death sentences, her appeals started soon after she was processed, had donned a cream-colored jumpsuit and was locked in her cell, logged in as Georgia Department of Corrections inmate number 0000357507. Appeals are automatic to the Georgia Supreme Court. Not even a month later, her lawyer filed a motion for a new trial. It was denied ten months later and Kelly Gissendaner filed a notice of appeal to the Georgia Supreme Court on September 24, 1999. The brief was filed in December.

Her argument was straightforward and oft-seen. She claimed the judge erred in not moving the trial to another county and that the jurors were selected in an unfair way: too few blacks, too limited questioning. She claimed nine of the twelve jurors should not have been seated because they expressed willingness to impose a death sentence. She also charged the prosecutors had defamed her and her attorneys with some of their comments, including calling her "evil." Kelly Gissendaner also declared the electric chair cruel and unusual punishment. She said her death sentence was far too severe when held against others. After all, she did not heave the nightstick or plunge the knife. The Georgia Supreme Court rejected all of her claims and refused to rehear the case in July 2000.

Our review of the sentences imposed in similar cases in Georgia reveals that the death sentence imposed in Gissendaner's case, considering both the gravity of the crime and the depravity of her character, is not disproportionate, the court wrote.

The U.S. Supreme Court refused to hear the case in February 2001.

Her execution was set by a Gwinnett County Superior Court judge for noon, January 15, 2001. It was standard procedure, just as it was

standard procedure for an inmate to sue the
warden of the prison, in what is known as a state
court habeas corpus action, and for the execution date to be stayed. Typically, the inmate must
show either that his attorney was incompetent
or that the trial was unfair. It is known as post-
conviction relief.

In Kelly Gissendaner's case, the new court fil-
ings would alarm Doug Gissendaner's parents,
but did not surprise the lawyers and other trial
veterans. Filed in December 2001, at its root, it
was intended to show Kelly Gissendaner's attorneys had been ineffective, inadequate, and therefore her constitutional rights were violated. She
had not had proper counsel, according to the
filing. Prosecutors had erred in such a way as to
deny her a fair trial, she claimed.

Her new attorneys, appointed by the court,
placed hundreds of pages into the record. The
records included affidavits of psychologists and
Kelly Gissendaner's family alleging a history of
sexual and physical abuse beginning when she
was a young girl.

Mindy S. Rosenberg, a Sausalito, California, psychologist who has taught at the University of
Denver, Yale University and the University of California, Berkeley, offered a chilling look at Kelly
Brookshire Gissendaner's twenty-nine years before
her husband was murdered. Rosenberg looked at
a large number of Kelly Gissendaner's records:
school, health, military, prison. She reviewed her
interviews with police and those of Greg Owen.
She spent fourteen hours with Kelly Gissendaner
at Metro State Prison in April 2004, and more time
with Kelly's mother, aunts, cousins and friends.

She found a world as sinister as any movie.

Domestic violence centered Kelly Gissendaner's life. It was in her home, her extended family and in her community. She watched her father beat her mother. She watched her mother fight back. Fistfights. The parents divorced, and days later, Maxine brought home a stepfather, Billy Wade, for Kelly and her younger brother, Shane. He cheated on Maxine, according to the affidavit. He beat her in jealous rages. He held her down and sat on her while the children watched. The stepfather drank and then drank more. He used speed and smoked pot. He'd pass out on the floor, but not before he pushed Maxine down on the floor or up against a wall. Punch. Spit. Claw. Choke. He was like an animal. And she would do the same to him. Blood trickled down their faces and flowed from their arms. Kelly watched it all, the psychologist said.

An aunt killed herself. Another aunt's boyfriend killed himself. An aunt and a cousin tried to kill themselves. Twice.

When Kelly was three or four, her stepfather's nephew who was eight or nine came over to play. When Maxine gave Kelly a bath that night, she noticed Kelly's genital area was red and raw. The playmate had done it with his finger, Kelly told her mother.

"When I confronted [his mother], she jumped up and called me a bitch and we got into a fight. We both had on wigs and they both went flying. His father tried to intervene, but I kicked him and he doubled over."

No charges were filed.

Kelly was ten the first time her stepfather sexually abused her, according to Rosenberg's report filed with the court. Kelly was in the fifth grade.

Maxine Wade worked at night and Kelly was home with her stepfather. The first time he abused her, she was taking a bath.

"I need to make sure you're all right down there," he told her. He took her into his bedroom and penetrated her with his fingers. He said he wanted to make sure no one was messing with her. The second time, the stepfather was in the bathroom and he called Kelly in to wash his back. He fondled her and then made her rub his penis.

"I'll kill you if you ever tell anyone about this," he told her.

Not long after, Kelly was raped by a friend's stepfather after he asked her to come over and clean his house. She told no one about it.

The abuse by Billy Wade continued. The stepfather abused her in the room he shared with her mother, in her own room and in her brother's room, according to the report. When Maxine bought a king-sized bed, the stepfather said he didn't like it. He was going to sleep in Kelly's room with her. And the abuse took place every night after that. For six months. Her stepfather told her it was something she had done that made him want to have sexual relations with her. Her mother did not know. Although in her interview with Rosenberg, she said, "I should have known something was terribly wrong," because her husband wanted to go into Kelly's room while Kelly was sleeping and have sex with Maxine.

"I was so wrapped up in my own problems," Maxine told Rosenberg. "I had such stress living with Billy Wade—constant nightmares, jumping and being startled—I was so nervous that I had to take Ativan just to cope with it all."

Maxine finally left her husband, but Kelly

continued to be victimized, according to the report. While visiting her grandmother in Alabama, she was molested by a twenty-six-year-old. He made her perform oral sex on him, he did the same to her. She was twelve. The abuse continued for three years, every time she visited. The same man reportedly molested two of Kelly's cousins. That revelation came out at their grandmother's funeral.

Kelly Gissendaner told Rosenberg she was raped while she was in high school by a twenty-seven-year-old she had been dating for about a month. A month later, she realized she was pregnant. Maxine Wade did not know about the pregnancy for six months, but when she learned of it, she went to the man's trailer and threatened to file charges. Kelly was a minor.

The man threatened to call the police and Wade said, "Go ahead, I'll get out of jail before you do." She told him never to try to see Kelly or the baby. Brandon was born two weeks after Kelly graduated from high school. He never knew his father.

Kelly Gissendaner also alleged that Greg Owen raped her in the spring of 1996 after she had broken up with him. She claimed Owen called at all hours of the night and stalked her. He'd pull his Trans Am into the driveway and just sit there.

"He reminded me of Charles Manson," Kelly told Rosenberg.

Kelly asked him to return her belongings and he showed up one night at her mother's trailer. Her mother was not home and the children were asleep. She claimed he raped her. No charges were ever filed and Owen denied it happened.

Rosenberg said Kelly Gissendaner's response

to sexual abuse was similar to that of most other women. She shut down emotionally.

"I went into a little room in my mind where I could shut it out and then it was happening to someone else," she told Rosenberg. Dr. William Bernet, the director of forensic psychiatry at Vanderbilt University, in Nashville, Tennessee, who examined Kelly Gissendaner as well, said she told him the room was sometimes white and airy. Sometimes it was a field of flowers and there was always a door that could be locked. She described the room as peaceful. No music. No talking. Quiet.

It was a "place where a wall goes up around me and I am protected," she said.

She regularly felt fear, depression, guilt. She had stomachaches. She couldn't sleep. She picked her skin, bit her fingernails.

"There was a tape going through my mind, saying, over and over, 'Why is this happening to me? How can I get away?' and other times, I stopped thinking and felt paralyzed," she told Rosenberg.

She wanted to die. In high school, she took her mother's pistol to bed with her and debated whether to kill herself. She decided not to use the gun when it occurred to her she might "screw that up, too, and become a vegetable." She felt ashamed and helpless.

Rosenberg's report offered a detailed analysis of Maxine's family of eight siblings in Gadsden, Alabama. Poverty, alcoholism, suicide, sexual and physical abuse offer the thread that ties all the relatives together.

Rosenberg found that Kelly suffered from "impairment in several domains of brain functioning."

Constant stress over many years had caused problems with attention, memory and interacting with others. Rosenberg believed Kelly Gissendaner suffered from post-traumatic stress syndrome.

She also said Kelly Gissendaner struggled with all the sexual relationships in her life, as do most victims of sexual abuse. Victims often distrust men generally. They have many brief and superficial sexual relationships. They tend to be too dependent or to make their partners more than they really are.

She had trouble sustaining intimacy and closeness in her relationship with her husband Doug, and their relationship suffered numerous ups and downs, Rosenberg wrote in her report. When she and Doug grew closer, Kelly sabotaged the relationship, common for people who were victims of long-term sexual abuse, Rosenberg said.

At the time Kelly Gissendaner went on trial, information about the psychological problems of sexually abused women was readily available, Rosenberg said. Such information, she said, should have been presented during the penalty phase of Kelly's trial.

Also included in the appeal was a two-page handwritten affidavit of Gregory Bruce Owen. He claimed there was an accomplice, but it wasn't Kelly Gissendaner.

The police never believed that I was the only one, the statement said. He did not see any reason to tell them who was involved, and he still didn't. He also rescinded some of his testimony against Kelly Gissendaner. He said she did not give him the knife, that she did not go to see Doug's body. He said those things because police threatened him with the death penalty.

I really don't care what happens to Kelly, the statement declared. *I am only making this statement because it is true.*

The statement says he did not write it, but he read every word and *it is all true.*

The case would be heard in Georgia Superior Court by Judge H. Gibbs Flanders Jr., a cum laude graduate of Georgia Southern University and of the University of Georgia School of Law. He was fifty when he heard arguments in the case in December 2004 and had been practicing law since 1979. Wiley testified, as did other officers of the court. Wilson and Reilly, too. Wiley denied Gissendaner's claims that the prosecution team told Owen what to say. Wilson said he knew of Gissendaner's claims of abuse, but he did not use it in the sentencing phase as a matter of legal strategy. He knew the prosecution could rebut it easily. There was no independent corroboration it had happened.

The prosecution had witnesses they could call, not the least of whom was her brother, to say she had a normal childhood. She was not abused. She was not beaten.

"We tried to show Kelly in the best light we could," Wilson testified.

Doug and Sue Gissendaner Sr. stayed in the courtroom to hear every word. They vowed they would be there whenever their son's murder was discussed. Every appeal, every decision. Kelly Gissendaner was there, too, wearing a prison-issued beige jumpsuit. There was no jury and therefore no need to look the part of a suburban housewife, as she had during the trial. She was a convict and the judge had seen plenty of them. She looked heavier than she had during the trial.

Her brown hair was longer in the back, scraggly. Wispy bangs played at her forehead. Her skin appeared splotchy. She looked more mannish than they had seen her in the years she lived with their son. Tired and sullen, she sat quietly as the testimony swirled around her. Clearly, the solitary sameness of prison life had not been easy.

In March 2007, almost nine years after Gissendaner was sentenced to die, Flanders's fifty-three-page ruling came down. One by one, Flanders picked apart Kelly Gissendaner's claims, some because they had been dealt with by another court already.

The court considered her claim that prosecutors were guilty of misconduct because they did not give Kelly Gissendaner copies of their notes from their interviews with Greg Owen. The notes show that Owen told prosecutors the car was burned with kerosene, not gasoline, and that Owen bought it. Owen also told prosecutors that Kelly Gissendaner took him to the scene and that the knife was not under her seat but in her trunk. Owen told them he got rid of the evidence the week after the murder by putting his clothes, knife, stick, watch and ring in a trash bag and threw it away. The notes also included a reference to *why not tell defendant there,* with regard to Owen's later claim that Kelly Gissendaner viewed the body. She alleged this meant prosecutors coached Owen, that they put ideas in his head.

Flanders ruled none of the statements could clear Gissendaner.

Whether petitioner gave directions to the crime scene or took Owen to the crime scene, she still, according to Owen, picked the crime scene. In fact the withheld state-

ment is more inculpatory than the testimony at trial,
Flanders wrote in the ruling.

The accelerant was used to cover the crime, he
said, no matter who provided it and was not part
of the actual killing. Likewise, if Gissendaner
viewed the body, it was after the fact.

Flanders said, however, the information should
have been given to Kelly Gissendaner. On the
claim that Owen was coached, Flanders said he
could not find evidence that it happened. It was
unclear in the notes who made the statement or
what context it was said. It was impossible to know
what it meant.

*In fact, although Owen seeks to recant some of his
trial testimony in this proceeding, even he still main-
tains that no one told him to change his story, but that
he did so based on what he believed they wanted to hear.*

Flanders explained that a petitioner would be
entitled to a new trial if the withheld information
would have caused a different outcome. He said
that would not have happened in this case. The
evidence did not rest solely on Owen's testimony.
He summed up the state's case quickly: phone
records, testimony of a confession to a friend,
Leicht's testimony that Kelly Gissendaner wanted
to use her husband to get the house and then
get rid of him, and the letter and diagram to
McDuffie.

About Owen's recanting some of his testimony,
Flanders pointed out that Georgia Supreme Court
rulings give more credibility to trial testimony than
to recantations after the fact. There was no evidence offered by Kelly Gissendaner, Flanders said,
that it was impossible for her to have given Owen
the murder weapon, for her to have gone to the

crime scene or for him to have committed the crime without *an alleged third person.*

The court does not find that Owen's recantation proves the total falsehood of his trial testimony. The court finds it to be one more story told by a witness prone to telling multiple stories. Also, even if Owen's testimony proved to be false, there was no evidence that prosecutors knew it.

Kelly Gissendaner claimed her trial lawyers improperly represented her and offered forty-seven instances that covered every aspect of the trial, from getting money to bring in expert witnesses to improperly questioning jurors to not giving her counsel on a possible plea. She also claimed her lawyers did not properly investigate her mental health and background, that they lacked the experience necessary to handle such a case and did not develop a coherent or consistent theory of the case.

Flanders said a defendant must show not only that a trial counsel's work was deficient, but that the performance was so bad it denied the defendant a right to a fair trial. The defendant must show that the lawyer's work was so error-ridden that the jury would not have convicted her or recommended death had she had better counsel.

Owen got a life sentence with a stipulation not to seek parole for twenty-five years. Kelly Gissendaner was offered the same. She turned it down because she believed she was less culpable than Owen. Her lawyer explained all the possible sentences and she did not say she wanted to take the plea, Flanders said in the ruling.

Petitioner had an opportunity to resolve her case prior to trial, Flanders wrote. Her lawyers were under no obligation to convince her to take the deal. Likewise, a defendant who turns down a deal should know there is a risk of a harsher sentence—should she be convicted.

Her lawyers were able to keep certain evidence out of the hearing of the jury, Flanders pointed out, including the fact that Kelly Gissendaner told police she pretended to be sick the Sunday before her husband died so she could have sex with Owen while her family was at church.

Kelly Gissendaner's lawyers did get money for expert witnesses, including a doctor to conduct psychological testing. They also hired a jury selection expert, a DNA expert, handwriting analyst and an investigator, who interviewed dozens of people and studied the physical evidence the prosecution would seek to admit. He also looked for the third person believed to have been part of the crime. He centered on someone Owen knew, but he could not establish that he was involved.

Reilly, who was responsible for planning who would testify in the sentencing phases—should Kelly Gissendaner be convicted—interviewed dozens of her family members, including her parents, brother, numerous aunts and uncles and friends. He was in regular contact with Kelly Gissendaner's mother. She told him about her violent past, about her suspicions that her daughter had been molested and that she did not know Kelly was pregnant during her senior year in high school for six months. Her mother said the father of the baby was twenty-seven but did not allege the pregnancy came about as a result of date rape. The lawyers decided not to use the information because there was no record, either through police reports or a doctor, that it had happened. They believed the prosecution would use that against them, they said.

Kelly had not been hospitalized and had not received mental-health counseling.

Flanders noted in his ruling that Wilson attacked the credibility of the state's key witnesses. He also said seven witnesses testified during the sentencing phase as to Kelly Gissendaner's good character. The lawyers presented witnesses who talked about her relationship with her children, her military record and lack of serious criminal record before being arrested for her husband's murder.

Flanders reviewed the reports from the doctors who evaluated Kelly Gissendaner. Psychiatrist William Bernet found that Kelly suffered from among other things post-traumatic stress disorder and depression. He said she was passive, dependent and submissive, and therefore unable to mastermind such a crime. The other two doctors agreed.

Although trial counsel could have reasonably chosen to present such evidence, trial counsel made a reasonable strategic decision not to present such evidence, Flanders wrote. *It is noted that the very concerns that trial counsel expressed in presenting the allegations of sexual abuse to the jury in the sentencing phase are the same type issues Respondent argued in their brief to discredit and impeach Petitioner's experts, i.e. the lack of corroboration, the inference that Petitioner is a liar, the unreliability of the expert's basic information and consequently their conclusions.*

He said the allegations were largely uncorroborated. And some of the information was conflicting. One witness called a grandfather an abusive monster, another that he was a great man. Kelly Gissendaner's brother said he did not believe the abuse allegations.

Flanders ruled that Wilson and Reilly thoroughly picked apart Owen's inconsistencies, including his initial lies to the police and that he did not implicate her until he learned she had been seeing other men.

The court cannot conclude that trial counsel performed deficiently in challenging the testimony of Owen, Flanders wrote. *Trial counsel's cross examination established that Owen told multiple and contradictory stories and that he was still adding details to his story just before trial.*

Flanders also said there was no evidence that uncovering more lies told by Owen would have changed the outcome of the trial.

Considering trial counsel's representation as a whole, the court does not conclude that counsel rendered deficient performance. Even if the court were to conclude that counsel's performance was deficient there is not a reasonable probability that but for this performance the result of the Petitioner's trial would have been different.

DENIED.

Typically in Georgia, it takes twelve years for a death sentence to move through the appeals process. Gissendaner must now move to federal court for relief.

Doug and Sue Gissendaner Sr. believe her habeas corpus appeal was all lies. Why would she keep such victimization secret? Why would someone not have known? They believe it is more of their former daughter-in-law's manipulation to get herself out of trouble, a trend they saw over and over in her dealings with their son.

Belinda Owen who went back to her maiden name after her divorce says she does not believe her brother's affidavit. All sorts of threats and violence take place in America's prison system. There was no telling who talked to her brother and what they offered or threatened. She's never asked him to tell her what happened that night. She has told him she will listen when he is ready to talk.

Epilogue

Chapter 25

In 2007, there were 51,250 adults incarcerated by the state of Georgia. Two percent—or 105—were under death sentences. That included 104 men on death row at the Georgia Diagnostic and Classification Prison, in Jackson. And that included one woman: Kelly Gissendaner. She remained forty-five miles away at Metro State Prison. Georgia has no actual death row for women. Officials decided to house her in a special unit created for inmates who cause trouble, because she could be segregated easily from other inmates. Four cells. She's in one at the end of the hall behind a metal gate that is kept locked.

Since 1976, when the U.S. Supreme Court upheld Georgia's death penalty, twenty-nine men have been executed. The state changed the law making lethal injection the method of execution, but it was for crimes committed after 2000. If Gissendaner loses her appeals, she will face the electric chair at the Jackson prison, the first woman to die for a crime in Georgia since 1945. Five other women have been sentenced to die in

Georgia, but their sentences were reduced to life by an appellate court.

In an interview with a reporter from the *Atlanta Journal-Constitution* in 2004, Kelly Gissendaner said she did not understand how she could be facing death, when Greg Owen will be eligible for parole one day.

"I deserve to be here," she said. "But I don't deserve to die."

The Atlanta newspaper reported Gissendaner lives in a twelve-by-nine-foot cell in D building, with everything she owns kept inside a small metal locker on the wall. Shampoo, soap, deodorant, kosher dill pickles, Cheetos, crackers. Ten CDs. She likes Melissa Etheridge, Usher and Ruben Studdard, the newspaper said. Furniture: metal, bolted to the floor. She watches *CSI* and reality shows on a thirteen-inch television set. She gets up at five o'clock every morning, gets an hour on the yard, during which she usually walks the track. A prison employee plays cards or bingo or exercises with her for another hour, three times a week.

Carlos Campos, the Atlanta reporter who interviewed her, said she described a Christmas card from a dozen men on Georgia's death row as a cherished possession. They share the same life.

"We may not be blood related but those are family," she is quoted as saying.

Danny Porter, the district attorney, said he believed from a legal standpoint there were no errors in Kelly Gissendaner's case.

"We would expect the sentence to be carried out," he said.

Prosecutor Phil Wiley said he has had communication from Kelly Gissendaner's lawyers asking if he would agree to a life-without-parole sentence. Out of the question, he responded. She threatened to kill witnesses and that he does not forgive.

In the years since her husband was murdered, she has taken a new look, harder still than the steely mother who was put on trial in late 1998. Her black hair falls barely past her neckline in a mullet style. Her wire-rimmed glasses are old-school style. She took back her maiden name: Brookshire. She sought pen pals through a Web site run by the Canadian Coalition Against the Death Penalty.

I am a gay white female, looking for the same to share letters with and to get to know one another, she wrote. *And learn more about each other. I am 5' 10½", 160 lbs, brown eyes and black hair. I am on Georgia's death row for a crime I did not commit. I'm looking for someone to write who loves to read, loves the outdoors, and who loves to write.*

On the Web page, she wrote about the inhumanity of capital punishment and several times proclaimed her innocence and that of others, unnamed, in prisons around the country.

If you are one of the lucky ones, you'll get visits from family and friends, she wrote. *You'll learn you want to see them no matter how much you hurt from missing them once they are gone. During the time you spend with them, you might even start to feel human again. But as soon as you do, it's time for them to leave without you. You watch your children grow older over the years. That becomes your calendar. The days drag, most of the time leaving you with too much time to think, and you hope and pray that the day will come when someone will see that maybe there was a mistake and something will be done to set you free before you take that final walk that will end your life.*

She wrote that a lesson from prison is you can't be who you were on the outside if you want to survive.

You ache for companionship, but you try not to get close to anyone because people come and go so much inside the system, she wrote. She said loneliness, not a cell, had become her harshest punishment. Like all death row inmates, she was not allowed to mingle with other prisoners.

She said she doesn't believe the death penalty is a deterrent. Countries with the death penalty have higher murder rates than those that don't. And the cost of taking a case from arrest to execution is always more than $1 million. Keeping a murderer in prison for life, much less.

The women on death row in America often had ineffective legal counsel and were victims of misconduct by prosecutors or law enforcement, according to a 2004 report by the American Civil Liberties Union. More than half have suffered regular, ongoing physical abuse by family members or spouses.

Half of the women acted with at least one other person, but in most of those cases, the co-defendant received a sentence other than death—even in cases where they appeared to be equally culpable. Many women live in almost complete isolation, which puts them at a serious risk of developing mental illness, or exacerbating existing mental illness.

Her oldest son, who in 2007 was twenty-one, lived with her father Larry Brookshire. The younger children, seventeen and fourteen, were cared for by her mother. The Gissendaners saw Kayla regularly, watching her softball games and talking to her on the phone. They tried to remain a positive force in her life. They want her to know something of her father, of his goodwill, his ease and how much he loved her and her brothers.

The children visited their mother in prison twice a month, according to the Atlanta newspaper. She also talked to them by phone, praising good grades and athletic prowess. She described herself to the reporter as a good mother. She did not respond to letters sent requesting interviews.

It took a long time to sell the house on Meadow Trace, and many of the neighbors who were there when Doug and Kelly moved in have moved on. It takes time for a house to be restored after a tragedy.

"Nobody even talks about it anymore," said neighbor Brett Brantley, one of the few in the subdivision who knew the Gissendaners.

In 2007, Greg Owen had served ten years of a life sentence at Telfair State Prison, in Helena, a community in the southern part of the state. After twenty-five years, he'll be eligible for parole. He calls his sister Belinda on Sundays, Wednesdays and Fridays, and despite the expense of collect calls from jail, she always answers. She drives the two hundred miles to visit with her brother once a month.

"There's things he didn't tell anybody," she said. "He's ready to tell."

She wouldn't elaborate, but she believed the information could get him paroled.

Belinda has maintained that Kelly Gissendaner killed her husband and set up Greg, whose only involvement was to help her burn the car.

"There was no fear in his body," Belinda Owen

said of Doug Gissendaner. "No way in hell is anybody going to be in the woods like that." To her, that meant Doug knew his assailant and he did not know Greg Owen. If a stranger had attacked him, he would have been afraid.

Doug was a bigger man than her brother and could have fought him off, Belinda Owen said.

Like her mother, she is waiting for the day her brother is paroled. She sends him a subscription to *High Performance Pontiac* and makes sure his 1975 teal blue Trans Am is cared for at his aunt's house. His pit bull named Toby has died since he has been in prison. Belinda took him aside in a corner of the prison visitation room to tell him. He couldn't let the other inmates know he was crying, much less for a dog.

Belinda is raising her sister's children and tells them about their uncle Greg. They know he is in prison, but she tells of his gentleness. At every one of the children's birthdays, the biggest present is from Greg. He laments that he's not there to throw the baseball around with his nephew.

Myrtis Owen made her son the beneficiary of her 401k and the stock in Merry Maid, where she works. She's not certain she'll be around when he gets out of prison and wants to be sure he has the means to start his life again.

When she heard the news of his arrest, she had two thoughts. "He should have lawyered up."

And. . . .

"I had already lost a son and you're sitting there telling me I'm going to lose the only son I have left," she said.

Like Belinda, she said Greg was under the influence of marijuana the night he was questioned by police. She wonders whether he would say what he did if he had not been. But that is revisionist history. It does no good. She concentrates on her work and her grandchildren and tries to stay positive about her own health despite rheumatoid arthritis.

Bruce Owen died in 2002. Greg was not allowed to attend the funeral. Belinda made all the arrangements for her father. The graveside service pained her. So few people showed up, but she was grateful her mother agreed to come. Bruce Owen had lived with his daughter off and on for the six years before he died.

"My dad was the only person who loved me like he did," Belinda said. He had transformed from an overbearing presence to a meek, whittled-down-to-nothing man in the years since her mother divorced him. Half of his stomach was removed due to a bleeding ulcer. He was drinking heavily. She forbade it in her house and then would kick him out when she found beer cans under his bed. The last time, she caught him stealing money from her purse.

"I'm done," she screamed at him. "If you're not going to get help, I'm not doing this anymore."

Finally his health problems became so severe, he was sent to hospice to die. And then he did. He was fifty-two.

Doug Davis, the lead investigator in the case, moved from murder investigations to an administrative job managing the hundreds of cars in

Gwinnett County's fleet. He planned on retiring by the end of 2008. His wife retired in 2007. It was time to spend uninterrupted time with her.

When he thinks of the case, he remembers Kelly Gissendaner as a ruthless woman. He feels sorry for the Gissendaner family. He never turned up anything bad about them or their son in all his investigation.

James Bell, the Georgia Department of Natural Resources sergeant who found Doug's car and body, is now a captain with the department, responsible for teaching hunter safety. He got a Christmas card every year from Sue Gissendaner's mother until she died. It meant a lot to him that she remembered. It meant a lot that he could help the family, if only to let them know what happened to their son.

"It was a major part of my life," he said. "Even in law enforcement, you don't think of people being that way."

Phil Wiley continues to work in the district attorney's office. He's been promoted to chief ADA, second in command of one of Georgia's busiest prosecutor's offices. Co-counsel George Hutchinson resigned in November 2004 to become a magistrate judge in Gwinnett County. Nancy Dupree retired at Thanksgiving in 2006. She had been with the DA's office for twenty-three years.

Wiley said when the time comes, he'll go watch Kelly Gissendaner die.

"Our feeling is, if you've got the guts to ask the

jury to do it, you should have the guts to go watch it," he said.

He has seen one death sentence carried out—by lethal injection. He and Danny Porter watched a man convicted of killing a liquor store owner after a bank robbery. Wiley called it a humbling experience but humane to the condemned.

"His head turned over. His color went gray and he was dead."

Thomas Dunn, the lead attorney with the Office of Georgia Capital Defender, asked Wiley to see if the Gissendaners would agree to a lesser charge. They said emphatically they would not talk to anyone representing their son's murderer. They just wanted to be left alone. They know they face many more years of appeals. More hearings. More legal-brief reading. More anguish. They are prepared and resolute. They know Kelly Gissendaner may get off death row, but they want to be sure she never gets out of prison.

For several years after the murder, Doug and Sue Gissendaner remained in the house where they raised their children, but they decided they wanted to be closer to their daughters. They bought a house on a lake in Alabama. Both Lee and Jennifer married—Lee about eight months before her former sister-in-law was sent to death row. They have had children of their own. And they yearn for their older, sensitive and generous brother to be part of their children's lives. He would have been an amazing uncle.

The Gissendaners also became involved in the Homicide Support Group hosted by the Gwinnett County Victim Witness Program. Stan Hall, the program director, said the organization allows people who have lost a loved one in a murder to talk about their grief. Some of the families talk about murders that took place as long as twenty years ago, others newly raw.

For several years, Sue Gissendaner made a memorial wreath to hang in the district attorney's office during National Crime Victims' Rights Week. Hall said the Gissendaners played an important role.

"We have used them as our models many times," he said. "They are the most typical American family you'll ever want to meet."

There was nothing in Doug's life that would make anyone think his end would come as it did. "Way down-to-earth people" was how Hall described them.

For a time, the elder Doug Gissendaner continued to travel the highways and interstates of the South, selling self-lubricating bearings. Time on the road was tough. It gave him more time to think of his son, Doug.

In Gratitude

This book has been a long time coming and for that alone I wish to thank Kensington editor Michaela Hamilton, whose patience wore thin as would be expected of any reasonable person. Michael Shohl did the heavy lifting on the editing and made this a much more readable and interesting book. Melissa Blanton served as a keen-eyed copy editor.

To the Gissendaner family, I express sincere sorrow for their loss. Their son and I share a birth date. He was born the day I turned twelve. I came to know him through the people whose lives he touched, many of them touched by him after he died. As more than one investigator said, they never uncovered anything bad about him. I've written four of these true crime books now, and I always look for a hero. I don't always find one. This time, I found Doug.